Homoerotic Poets of the Italian Trecento

THE WILLIAM AND KATHERINE DEVERS SERIES
IN DANTE AND MEDIEVAL ITALIAN LITERATURE

Laura Banella, Zygmunt G. Barański, and Theodore J. Cachey, Jr., editors

RECENT TITLES

VOLUME 27
*Homoerotic Poets of the Italian Trecento:
The Complete Poems of Meo dei Tolomei,
Cecco Nuccoli, and Marino Ceccoli*
- Fabian Alfie

VOLUME 26
*American Dantes: Traditions,
Translations, Transformations*
- Edited by Zygmunt G. Barański
and Theodore Cachey, Jr.

VOLUME 25
The Early Printed Illustrations of Dante's "Commedia"
- Matthew Collins

VOLUME 24
Petrarch's Penitential Psalms and Prayers
- Francesco Petrarca,
edited and translated by Demetrio S. Yocum

VOLUME 23
Dante's "Vita Nova": A Collaborative Reading
- edited by Zygmunt G. Barański
and Heather Webb

VOLUME 22
*Manuscript Poetics: Materiality and Textuality in
Medieval Italian Literature*
- Francesco Marco Aresu

VOLUME 21
Dante's Multitudes: History, Philosophy, Method
- Teodolinda Barolini

VOLUME 20
Dante's "Other Works": Assessments and Interpretations
- edited by Zygmunt G. Barański
and Theodore J. Cachey, Jr.

VOLUME 19
Liturgical Song and Practice in Dante's Commedia
- Helena Phillips-Robins

VOLUME 18
Dante and Violence: Domestic, Civic, and Cosmic
- Brenda Deen Schildgen

VOLUME 17
*A Boccaccian Renaissance: Essays on the Early Modern
Impact of Giovanni Boccaccio and His Works*
- edited by Martin Eisner and David Lummus

VOLUME 16
*The Portrait of Beatrice: Dante,
D. G. Rossetti, and the Imaginary Lady*
- Fabio A. Camilletti

VOLUME 15
*Boccaccio's Corpus: Allegory, Ethics,
and Vernacularity*
- James C. Kriesel

VOLUME 14
*Meditations on the Life of Christ:
The Short Italian Text*
- Sarah McNamer

VOLUME 13
*Interpreting Dante: Essays on the
Traditions of Dante Commentary*
- edited by Paola Nasti
and Claudia Rossignoli

VOLUME 12
*Freedom Readers: The African American Reception
of Dante Alighieri and the
"Divine Comedy"*
- Dennis Looney

VOLUME 11
Dante's Commedia: *Theology as Poetry*
- edited by Vittorio Montemaggi
and Matthew Treherne

VOLUME 10
*Petrarch and Dante: Anti-Dantism,
Metaphysics, Tradition*
- edited by Zygmunt G. Barański
and Theodore J. Cachey, Jr.

VOLUME 9
The Ancient Flame: Dante and the Poets
- Winthrop Wetherbee

VOLUME 8
*Accounting for Dante: Urban Readers
and Writers in Late Medieval Italy*
- Justin Steinberg

VOLUME 7
*Experiencing the Afterlife: Soul and Body in Dante
and Medieval Culture*
- Manuele Gragnolati

HOMOEROTIC POETS OF THE ITALIAN TRECENTO

The Complete Poems of Meo dei Tolomei, Cecco Nuccoli, and Marino Ceccoli

FABIAN ALFIE

University of Notre Dame Press
Notre Dame, Indiana

Copyright © 2026 by the University of Notre Dame

Published by the University of Notre Dame Press
Notre Dame, Indiana 46556
undpress.nd.edu

All Rights Reserved

Published in the United States of America

Library of Congress Control Number: 2025946663

ISBN: 978-0-268-21058-8 (Hardback)

ISBN: 978-0-268-21059-5 (Paperback)

ISBN: 978-0-268-21061-8 (WebPDF)

ISBN: 978-0-268-21060-1 (Epub3)

GPSR Compliance Inquiries:
Lightning Source France, 1 Av. Johannes Gutenberg, 78310 Maurepas, France
compliance@lightningsource.fr | Phone: +33 1 30 49 23 42

ABOUT THE WILLIAM AND KATHERINE DEVERS SERIES IN DANTE AND MEDIEVAL ITALIAN LITERATURE

The William and Katherine Devers Program in Dante Studies at the University of Notre Dame supports rare book acquisitions in the university's John A. Zahm, C.S.C Dante collections, funds a visiting professorship in Dante studies, and supports electronic and print publication of scholarly research in the field. In 1995, in collaboration with the Medieval Institute at the university, the Devers program initiated a series dedicated to the publication of the most significant current scholarship in the field of Dante studies. In 2011 the scope of the series was expanded to encompass thirteenth- and fourteenth-century Italian literature.

In keeping with the spirit that inspired the creation of the Devers program, the series takes Dante and medieval Italian literature as focal points that draw together the many disciplines and lines of inquiry that constitute a cultural tradition without fixed boundaries. Accordingly, the series hopes to illuminate this cultural tradition within contemporary critical debates in the humanities by reflecting both the highest quality of scholarly achievement and the greatest diversity of critical perspectives.

The series publishes works from a wide variety of disciplinary viewpoints and in diverse scholarly genres, including critical studies, commentaries, editions, reception studies, translations, and conference proceedings of exceptional importance. The series enjoys the support of an international advisory board composed of distinguished scholars and is published regularly by the University of Notre Dame Press. The Dolphin and Anchor device that appears on publications of the Devers series was used by the great humanist, grammarian, editor, and typographer Aldus Manutius (1449–1515), in whose 1502 edition of Dante (second issue) and all subsequent editions it appeared. The device illustrates the ancient proverb *festina lente*, "Hurry up slowly."

Laura Banella, Zygmunt G. Barański, and Theodore J. Cachey, Jr.,
editors

ADVISORY BOARD

Albert Russell Ascoli, Berkeley

Teodolinda Barolini, Columbia

Piero Boitani, Rome

Patrick Boyde, Cambridge

Alison Cornish, New York University

Christopher Kleinhenz, Wisconsin

Giuseppe Ledda, Bologna

Simone Marchesi, Princeton

Kristina M. Olson, George Mason

Lino Pertile, Harvard

John A. Scott, Western Australia

Heather Webb, Yale

Dedicated to
Steven Botterill
(1958–2017)

CONTENTS

Acknowledgments   xi

Introduction: Homoerotic Poets: Meo dei Tolomei,   xiii
Pseudo-Cecco Angiolieri, Cecco Nuccoli, and Marino Ceccoli

PART 1
Siena: Poets of Chigiano L.VIII.305 and Related Manuscripts

One	Meo dei Tolomei	3
	Poems by Meo dei Tolomei	4
	Meo dei Tolomei: Poems of Debated Attribution	54
	Poetry Addressed to Meo dei Tolomei	64
	Poetry Influenced by Meo dei Tolomei	68
Two	Pseudo-Cecco Angiolieri	71

PART 2
Perugia: Poets of the Vatican Barberiniano Latin 4036 Manuscript

Three	Cecco Nuccoli	83
Four	Marino Ceccoli	161
	Works by Marino Ceccoli	162
	Works Written to Marino Ceccoli	236
	Notes	243
	Bibliography	267
	Index	283

ACKNOWLEDGMENTS

No study takes place in a vacuum, and that is certainly true of these translations. Were it not for the assistance I received from many individuals over the years, this book would not have seen the light of day. But there are several people who stand out as deserving special thanks. First, I want to acknowledge Albrecht Classen, professor of German at the University of Arizona, who helped with Cecco Nuccoli's verses in German, and Philip Waddell, associate professor of classics at the University of Arizona, who provided me crucial assistance with Marino Ceccoli's Latin epistles. In addition, Aileen Astorga Feng, associate professor of Italian at the University of Arizona, and Nicolino Applauso, visiting assistant professor of Italian at Loyola University Maryland, gave me crucial feedback about the poetic traditions of the late Middle Ages and early Renaissance. Denis Provencher, professor of French at North Carolina State University, and William L. Leap, professor emeritus of anthropology at American University, offered unique insights into queer linguistics and how they could be adapted to the homoerotic poetry of the trecento. Special thanks are offered to Antonio Lanza, Donato Pirovano, Claudio Ciociola, and GLU editions for allowing me to reproduce the original poems for the facing-page translations. Finally, this book would not have been possible without the feedback and assistance of the editors and anonymous readers of the University of Notre Dame Press.

INTRODUCTION

Homoerotic Poets

Meo dei Tolomei, Pseudo-Cecco Angiolieri, Cecco Nuccoli, and Marino Ceccoli

FROM SIENA TO PERUGIA

The Literary Culture of Fourteenth-Century Perugia

A sole manuscript, Barberiniano Latin 4036 of the Biblioteca Apostolica Vaticana in Rome, preserves the works of a group of poets unattested elsewhere. Compiled in Perugia before 1353, it consists of seven fascicles of folios numbered from 1 to 196, and although it was transcribed by several individuals, one of them, Gino Guidinelli da Castro San Piero, was the notary who drew up the document contained at the end of the codex.[1] The primary poets therein were Neri Moscoli, Cecco Nuccoli, and Marino Ceccoli, but other writers, such as Cucco di Gualfreduccio Baglioni and Cionello, also contributed. Historical references in their lyrics indicate these writers were active in the 1330s. Like Gino Guidinelli, the poets were notaries, suggesting that Barberiniano Latin 4036 was the anthology of the lower aristocracy of Perugia.[2] By all appearances, they were on the fringes of the broader literary movement of northern Italy in the fourteenth century, having neither immediate predecessors nor followers.[3] None of them wrote in Tuscan, which at the time was evolving into the standard medium for literary works, but in the Perugian dialect, further restricting their readership.[4] Were it not for this manuscript, these authors would have left virtually no traces on Italian literature.

xiv   Introduction

The writers of Perugia did not operate in complete isolation from the broader literary developments in Italy, however. On the contrary, their lyrics show that they kept abreast of the more famous Italian authors. For instance, Neri Moscoli recalls the poetry of the *dolce stil nuovo*, the philosophical and spiritual love poetry of Florence of the late 1200s;[5] he also echoes the experimental *rime petrose* by Dante Alighieri (1265–1321) and some passages of *Inferno*.[6] Cucco di Gualfreduccio Baglioni demonstrates the influence of the *stilnovista* Lapo Gianni (d. ca. 1328), and Cionello evokes Onesto Bolognese (ca. 1250–ca. 1300).[7] Furthermore, two other poets, Cecco Nuccoli and Marino Ceccoli, are thoroughly steeped in the comic literature of the age: Mario Marti amply demonstrated in his anthology that they repeatedly invoke the sonnets of Meo dei Tolomei and those by Cecco Angiolieri of Siena (ca. 1260–1312).[8] Like Tolomei and possibly Angiolieri, Nuccoli and Ceccoli also wrote about love and sexual attraction to other men, and it is thanks to that subject matter that Nuccoli and Ceccoli are best remembered today.[9]

Homoerotic literature was not unheard of in the Middle Ages, but it was uncommon. More so than their predecessors, however, Nuccoli and Ceccoli explore quite broadly the poetics of same-sex desire in fourteenth-century Italian literature. It is important to remember that these poets wrote about a range of topics, not merely same-sex attraction. When speaking about medieval poets, it is a common error to reduce them to their one "typical" style, and then to interpret all their works by the light of that style. Yet the writers of the Middle Ages—not only those represented in this book—were multifaceted human beings who used poetry to comment on a range of matters over the course of years, if not decades. It is necessary, therefore, to approach each poem on a case-by-case basis and not assume that the writers were monotonal in their literary productions.

Cecco Nuccoli and Marino Ceccoli are probably the most famous authors of Perugia in the trecento. The Perugian city-state, situated on a cluster of hills at an altitude of almost 500 meters, dominated the Tiber valley to the south, the plains of the Umbrian valley to the east, and the valleys of the Trasimeno and Chiana to the west.[10] The valleys supplied the city with grain, but they were prone to flooding, and Lake Trasimeno provided it with nearly 5,000 *quintali* of fish per year.[11] Perugia sat on several lines of communication running north–south along the Italian peninsula, connecting Rome with the major centers of trade.[12] By 1285, the population of Perugia was estimated to be between 33,000 and 34,000, making it an important city in central Italy.[13] From the perspective of economic and political influence, citizens of Perugia could be called anything but marginalized, yet Perugian citizenship conferred little status to them as literary figures. Despite its political and economic importance in central Italy, medieval Perugia was not a major center of literary production.[14] Hence, Nuccoli and Ceccoli in some ways epitomize the literary status of all the writers of Perugia at the time, because they absorbed the greater movements while at the same time remaining relegated to the sidelines somewhat.

The Medieval Literature of Love

The principal subject matter of Nuccoli's and Ceccoli's poems only further places them outside the norm. Love literature dominated the poetry of the thirteenth and fourteenth centuries, but most men wrote about their attractions to women. The earliest approaches to love, the *fin'amor* pioneered by the Occitanic troubadours in the twelfth century and transmitted through Italy by the Sicilian school in the thirteenth century, presented love as a type of aristocratic service in which the lover treated the lady as a feudal superior.[15] Love was treated as something exclusive to the aristocracy, and as such it reflected their values.[16] Indeed, at times devotion to the lord was expressed in terms quite similar to those of love literature, rendering it difficult to distinguish between expressions of passion and assertions of fealty.[17] The conventions of *fin'amor* resulted in a reversal of the social hierarchy that subordinated the male lover to the woman, and many writers depicted their abject conditions relative to the beloved to describe their amorous pains.[18] Yet most writers in the troubadouric tradition also cast same-sex desire as uncourtly.[19]

By the turn of the fourteenth century, the amorous literature tradition in Italy had evolved. A number of Tuscan poets, often designated as the *dolce stil nuovo*, began describing passion as distinct from aristocratic birth.[20] The writers of the new style about love, such as Dante Alighieri, Lapo Gianni, Guido Cavalcanti (ca. 1250–1300), and Cino da Pistoia (1270–1337), were educated city dwellers, versed in the teachings of scholastic philosophy, with little in common with the noblemen of medieval courts. Generally speaking, the poets of the *dolce stil nuovo* came from wealthy backgrounds but not from the high aristocracy, and therefore they asserted that the lover's inner nobility was more important than the traditional notion of nobility derived from blood.[21] In so doing, they started the process of separating the discourses of love from those of social rank. There is much debate as to what the *dolce stil nuovo* was or even if it constituted an actual movement at all.[22] For instance, Marco Berisso argues that they were poets united primarily by historical developments, since all of them came of age in Tuscany in the aftermath of the Battle of Campaldino in 1289.[23] Still other critics see the poetry of the *dolce stil nuovo* as depicting the lover's desire for the lady in terms reminiscent of the soul's meditation on vice and virtue.[24] What is beyond debate is that the poets of the *dolce stil nuovo* exerted a marked influence on the poetry of central and northern Italy of the early decades of the trecento, inspiring a number of imitators.

Cecco Nuccoli: Overview

It is unclear why Nuccoli and Ceccoli composed poems about homoerotic love and sex, but they seemingly were expressing their personal passions, at least in part. Corroboration of their actual emotions is lacking, however, because almost no biographical information about them is extant. No documentation at all exists about Cecco Nuccoli (d. ca. 1350), so all that is known about him is derived from his poetic corpus, a collection of twenty-eight sonnets, some written in correspondence with other individuals.[25] In them, he complains about the pains of love for a man he calls "lord" (*signore*), possibly taking inspiration from Occitanic love poetry in which the poets sometimes referred to their beloved as "my lord" (*midons*):[26] "Ever since I lost my soul in your sweet face, / and I bound it up in your behaviors, / oh, my lord, guide and light of my life, / will I ever see you before I die?" (Nuccoli, sonnet 1.1–4). Elsewhere he begs for forgiveness from this man (sonnets 2 and 20), and later suggests that the "lord" lives in a cloister: "I'll have you know this, my dear lord, / that while I live, I will belong to you, / because you gave me such great comfort in the cloister / when your eyes turned toward me" (sonnet 25.1–4). Nor is this the only reminiscence of troubadouric verse in his lyric production. In other sonnets, Nuccoli decries the cruelty of a specific individual, Trebaldino Manfredino. Nuccoli spells out Trebaldino's name in an acrostic (sonnet 8), and he proclaims that he is in love with the letter *T*: "I am so strongly in love with 'T' / because it's the beginning of the lovely name" (sonnet 24.1–2). It is not clear if Trebaldino is the same person Nuccoli calls "my lord," or if they are different people altogether. Whatever the case, Nuccoli writes love poetry for men from the disempowered position of the courtly lover who begs for mercy from his beloved. With no discernable traces of ironic distancing, Nuccoli appropriates the tropes of *fin'amor* to express his adoration for other men. Through these sonnets, Nuccoli translates his sentiments toward other men into the recognizable style of troubadouric love poetry.

Complicating matters, in other sonnets Nuccoli depicts his passion using a distinctly comic style. He criticizes Trebaldino's mother, Rabeluccia (or "Luccia"), because she impedes the lover's advances on her son, portraying her as the stereotyped old woman of medieval misogynistic literature:[27] "Luccia, that slut, moves above / her son to cause me a new type of torture, / always telling me: 'I won't make room / for you to speak, thief, with the man who makes you burn'" (Nuccoli, sonnet 10.5–8). Significantly, he evokes the medieval ideology of the tavern as a locus of sex, gluttony, gambling, and sin, which is a commonplace of comic literature:[28] "You're in Perugia, with Ciamprolino and the dice / in the tavern with bursting purses" (sonnet 17.12–13). Furthermore, Nuccoli writes openly about sexual matters, in one sonnet implying the act of fellatio, a subject matter relatively uncommon in medieval culture:[29] "tell me where to come, and suck on my beak" (sonnet 11C.17). The use of the comic style to depict homoerotic yearning might appear incongruous, but Steven Botterill noted that for Nuccoli the comic and the autobiographical were joined together.[30] For Nuccoli, the personal subject matter and its stylized medium were not at odds, but rather he employed the comic style to give himself the room to discuss sexual attraction to fellow men.

Marino Ceccoli: Overview

The other poet to write extensively of same-sex attraction in Barberiniano Latin 4036 is Marino Ceccoli, who left a literary production of twenty-five sonnets, two epistles in Latin, and a *canzone*.[31] More is known about Ceccoli because the manuscript contains rubrics for his poetry, some of which provide insights to his life.[32] Moreover, decades after the compilation of Barberiniano Latin 4036, Ceccoli appears in a historical document. On 19 September 1366, the commune of Perugia sent him to Florence, accompanied by Tonio Falcucci, to sign an agreement against the employment of mercenary companies.[33] Three years later, on 2 January 1369, the Florentine humanist Coluccio Salutati (1331–1406) addressed an epistle to him requesting his assistance in acquiring the chancellorship of Perugia. Despite these later documents, precedence should be given neither to him nor to Nuccoli, because no evidence clarifies who influenced whom; Ceccoli is placed after Nuccoli in this book only because some documentation of Ceccoli's life is later than that for Nuccoli.

However, the homoerotic poetics of Nuccoli and Ceccoli show strong similarities to one another. Numerous textual resonances link the two poets, demonstrating a state of mutual influence. Like Nuccoli, Ceccoli repeatedly depicts the pains of love for a man he calls "lord" (*signore*): "Since you chase me off without pity, / at least tell me, lord, what road I should take, / for I don't know where I am nor where I should go, / and I'd willingly die in your arms" (Ceccoli, sonnet 6.1–4). His suffering knows no bounds: "My lord, I now remain so destroyed / that I can no longer endure your wounds" (sonnet 8.1–2). Like Nuccoli, he begs for mercy: "Oh, see now that I myself will come / and I'll throw myself prone at your feet / and I'll weep so much about my faults / until I pay remission for my crime" (sonnet 7.1–4). As Nuccoli does, Ceccoli at times echoes the commonplaces of Occitanic love literature.

In other sonnets (1, 2, and 3), Ceccoli decries the cruelty of "that man" (*tal*), but he does not specify if he refers to the same individual he elsewhere calls "lord." In so doing, Ceccoli may refer to other homoerotic poetry of Siena from earlier in the century questionably attributed to Cecco Angiolieri (ca. 1260–1312). Since the homoerotic poems have not been embraced as authentic by Angiolieri critics, the author of them is listed herein as pseudo-Cecco Angiolieri. In two sonnets, the pseudo-Angiolieri poet complains of a cruel man in a manner almost identical to Ceccoli in the 1330s (*cotale*). Ironically, one of the manuscript rubrics notes that Ceccoli composed a sonnet as a defense against the accusation of sodomy (see his sonnet 5A). Given the repeated references to same-sex attraction in his literary production, it is not clear what to make of his denial in this instance. Perhaps he simply wanted to avoid the judicial punishments, or merely the social shame, that the accusation of sodomy might bring. Or perhaps the statement is a bona fide refutation of the charge, and he did not, in fact, participate in the specific sodomitic activities as accused. Given the current state of information about Ceccoli, a consistent picture does not emerge in this regard.

Meo dei Tolomei: Overview

Nuccoli and Ceccoli developed their homoerotic poetics from the examples of writers from several decades earlier. One predecessor in particular stands out. Several facts are known about the life of the Sienese poet Meo dei Tolomei, referred to as "Meuccio" in the literary manuscripts (also spelled "Meuzzo" and "Meuçço"). He was a member of the powerful Tolomei family, the son of Simone Tolomei, nicknamed Sorella. In the archives, Meo's name first appears along with that of his brother, Mino, nicknamed Zeppa, in two documents dated 19 and 30 January 1279. At that time, Meo was acting as the representative for the Tolomei family, suggesting both that his father was already dead and that he had reached the age of maturity, but his brother had not; thus, the date of Meo's birth has been extrapolated to circa 1260. In 1280, three documents place Meo at the center of peace accords between the Sienese Guelphs, the party in support of the papacy for political supremacy, and the Ghibellines, who rejected the popes' claim in favor of the Holy Roman emperors: (1) ratification of the peace accord on 13 October and (2) on 17 October; (3) oaths taken by three powerful families, the Tolomei, the Salvani, and the Guinigi, to uphold the peace agreement, on 31 October. The next documentation for Meo is on 7 May 1285, when he married Mita di Bindino, a member of the Salvani family, in an apparent overture to solidify the peace between the rival clans of the Salvani and the Tolomei. Throughout the 1290s, Meo's brother, Mino Zeppa, also became active in the politics of Siena, eventually eclipsing the poet in wealth and status. On 19 March 1295, Meo sold a vineyard to his brother suggesting the poet's economic decline relative to Mino; by 1299, Mino Zeppa was appointed *podestà* of San Gimignano. Decades later, Giovanni Boccaccio made Mino Zeppa the protagonist in tale 8.8 of the *Decameron* (ca. 1351).[34] In it, Mino Zeppa discovers that his close friend, Spinelloccio, has been having an affair with his wife; in retribution, Mino Zeppa locks Spinelloccio in a chest upon which he has sex with Spinelloccio's wife.[35] The final documentation of Meo dei Tolomei's life is dated 3 June 1310, when he hired an attorney to defend him against some accusations, now unknown.[36] No information exists about the exact date of Meo's death.

Meo left a poetic corpus of eighteen sonnets and one *caribetto*, a multistrophic poetic form with an irregular structure. In addition, he may be the author of another four sonnets of debated attribution. As a poet, Meo dei Tolomei was highly engaged with the literary movements of his age. One of his sonnets is the reaction to a poem by Guido Cavalcanti (poems 23A and 23B in Tolomei's corpus). He may have been the recipient of two occasional poems addressed to "Meuccio," one by Dante Alighieri and the other by Cino da Pistoia (poems 24 and 25 in Tolomei's corpus). In other words, Tolomei possibly interacted with some of the great writers of the times, including the author of the *Divine Comedy*. Meo excelled in the comic style, mastering the technique of *vituperium*, the second- and third-person insult and invective against other individuals.[37] There are three principal targets of his harangues: his brother, Mino Zeppa, a coward who works to defraud Meo of his inheritance; his mother, who acts in concert with Mino Zeppa and wants to kill Meo; and ex-lover Ciampolino. It is the poems about the last individual that seemingly influenced the Perugians to write about same-sex attraction in the 1330s.

Before proceeding, we must examine closely the term "Ciampolino," because it is under some debate. The editors of the poets I cite in this book are not in consensus, with Meo dei Tolomei's "Ciampolino" treated as a name, but Nuccoli's "ciamprolino" considered a noun.[38] The *Grande Dizionario della Lingua Italiana* defines "ciampolino" both as a type of pear and as a diminutive of the name "Giampaolo" (i.e., Little Gian Paolo or Little Jean-Paul).[39] The latter will be somewhat familiar to readers of canto 22 of Dante's *Inferno*, which alludes to Ciampolo of Navarre (vv. 48–54). Furthermore, it is clear that Meo dei Tolomei consistently intends Ciampolino to be a person;[40] so too does Cecco Angiolieri in the sonnet "I could so live without love" (see sonnet 26 in my chapter 1, on Meo dei Tolomei), where he portrays him as a gambler. Hence, it is probable that, whatever else was intended, for the poets of Siena, Ciampolino was a proper name.

Conversely, the editor of Nuccoli, Franco Mancini, glosses "ciamprolino" as a euphemistic term from the penis, perhaps derived from *ciampa*, that is, a paw, or more generally, a leg (*zampa*). *Tesoro della lingua Italiana delle Origini* (*TLIO*) similarly defines "ciampolino" as a slang term for the penis, citing only one source for that definition, specifically "ciamprolino" from Nuccoli's sonnet 17, which I cited above.[41] Because of its singular citation, it appears that *TLIO* arrived at its definition via Mancini's gloss. An informal meaning for "ciamprolino" such as this is not out of the question, but it also is not corroborated by other texts. Neither "ciampolino" nor "ciamprolino" appear as any form of sexual terminology in Valter Boggione and Giovanni Casalegno's *Dizionario storico del lessico Italiano*, Giovanni Casalegno's *Brutti, fessi e cattivi*, nor in the listing for "ciampolino" in *Grande Dizionario della Lingua Italiana* (there is no listing for "ciamprolino").[42] For the purposes of my translations in this book, therefore, both "Ciampolino" and "Ciamprolino" will be treated as proper names. In saying this, I do not intend to imply that the poets intended the very same person, nor even that there was not also a slang usage to the name.[43] In fourteenth-century Italy, "Ciampolino" might well have connoted the penis; one need only think of the modern-day "Dick" or the British usage of "John Thomas" to see how a term can be at once a proper name and a slang euphemism. Given the poets' consistent depictions of Ciampolino/Ciamprolino as sexually attractive men, this is exactly what I think they are doing. Furthermore, in my opinion, the other similarities in their respective poems containing Ciampolino/Ciamprolino only underscore the direct influence of Meo dei Tolomei upon Nuccoli.

Of the sonnets in Meo dei Tolomei's Ciampolino cycle, one poem provides the clearest statement about the former relationship between the two men. He writes: "I cut my heart off from you, Ciampolino. . . . Be assured that I'd know how to eat partridges, /and gamble, and desire the masculine / just like you do" (Tolomei, poem 13.1, 7–9). The *Grande Dizionario della Lingua Italiana* cites Meo dei Tolomei's poem to assert that the phrase "to desire the masculine" (*voler lo mascolino*) (v. 8) was an expression that connoted male same-sex activity in the late Middle Ages and Renaissance.[44] In that passage, Meo indicates that his defunct relationship with Ciampolino was undoubtedly sexual in nature. In another sonnet, Meo is less explicit, but he still proclaims that he believed the two men were united in love: "I made myself into a Ciampolino / believing that I was loved by him; / and we were, though two, one for my part, / and in his mind, 'Piero,' 'Giovanni,' and 'Martino'" (Tolomei, poem 17.1–4). He reiterates Ciampolino's faithlessness, associating with his other enemies, his brother and mother: "My mother tricked me, and Ciampolino / didn't keep hold of his belt" (Tolomei, poem 16.1–2). As does Nuccoli, Meo dei Tolomei appears to combine autobiographical statements with the typical comic style. At the same time, Meo adds an additional facet to his self-presentation. Throughout the five sonnets, Meo consistently portrays his love relationship with Ciampolino as over, and an observation by Alistair Minnis may help make sense of that fact. In discussing *auctoritas*, the clout and prestige of culturally influential individuals, Minnis determined that "an *auctor* may not be *in* love; he has to be *out* of love to be utterly acceptable."[45] Minnis's observation may be applicable to Meo and other similar poets of same-sex desire. To say that the relationship has ended may have provided sufficient distance from the material, giving Meo plausible deniability if someone should protest about his sexuality.

Tolomei's portrait of Ciampolino does not univocally focus on their sexual relationship. In several instances, he describes Ciampolino as impoverished as a result of gambling (e.g., Tolomei, poem 13.8). At one point he writes: "now go, and trust a man who has gambled!" (poem 17.14). In so doing, Meo evokes the medieval ideology of the tavern in this poetic corpus. As a concept, the tavern was the locus of all that was negative in the world, a type of symbolic anti-church where one drank, diced, caroused with prostitutes, and awoke the next morning atop a dunghill, robbed and stripped bare.[46] It was viewed as "the devil's church," and in Italy the term "tavern-keep" was often associated with that of "pimp."[47] According to Martha Bayless, across numerous texts in the Middle Ages the tavern was the standard literary convention for the depiction of irreligious practices and for comic impiety.[48] In fact, in colloquial Italian at the time, the word "ribald" denoted a man who had been stripped down to his undergarments while gambling; it indicated someone for whom gambling and prostitution were linked.[49] Certainly, the notion of a ribald stands behind Meo's portrait of Ciampolino, however imperfectly. Ciampolino is unwisely squandering his money—and robbing from Meo—by engaging in foolish practices at the tavern. In short, Meo was central to the tradition of comic poetry in the medieval vernacular.

The Antecedent, Cecco Angiolieri

Despite his centrality, in the modern age Meo dei Tolomei was not seen as a distinct writer but was conflated with Cecco Angiolieri for decades. Meo's poetry appears in three extant literary codices: (1) Chigiano L.VIII.305 and (2) Barberiniano Latin 3953, both in the Biblioteca Apostolica Vaticana in Rome, and (3) Escorialense e.III.23 at the Real Biblioteca de El Escorial in Madrid. Each of these manuscripts is essential for both medieval comic poetry and for the poetry of the *dolce stil nuovo*.[50] Furthermore, one poem ascribed to Meuzzo Tolomei de Siena also appears in Barberiniano Latin 3953.[51] The majority of Meo's work, twenty sonnets, is found in Chigiano L.VIII.305, in several large sections of Sienese poetry, which were probably transcribed from a lost source.[52] Chigiano L.VIII.305 was compiled around the middle of the 1300s (ca. 1340), but the missing Sienese source was likely from decades earlier.[53] Chigiano L.VIII.305 is important, but it is problematic because all the poems in the Sienese sections of the codex, including Meo's, are anonymous. Meo's verse is scattered among the verse of other poets therein, particularly that of Angiolieri, for whom the manuscript is also the primary source. Starting in 1880, the editors who published Angiolieri's corpus assumed that all the anonymous poetry in the Chigiano manuscript was his, and therefore they wrongly attributed Meo's sonnets to him.[54] For years afterward, Meo's insulting poems were mistakenly absorbed into Angiolieri's poetic production. Chigiano presents the largest number of these Sienese poems, but it required other manuscripts to determine the proper attribution.

In 1915, the Escorialense e.III.23 manuscript came to the attention of Italian scholars, and alongside sonnets by Angiolieri it contains five poems attributed to "Meuçço di Tallomei da Siena," and one to "Meo de scemone fratel de messer Min Çeppa."[55] The clear attributions in Escorialense e.III.23 indicated that the insulting poetry about Mino Zeppa, Ciampolino, and "mother," heretofore ascribed to Angiolieri, actually belonged to another poet entirely, Meo dei Tolomei. In 1934, Adele Todaro published a study of Escorialense e.III.23, and for the first time Meo's verse was separated from Angiolieri's; two years later, Todaro published an analysis of Meo's *caribetto*, found only in Escorialense e.III.23, thereby fully establishing Meo's poetic corpus as we currently know it. Thus, it was only in 1936 that Meo dei Tolomei came into the light as a poet in his own right.

The twentieth-century editorial mixing of Meo's poetry with Angiolieri's is ironic, because as a poet Meo was indebted to Angiolieri, who left a corpus of more than 100 sonnets, predominantly in the comic style. The majority of Angiolieri's verse satirizes the love tradition, but he also complained about his poverty, and he wrote a series of sonnets denigrating other individuals, most notably his father, Angioliero; he also engaged in several insulting correspondences, including three sonnets addressed to Dante Alighieri. Angiolieri left an indelible mark on Meo's poetry. Meo rewrote one of Angiolieri's sonnets, "I'm so thin that I'm almost transparent," retaining the first two verses, but altering the following twelve lines (poems 1A, 1B, and 1C in Tolomei's corpus; two extant versions of Angiolieri's poem are also translated herein).[56] The similarities between the poetics of Angiolieri and that of Meo go far beyond one particular sonnet, however. Mario Marti notes that the technique of vituperation frequently challenges the tightest familial bonds, and Marti's observation can be applied to the writings of both Sienese authors.[57] Angiolieri pillories his own father, while Meo repeatedly reviles both his mother and his brother.[58] Marti employs the analogy of a competition when comparing the antimaternal poetry of Meo to the antipaternal verse of Angiolieri; the two poets, Marti writes, attempted to outdo one another with increasingly outrageous statements and curses.[59] Meo also composes several poems as comic dialogues (Tolomei, sonnets 7 and 18), a technique developed extensively by Angiolieri.[60] Yet the literary influence was not one-sided: Angiolieri also included Meo's enemy, Ciampolino, in a list of degenerates in "I could so live without love" (sonnet 26 in Tolomei's corpus). Thus, Meo was not a mere imitator of Angiolieri, but the latter exerted some influence over Meo. Indeed, Meo needs to be seen as a companion to Angiolieri in the comic poetry of medieval Siena.

To some degree, all the poets I cite in this book operated in the shadow of Angiolieri.[61] In a sonnet critical of his father, "There are three things that give me delight," Angiolieri lists his pleasures as "woman, the tavern and a game of dice" (v. 3).[62] In an anti-Ciampolino sonnet, cited above, Meo mimics that verse, asserting that he will enjoy the pleasures of fine foods, gambling, and "the masculine" (Tolomei, sonnet 13.7–9). Decades later, Nuccoli addressed a sonnet to an unknown recipient, enumerating the delights of

Perugia: "You're in Perugia, with Ciamprolino and the dice / in the tavern with bursting purses" (Nuccoli, sonnet 17.12–13). Through these verses an undeniable chain of influence runs from Angiolieri through Meo to Nuccoli, and this is not the only trait of Angiolieri's poetics in Nuccoli's lyric production. In another sonnet, Nuccoli complains of someone who has offended Monna Raggia, saying he would scratch the villain with both hands (sonnet 7A.4), a statement that echoes Angiolieri: "I'd scratch her up and down with my ten fingers."[63] Additionally, Nuccoli depicts his lover's rude statement, "Go and may you be killed!" (Nuccoli, sonnet 16.16), again taken directly from Angiolieri's poetry: "Go and get yourself impaled!"[64] Beyond the citation of specific passages, however, Angiolieri served as an example of the artistry involved in comic literature. He famously developed a poetic persona, building upon personal factors to develop a fusion of autobiographism and comicality.[65] He set an example, therefore, that the other poets would build upon to discuss their sexual attraction to other men. The lessons they learned from Angiolieri's poetic persona go beyond homoeroticism—Meo, Nuccoli, and Ceccoli all combine various autobiographical elements with the comic style.

Pseudo-Cecco Angiolieri

Because Cecco Angiolieri's poetry has been available to English readers for decades, his complete corpus does not appear in this book. However, four sonnets of dubious attribution that discuss the poet's love for another man are relevant to the topic at hand and therefore they have been included. In two of the sonnets, the pseudo-Cecco Angiolieri poet complains about a former lover from Corzano named Corzo (or Corso). The Corzo poems show strong similarities to Meo dei Tolomei's complaints about Ciampolino. In the other two poems of questionable attribution to Angiolieri, the poet writes about a painful passion about a man (*tal*), and elements therein, such as references to medieval medicine, resemble Meo dei Tolomei's poetic corpus. As with Nuccoli and Ceccoli, however, it is not possible to determine if the pseudo-Angiolieri poet influenced Tolomei, or vice versa. In addition, other textual resonances link pseudo-Angiolieri to the writings of the Perugian poets; for instance, in a *tenzone* (poetic correspondence) with Cecco Nuccoli, Cucco di Gualfreduccio Baglioni recalls the *incipit* verse of one of the sonnets (sonnet 13A of Nuccoli's corpus). Hence, despite being found in the appendix to Cecco Angiolieri's edition, the four sonnets exerted a degree of influence over the poetry of the early trecento.

The Sienese Influence on the Perugian Poets

Interestingly, the four pseudo-Angiolieri sonnets appear solely in the section of the Chigiano L.VIII.305 manuscript transcribed from the lost Sienese source. Indeed, as I show in footnotes throughout this book, all of the poems by Meo dei Tolomei and Cecco Angiolieri—authentic and of questionable attribution—that are directly quoted by Cecco Nuccoli and Marino Ceccoli can be found in the folios of the Chigiano L.VIII.305 manuscript, and the majority of them only appear there (*unici*).[66] In other words, the extant evidence strongly indicates that the Perugians had access to the Sienese source for Chigiano L.VIII.305 in some guise. This is not to suggest that the Sienese source consisted of a single codex that ambled about Italy, first to Perugia and then eventually to the scribes responsible for Chigiano L.VIII.305. Rather, it is more likely that multiple copies of it were made, and one of them was brought to Perugia; alternatively, a Perugian might have traveled to Siena and been exposed to it there. However it happened, awareness of its poetry was probably brought ninety kilometers east from Siena, one of the centers of Italian literature with a strong tradition in comic poetry, to Perugia on the distant shore of Lake Trasimeno. There it inspired the notaries Nuccoli and Ceccoli, who wrote of their real-world attractions to men using the comic style. Because there is good reason to believe that Nuccoli and Ceccoli knew the Sienese source in some fashion, it is used as the organizing principle of this book, which tells the story of how one source for the manuscript Chigiano L.VIII.305 probably influenced the writings found in another manuscript, Barberiniano Latin 4036.

Specifically, this book represents a probable chain of influence between the four poets whose lyrics have never appeared in English (except where noted). It traces the development of the homoerotic motif in Italian medieval poetry, beginning with the two Sienese writers in the Chigiano L.VIII.305 manuscript, Meo dei Tolomei and pseudo-Angiolieri. It then concludes with the two Perugian poets whose poetry from the 1330s was collected in the Barberiniano Latin 4036 manuscript, Nuccoli and Ceccoli. Because the poets presented here have never been translated in their entirety, I have rendered their complete literary productions into English. In the case of Meo dei Tolomei, his vituperations of Ciampolino sit alongside those against his mother and brother, and his entire lyric production forms a seamless whole. For the Perugian poets, the homoerotic lyrics are but one facet of their broader literary aims. In addition, I have translated the manuscript rubrics of Vatican Barberiniano Latin 4036, and they are of particular importance for Ceccoli. Moreover, I have incorporated Ceccoli's correspondence, including the epistle from Coluccio Salutati. By presenting all the available documents, the fullest picture of these fascinating writers can emerge.

Sodomy in the Italian Middle Ages

Male–Male Sexuality

Same-sex desire, when it was acknowledged in the Middle Ages, was configured in a manner different from that of the modern world; to make sense of the poetry, a clearer understanding is required of the medieval concept of sodomy, as it was termed. Historians of sexuality stress that it is important to avoid the anachronistic term "homosexual" (for that matter, "heterosexual" should be avoided too);[67] in the Middle Ages, sodomy consisted of a series of prohibited acts that anyone could commit. Scholarship has grappled with the question of what to make of people whose primary orientations were to their own sex. Some have taken an essentialist position, stressing the continuities between medieval sodomy and modern-day homosexuality; others proposed a constructivist approach, asserting that the cultural matrices of the different historical periods resulted in differing sexualities.[68] Amy H. Hollywood describes the extremes of the two approaches as either "mimetic identification [of the present] with the past" or "radical alterity."[69] The consensus is now emerging that the extremes of both opinions should be avoided. Robert Mills says that medieval sodomy and modern-day homosexuality cannot be strictly identified with one another, nor should they be considered as fully distinct from one another.[70] Complicating both attitudes are literary texts that present historical sexualities in manners at once both familiar and alien to twentieth-century readership, thus bridging both positions.⁷¹ The poems by Meo dei Tolomei, pseudo-Angiolieri, Nuccoli, and Ceccoli are further examples of such literature. What follows, then, is an overview of the understanding of male–male sexuality as conceptualized during the fourteenth century.

The Preceding Literary Tradition

To begin, none of this discussion is intended to suggest that the four writers discussed here were the only people—or even the first people—to treat same-sex desire among men in Italy during the Middle Ages.⁷² On the contrary, for centuries throughout Europe there was a large body of erotic literature in Latin written by and about men.⁷³ It may be that the Latin tradition was itself related to the twelfth-century Arabic genre of *mujūn*, licentious love poetry that, according to Jerónimo Méndez, subsequently influenced troubadouric poetry and the French fabliaux;⁷⁴ *mujūn* treated comic topics such as drunkenness and sexuality, including homoeroticism. Broadly speaking, thirteenth-century Italian literature about homoeroticism followed two basic approaches, expressing either hostility or positivity.⁷⁵ Both approaches are found in the poetry of medieval Italy. Some writers treated the topic of sodomy as an accusation, in accordance with the many teachings against sodomy, from sermons to philosophical writings, which were prevalent throughout Europe.⁷⁶ The stigma attached to sodomy may explain why Ceccoli denied the accusation. Insulting poetry exemplifies the tendency for the popular culture to transform juridical labels into insults.⁷⁷ The legal and theological term "sodomite" became so widespread that it passed into verbal insult and by extension to the literary vituperation typical of comic and satiric literature.

The Florentine poet Lupo degli Uberti insulted Guido Cavalcanti, illustrating the hostile approach to homoeroticism. Biographical facts about Lupo are unavailable, but he may have been a member of the Uberti, a powerful Florentine Ghibelline family. If so, he was an in-law to the object of his derision, Guido Cavalcanti, who had married the daughter of Farinata degli Uberti, whom Dante condemned to hell in canto 10 of the *Inferno*. Lupo replied to one of Cavalcanti's poems, "Within a copse I found a shepherdess," where he described himself falling in love with a young shepherdess.⁷⁸ Cavalcanti's poem constitutes his own version of the *pastourelle* genre, indicating that, though he was innovating upon the love tradition, he was still influenced by Provençal models.⁷⁹ In his response, Lupo asks Guido to correct the poem's inaccuracy: "Guido, I wish, when you wrote 'shepherdess,' / that you had said 'a strapping lad,'" (vv. 1–2). He then describes the young shepherd equivocally: "What a beautiful shepherd's staff he had" (Tuttor verghett'avea piacente e bella) (v. 5).⁸⁰ In the original language, Lupo uses the Italianized form *verga* of the Latin term *virga* for the shepherd's staff, a common euphemism at the time for the penis.⁸¹ He adds that the young man was blond and wore a short tunic (vv. 12–13). Hence, Lupo's comments on Guido's poem appear to be the pretense to deride Cavalcanti for his attraction to men, whether real or imaginary.

Furthermore, the Florentine poet Rustico Filippi (ca. 1230–ca. 1299) and the Sienese Iacomo de' Tolomei, nicknamed il Graffione (d. ca. 1290), both comic predecessors to Meo dei Tolomei, inveighed against the Sienese poet Niccola Muscia because of his purported sexual practices with men. Very little is known about Muscia, author of three sonnets, except that he lived in the last decades of the duecento.⁸² In his sonnet, Rustico Filippi draws a caricature of Muscia, who goes about proclaiming his sexual prowess to women; however, when he gets them alone, they are sorely disappointed, needing to masturbate him to keep him erect: "and then, when they arrive at that point, / they will grab it with both of their hands, / for to shake it well is such a delight!" (vv. 11–14). Similarly, the Sienese poet Iacomo de' Tolomei identifies several individuals for vituperation, including Muscia: "Muscia's a witch, a she-cat in human form, / who goes by night an suckles on people" (vv. 10–11). Iacomo portrays Muscia as if a succubus who wanders at night sucking men dry.⁸³ Here too, Iacomo may allude to fellatio. As with Lupo degli Uberti, Rustico Filippi and Iacomo de' Tolomei typify the hostile approach to discussing male same-sex attraction. Unlike Guido Cavalcanti, whose actual sexual practices can only be conjectured, Muscia expresses actual affection for another man, Lano. Hence, he may corroborate the accusations of sodomy leveled against him by Rustico Filippi and Iacomo de' Tolomei.

Muscia is important in this discussion because he also provides two examples of the counterpoised positive attitude toward sodomy in his verse. In one sonnet, "Two hundred saucers filled with diamonds," which he modeled on the Provençal genre of the *plazer*, Muscia enumerates the courtly gifts he would bestow on Lano.[84] In his second sonnet, "Red dates at the close of Lenten time," Muscia reiterates his intention to endow Lano with fabulous gifts, this time with items that cannot exist naturally, ripe plums in February and fresh almonds in January. He proclaims that he loves Lano more than any person loves life, and that they belong to one another (vv. 5–6). He then makes a startling assertion: "And I'm drawn to him like a magnet / draws iron, which is most natural" (vv. 8–9). In contrast to his imaginary gifts, his desires for Lano follow the laws of nature. By stressing its naturalness, he argues against the prevalent definition of sodomy as a crime against nature.[85] Thus, unlike the other writers who hurled "sodomite" as an insult, Muscia composed a first-person declaration of affection for another man. Interestingly, Muscia's poems are transcribed anonymously in the Sienese section of the Chigiano L.VIII.305 manuscript, and, like Meo dei Tolomei's sonnets, were also mistakenly attributed to Angiolieri at the end of the nineteenth century. It may be that he influenced the poets treated in this book, but if so they make no plausible textual references to him in their lyrics. In short, it is possible that the similarities in their subject matters are coincidental.

Theologians and Lawmakers

The hostile approach seen in the poetry of Lupo degli Uberti, Rustico Filippi and Iacomo de' Tolomei developed out of a centuries-long change in attitude toward sodomy. Until the eleventh century, same-sex practices were simply condemned as a subset of the sin of lust. Beginning with Peter Damian (1007–ca. 1073), theologians changed how they conceptualized sodomitic acts. Before Damian, sodomy had been at the center of disparate but overlapping discourses, which might have referred to anal intercourse between men, to any nonprocreative act, or merely those sex acts that should not be mentioned.[86] Damian defined sodomy instead as a crime against nature.[87] Dante, for instance, appropriates Damian's definition in his *Inferno*, situating the sodomites among those who commit violence against God or his offspring, Nature (*Inferno* 11.46–48). They spend eternity running beneath an infernal rain of fire in a sterile desert (*Inferno* 15 and 16). But Muscia pushed back against Damian's definition of sodomy as a crime against nature, which by the end of the duecento had become culturally predominant. Muscia is important for illustrating that the culture of the late Middle Ages was not monolithic in its condemnation of same-sex attraction.

In his thirty-first epistle, known as *Liber Gomorrhianus*, Peter Damian collapsed several sexual acts together under the heading of sodomy. He wrote about those men who "with their hands or with one another have practiced masturbation, or have sinned by ejecting semen within the thighs."[88] He then adds: "There are some who pollute themselves; there are others who befoul one another by mutually handling their genitals; others still fornicate between the thighs; and others who do so from the rear."[89] On the surface, what results from Damian's collection of sexual acts appears to be an "utterly confused category."[90] However, the singular through line of the sex acts he enumerates is the impossibility of procreation. For Damian, and subsequently for the culture of the following centuries, the defining characteristic of sodomy was any sex act with no reproductive potential.[91] By the fourteenth century, sodomy meant anal intercourse, oral sex, intercrural sex (i.e., between the thighs), and any other form of activity that resulted in ejaculation outside of the vagina; even solitary masturbation was a type of sodomy.[92] Any sex act opposed to begetting was illicit, irrespective of the partner.[93] As later elaborated by Thomas Aquinas (1225–74), all sexual behavior was supposed to be procreative; by definition, therefore, the wasting of semen in any way was contrary to nature.[94] As should be clear, all sex acts between men fell squarely within the definition of sodomy, but sex between men was only one subtype of it. During the thirteenth and fourteenth centuries, many people, perhaps most—and not merely those oriented to their own gender—engaged in sodomitic behaviors at some point.

Based on the change in conceptualizing sodomy, in the thirteenth and fourteenth centuries, legislation against sodomy prescribed increasingly harsh penalties for those found guilty.[95] Over the period of two centuries, sodomy went from being morally condemned to wholly criminalized across Western Europe.[96] The same was true in Italy. According to the 1310 statute of Siena, the sentence for sodomy was a fine of 300 lire, and if the convicted did not pay within a month, he would be suspended by his "virile member" in the Campo del Mercato. According to the 1325 statute in Florence, the punishments depended on the age of the offenders and the frequency of the offenses: a boy under the age of fourteen who voluntarily submitted to the act was to be beaten while driven naked through city, or fined 50 lire;

someone between the ages of fifteen and eighteen would need to pay the higher fine of 100 lire or suffer the same pains; and any adult convicted of the offense would be beaten by the bystanders while transported to prison, eventually to be burned at the stake.[97] The Florentine law also stipulated a 10 lire fine for composing or singing songs about sodomy.[98] The Perugian code of 1342 also provided different punishments: a fine of 200 lire for the first offense; 500 lire for the second, or burning at the stake if the fine was not paid; and burning at the stake for the third. Anyone proven guilty would also be publicly defamed "in word and deed": "E en tucte glie dicte case, cotale condannato sia infame d'enfamia de ragione e de facto e de ragione e de facto." Furthermore, clerics and those people not subject to the jurisdiction of Perugia would be fettered while the pope was consulted.[99] In the Italian communes of the trecento, legislation focused on a specific set of acts, and not on orientations or emotions.[100] Hence, Ceccoli's refutation of the accusation of sodomy, mentioned in the manuscript rubric, may not have been inaccurate. Irrespective of the sentiments he expressed in his poetry, it is possible that he never engaged in the sexual activities as charged.

Real-World Practices and Beliefs

It is important to treat any accusations of sodomy from the time with circumspection. As the concept of the sodomite developed, people came to treat it as an "Other." The accusation did not always reflect real-world sexual behaviors, but instead at times it became a type of generic "boogeyman."[101] As the decades passed, the negative connotations that accrued to the sodomite were then transferred to other classes of people in medieval society. R. I. Moore states that once the concept of an enemy of God became established, it could be applied to other common enemies.[102] Throughout the twelfth and thirteenth centuries, sodomy was frequently associated with Muslims, Jews, and heretics.[103] The poetic exchange between Cola di Messer Alessandri and Nuccoli (Nuccoli, sonnets 19A and 19B) illustrates the point fully. Cola di Messer Alessandri notes that the city of Spoleto has cast out its prostitutes, and, consequently, all its men have become sodomites: "to tell the truth, they've all become Patarines, / and habituated as unnatural sodomites" (19A.7–8). Cola capitalizes on the connection between the Patarine heresy and sodomy, erasing any distinction between the Spoletans' sexual practices and the heterodox creed. In his fragmentary response, Nuccoli replies in kind, saying that Spoleto has already been punished when it was laid low by Oddo degli Oddi, the captain of the Perugian forces during the war of 1322–24:[104] "If you recall well, the Spoletans / were well punished for their evil actions" (19B. 1–2). In their *tenzone*, Cola and Nuccoli treat "sodomite" and "heretic" almost as synonymous terms, assuming that the former activities necessarily presuppose the latter beliefs. If the Spoletans are sodomites, perforce they must also be heretics.

In addition, historians have questioned how frequently the severe judicial punishments for sodomy were enacted. The penalties appear to have been sporadic, particularly if there was no violation to the social order.[105] The repeated enactment of laws, with their harsh and symbolic penalties, instead speaks of a deep anxiety in the culture. Part of the anxiety may have stemmed from the prevalence of male same-sex practices in the community at large. Historian Michael Rocke examines the records of fifteenth-century Florence and demonstrates that the majority of men engaged in sexual activities with other men at some time in their lives; although Rocke's study focuses on a subsequent period, it begins in the fourteenth century and thus his findings can be applied to our poets under examination. Rocke notes that Florence was so strongly associated with sodomy that German slang reflected it, and in his sermons Bernardino of Siena (ca. 1425) called it a veritable custom of the city.[106] Rocke's study highlights that male–male sexual practices were not confined to an ostracized subset of the society but were commonplace among the entire male population of the medieval Italian communes.

Other historians have replicated Rocke's findings, applying them more broadly to medieval Italy. For centuries, male–male eroticism in the peninsula was centered on differences of age, with adult men having relations both with women and with adolescent males.[107] According to Randolph Trumbach, before 1700 many Italians presumed that normative sexuality consisted of masculinity desiring femininity, whether found in women or in the soft, hairless bodies of adolescent boys.[108] Trumbach describes a state of nearly universal (male) bisexuality in which most men had sex with other males, either with older men during adolescence or with adolescents during more mature ages. In other words, the societies in the Italian communes faced a type of cognitive dissonance wherein the ecclesiastical fulminations against sodomy contrasted with real-life sexual practices. Many men

xxxiv Introduction

had sexual contact with other men in private, but most of them did not challenge the antisodomitic discourse preached from the pulpits. Instead, they drafted the laws accordingly, but then engaged in a code of silence when it came to enforcement.

Cultural Anxiety

The legal strictures against sodomy, rather than clamping down on specific activities or emotions, were probably intended to reinforce the internal stability of the society.[109] Anna Clark writes that anxiety about social disorder tends to erupt during times of social crisis.[110] Some of the enforcement of the antisodomy laws varied according to who stood accused. After all, the cities allowed for the payment of fines, offering an alternative for those with the economic means to pay. Meo was a member of the powerful Tolomei family, for instance, and the Perugian poets were both notaries, that is, they were in reasonably comfortable positions; whatever their writings, they did not overtly challenge the structures of their communities. The emotions they described might have been out of conformity with the teachings of the dominant culture, but the roles they played in life were central to its power structures. In other words, the sentiments they expressed were marginal, even if the poets themselves may not have been.

Part of the cultural anxiety about sodomy at the time, moreover, stemmed from the belief that it caused people to transgress socially prescribed gender roles.[111] As long as the sexual conventions of the communes remained unchallenged, the laws against sodomy were primarily nominal. What drew the greatest scorn was not necessarily the notion of a man having sex with another male, but for a man to take the passive, "feminine" role while doing so, particularly with someone younger and thus less masculine than oneself.[112] It is in this regard that the comicality of some of the poetry may come to the fore. Lupo degli Uberti and Iacomo de' Tolomei constructed their vituperative sonnets around the accusations that Cavalcanti and Muscia were effeminate, for instance; an insulting poet would naturally hurl the most offensive accusation. Many of the first-person declarations seen in this book also do so, sometimes for comic effect. Nuccoli, Ceccoli, and pseudo-Angiolieri present themselves as traditional lovers, and a critique of amorous literature posited that love feminized a man.[113] Much as Cecco

Angiolieri weaved together biographical data and comic tropes to present an abject persona in his poetry, these writers too depicted themselves in thrall to other men. In short, our poets built upon the anxiety of gender nonconformity to create comicality in many of their sonnets.

One verse in particular deserves close attention in this regard. In a specific sonnet, Ceccoli decries the cruelty of love, saying that he will make a particular gesture for luck: "But I'll make a fig [*fica*] and say '*Castra!*'" (sonnet 17.9). To make the gesture of the fig one inserted the thumb between the index and middle fingers of the same hand. Yet the name of the gesture evokes the vagina (*fica*), giving the appearance in the poem that Ceccoli will transform his genitals into a vagina while exclaiming, "*Castra!*" (castrate!). In the economy of a single verse he seems to indicate that he will transition from one gender to the other. His gesture has an additional sexual connotation, and it was believed to have originated with Emperor Frederick I "Barbarossa" (1122–90); Frederick avenged himself on rebellious Milanese lords by requiring them to extract a fig from the anus of a mule with their mouths.[114] The gesture replicates the emperor's sexualized punishment of the traitors. Ceccoli's verse is deliberately ambiguous, appearing to imply that he will emasculate himself—literally—for the love of another man. Susan Signe Morrison describes the importance of gender fluidity to medieval comic literature: "The instability of bodily integrity fuels the comic mode."[115] Much of the sonnet is vituperative against love, situating it well within the comic style. Nonetheless, Ceccoli uses extremely subtle language to insinuate far more about himself and his same-sex attraction.

The passage from Ceccoli raises the question of how to interpret the same-sex material in the context of their comic styles. In the contemporary world, comic writing appears to undercut any authentic autobiographical content, and the modern presuppositions influenced critical interpretation. Citing the laws with their severe punishments, Mario Marti proposed that the poets were proclaiming their homoeroticism solely to satirize the literary love tradition in general, and the *dolce stil nuovo* in particular.[116] The historical information in Marti's time had not yet called into question the degree to which the punishments were enacted; furthermore, Marti simply could not accept as authentic the poets' assertions of attraction to other men.[117] Criticism on them has since changed over time and is now more accepting of their sexuality. Marco Berisso, for instance, offers the insightful interpretation of the poets as satirists publicly displaying their sexualities as a political strategy to underscore the incompetence of the upper aristocracy dominating Perugia.[118] Yet as this brief overview illustrates, no critical consensus has emerged about the fusion of personal sentiments and the traditional comic style by these poets.

Comic Homoeroticism

The more recent studies on medieval sodomy might provide a key for the interpretation of the comic homoerotic poetry of Meo dei Tolomei, Nuccoli, and Ceccoli. As should be clear, their poems challenge one of the powerful cultural prohibitions of the time, requiring them to discuss it in different manners. In other instances, the poets violated the linguistic taboos directly, using explicit language as part of their strategy. Meo, for example, insults his mother's sexuality, claiming that she has an ass "so hungry / that she has worn out all the pricks in the world" (Tolomei, poem 8.13–14). Of course, that she engaged in anal sex indicates that she, too, participated in sodomitical acts multiple times. Meo's poem contains one of the first attestations of the word "prick" (*cazzo*), transgressing the cultural proscription on obscenity.[119] Linguistically speaking, obscenities arise from body parts and physical activities that a culture deems inappropriate for public display.[120] Certainly that was true for the genitals in the late Middle Ages, and Meo certainly knew that fact when he composed his poem. When it came to the discussion of sex and other materials, Meo had no scruples against contravening a taboo. In other instances, however, the poets under examination approached their topics more circuitously.

Linguists have noted that people employ a large number of strategies when speaking about topics deemed "unmentionable," such as euphemism, register- and language-shift, and paraphrase.[121] Ridicule and humor can also be brought into play as a means to avoid verbal prohibitions.[122] William Leap studies queer linguistics in the twentieth century, exploring the language practices that people use to address a forbidden topic without explicitly breaching the norms.[123] Leap examines how people co-opt preexisting discourses to express what is socially forbidden: he considers "how language use creates moments of linguistic and sexual transgression as well as moments of linguistic and social compliance."[124] Leap's analysis provides a lens through which the homoerotic poets of the trecento can be understood. Angiolieri offered them the model of comical autobiographism, but his reasons for doing so were, strictly speaking, his own. Meo, Nuccoli, and Ceccoli may have appropriated Angiolieri's model of comic autobiographism to communicate something otherwise impermissible, namely, sexual attraction to other men. They presented themselves negatively—as willful sodomites—to be able to write about a taboo topic. The personas they constructed in their verse were exemplary of comic characters, irascible tavern-goers who flaunted their sexual appetites. Hence, we can see their poetry as conventional, using an established set of stylistic features from the troubadouric and comic traditions, and at the same time it is innovative, broaching an unconventional topic.

THE POETS' OTHER TOPICS

Meo dei Tolomei: Praise and Blame

It would be a mistake to interpret our poets here as exclusively homoerotic. On the contrary, their lyric productions deal with a number of topics beyond same-sex yearning, and it is necessary to take these topics into account. For example, nearly all of Meo's poetry consists of insult, and insulting literature had a long lineage in the Middle Ages. For centuries, medieval literary theorists had conceived of all literature as a subset of ethics, consisting of two diametrically opposed impulses: praising the virtuous (*laus*) or blaming the ignoble (*vituperium*).[125] The poetry of insult, like Meo's, fell squarely into the latter category, and it was viewed as serving the important social function of enforcing morality by exposing vice to public ridicule. It followed a specific set of rhetorical and stylistic rules, treating low material with low language. Since it was supposed to deride immorality, it needed to denote unacceptable behaviors, impulses, body parts, and corporeal excreta with direct language.[126] Such characteristics occur throughout Meo's poetry. He depicts the small-mindedness and treachery of his brother, Mino Zeppa, and alludes to their mother's whorishness in blunt language. To a great degree, therefore, his poetry exemplifies the teachings about *vituperium* in the late Middle Ages.

In his *Ars versificatoria* (ca. 1175), Matthew of Vendôme explained that the very descriptions of the characters themselves should communicate praise or blame to the reader. As one such example, Matthew offered the portrait of the old hag Beroë.[127] In it, he depicts her nauseating physical state, including her filth, parasites, foul odor, and bodily effluvia. For Matthew, the readers' disgust is the point, because it induces them to reject her and the immorality that she symbolizes. Matthew's depiction of Beroë constitutes one of the earliest examples of a subtype of the literary tradition, *vituperium in vetulam*, the insult and abuse of a stereotyped elderly woman. Afterward, the image of the horrible old woman became a cultural touchstone in both the Latin and vernacular literary traditions, appearing in texts as diverse as poems, prose narratives, sermons, and pamphlets.[128] She was an open symbol, able to personify whatever negative concept the writer wished to disdain.[129]

In a sonnet attributable to Meo, the poet engages with other Italian writers regarding *vituperium in vetulam*. The poem "Now look well, Ciampol, at this little old woman" is a reaction to the poet Guido Cavalcanti, who composed "Look, Manetto, at that little hunchback" (sonnets 23A and 23B in Tolomei's corpus).[130] In the first of the sonnets, Cavalcanti urges his addressee to reflect upon her ugliness, and his resulting laughter will cure him of his melancholy. In his poem, Meo encourages Ciampolo, perhaps the same man as his former lover Ciampolino, to meditate on the old woman's hideousness because that will drive out any feelings of love from his heart. The poet echoes the commonplace belief that a cure for lovesickness was for the lover to look upon—and perhaps have therapeutic intercourse with—an old woman, because her ugliness would counteract the man's fixation on the beauty of his beloved.[131] In this way, the sonnet stands as a corrective to the predominant form of poetry at the time, love literature.

Meo also crafts the insult of his mother in line with the *vituperium in vetulam* tradition. She does not treat her (presumably) first-born son as someone who will perpetuate the noble family's prestige, but as someone to be eliminated.[132] She is not a parent to be honored (Exodus 20:12), nor an elder in whom one can feel family pride, violating the ethos of medieval aristocracy. Similarly, Meo repeatedly accuses his brother of attempting to acquire his patrimony, impeding the proper descent of inheritance, a legal right central to the aristocracy.[133] Mino Zeppa is also a coward, who flees before enemies and sues for peace with people who have wronged him. In other words, Meo's insults gravitate toward the violations of the ethos of the nobility. Accusations of cowardice or of the failure to avenge a slight were affronts to a nobleman, such as a member of the Tolomei.[134] Hence, Meo's poetry reflected the society in which he lived. During the thirteenth and fourteenth centuries, the concept of the nobility was debated in the Italian communes, when changing economic and social realities challenged the traditional definition of aristocrats as possessing wealth and virtue.[135] From this perspective it can be seen that Meo treats his enemies, in part, as exemplary of the degeneracy of the nobility in his age.[136] Through the figures of his brother and mother, Meo's insulting poetry satirized the changes taking place in Italy at the start of the fourteenth century.

Meo dei Tolomei: Communal Culture

The culture of the communes has a prominent place in Meo's poetry. For example, he repeatedly introduces the episodes from the history of the Sienese city-state into his verse. In one poem (sonnet 12.12), he compares a dejected Zeppa to the frightened prisoners taken at the Radda castle, which Siena successfully besieged in 1230. Meo also refers to two significant historical personages in his corpus. In two sonnets (9 and 10), he mentions Capocchio, the famous alchemist and heretic whom Dante condemns to the *bolgia* of the falsifiers in *Inferno* (canto 29.124–39, and canto 30.1–30). Historical records indicate that Capocchio was burned at the stake in Siena for alchemy on 15 August 1293. In the first of the two sonnets, Meo depicts his brother trying to woo a woman with counterfeited coins that she identifies as Capocchio's (9.14); in the second, Mino Zeppa fears that he, too, will be executed like Capocchio (10.11). The latter poem also makes reference to Branca Doria, made famous by Dante, who places him in the ninth circle of hell among the traitors to guests (*Inferno* 30.134–47). Branca Doria, a Genoese politician, assassinated his son-in-law Michele Zanche during a feast in his home. In his sonnet, Meo again depicts his Mino Zeppa as fearful of being murdered like Michele Zanche (10.13). Thus, the historical references in Meo's poetry tie in with the masterpiece of the age, Dante's *Divine Comedy*.

Meo incorporates other aspects of fourteenth-century culture into his poetry, such as medicine and anatomy. Throughout his corpus he reflects the notion of the body as an enclosed system, consisting of four humors whose balance resulted in health.[137] For medieval thinkers, diseases had only three causes: the discontinuities of the body (i.e., wounds), the imbalance of the four humors, or the accumulation of harmful humors.[138] All three types of harm appear in Meo's poetry. His mother attempts to attack him, which would cause bodily discontinuity (Tolomei, poem 5); she recommends a diet that would exacerbate his melancholic disposition, bringing his humors out of balance (poem 4); and she tries to poison him (poem 3). In addition, in his poetic production he describes the properties of different plants and herbs, including fennel (10), and peaches and leeks (4). Medieval medicine was predominantly herbal,[139] representing a blend of erudite learning and folk traditions.[140] Not all treatments were strictly herbal, however, but also included metals, animal parts, human or animal milk, and urine or excrement.[141] Theriac, which figures in two of Meo's sonnets (4 and 12), was a compound of vipers' flesh and other ingredients, and it was used as an antidote to most poisons.[142] Theriac and other medicines are also listed in one of the pseudo-Angiolieri sonnets about Corzo (3.1–4), pointing to a connection to Meo's poetics. It is impossible to say with certainty the poet's background in medicine, but Meo's poetry indicates that he possessed some knowledge of the human body and its humors.

One sonnet in particular warrants closer scrutiny because of the insights it provides into the cultural understanding of illness and disability. Irina Metzler writes that because disability is a private matter, it frequently pertained to comic literature during the Middle Ages.[143] That is true in this sonnet, because it deals with vituperation, specifically of his mother. In "I was so fiercely sick the other day" (Tolomei, sonnet 3), Meo mentions that his ailment caused him to lose the power of speech (v. 2). Thus, at the outset of the poem he presents himself as temporarily disabled. Disability scholars have noted that, during the Middle Ages, there existed two predominant models of disability: a medical model, seeing the impairment as the absence of full health; and a religious model, with the impairment used as part of the narrative about a holy person who performs miracles.[144] Both models are at play in the poem. The poet subverts the medical model by portraying his mother's attempts to treat him with a potion—but it is really a poison (3.4–5). He then refuses to drink the concoction, communicating his intentions through gestures (3.7). By describing himself gesticulating, Meo may be alluding to real-world practices of the times, specifically to the finger alphabets that were developed by clerics to communicate with the ill.[145] Finger alphabets were also a form of sign language available to some members of the deaf community.[146] A more famous example of communicating through signs in medieval Italian literature occurs in the tale of Masetto di Lamporecchio in Boccaccio's *Decameron* 3.1; Masetto, feigning muteness, begs for food and offers to work at a convent through the use of gestures. As in that narrative, a fake miracle occurs at the end of Meo's sonnet 3, subverting the expectations of the religious model for disability. When his mother insists that he take a drink, he is able to break his silence and proclaim that he is in fact healthy (3.12). He provides no explanation as to why this occurs, again subverting the readers' expectations. Even though the sonnet is a comic insult of his mother, Meo imbues it with attitudes toward and beliefs about disability prevalent in his society.

We have already seen how Meo's verse contains elements from the oral culture of the age, but there are still others to discuss. In one poem (Tolomei, sonnet 6), the poet compares his brother's speed when retreating to that of Pier Fastello (v. 3). Sienese legend held that the founder of the Bandinelli family, Piero, nicknamed Fastello, participated in the First Crusade in 1096, but was reputed to have returned to Italy in a single night.[147] Furthermore, another lyric (Tolomei, sonnet 11) refers to several oral narratives. In that poem, he envisions how his brother would survive even the most violent attacks, first by claiming that were he decapitated he would still live on (11.1–2); in that statement the poet alludes to the game of "Uvil," which Roberto Wis argues is a linguistic variation on the name of Uliva, the saint. Uliva amputated her own hands rather than submit to her father's incestuous desires, but afterward the Virgin Mary miraculously restored them to her.[148] In a similar fashion, Mino's head would be reattached to his trunk. Meo then asserts that poison would not affect Mino at all, much as it did not bother Saint John the Baptist (11.7–8). Tolomei apparently conflates John the Baptist with John the Evangelist, who, according to Jacobus de Voragine, was able to drink poison safely when challenged to do so by the high priest at the temple of Diana.[149] Finally, he closes the sonnet by saying that if Mino were tossed into the ocean, he would become Nicholas the Fish (11.11–14). A man from Messina named Nicola Pesce or Colapesce (Nicholas the Fish) was cursed by his mother while swimming, causing him to be transformed into a fish; the legend of Nicholas the Fish is reported in several medieval sources, including the *Cronica* by Salimbene de Adam and the *Dittamondo* by Fazio degli Uberti.[150] Thus throughout his poetic corpus, Meo reflects the culture, history, and society of his times. He offers a window through which to view the living traditions of the Italian communes at the start of the fourteenth century.

Cecco Nuccoli: Literary Reminiscences

Of our poets, Nuccoli is probably the most focused on homoeroticism, but that is not to say that other topics do not appear in his verse. On the contrary, his poetry is immersed in the commonplaces of medieval comic literature. For example, he engages in a *tenzone* with Gilio Lelli, complaining about the loss of a colt while gambling (sonnets 3A and 3B of Nuccoli's corpus); thus he again evokes the comic ideology of the tavern. Several sonnets insult their recipients, illustrating Nuccoli's familiarity with the poetics of vituperation (e.g., Nuccoli, sonnets 18, 19A, and 19 B). He also complains about Trebaldino's mother, Rabeluccia, in terms reminiscent of the denigration of the old woman, *vituperium in vetulam* (sonnets 7A, 7B, and 10). We've already seen, furthermore, that Nuccoli—along with the others—was deeply influenced by Angiolieri's poetics. Moreover, Nuccoli crafts puns suggestive of sexual behaviors, often using metaphors about hawks and hawking: "when I go to the bird's roost to eat / I now leave my heavy arms at the door, / and with every hunt I slurp down / and swallow as does the wolf" (14A.10–13). In another sonnet, he describes Trebaldino as being bitten on the nose by a snake: "your Trebaldino / drank from that goblet, a snake struck him / on the nose and smeared him further. . . . / He went away touching his nose just so" (28A.2–4, 9). In this case, "nose" appears to be a metaphor for the Trebaldino's penis, a common euphemism at the time that also appears in the poetry of Meo dei Tolomei.[151] In these instances, Nuccoli follows the comic strategy of allusion, calling to mind illicit sexual activities without engaging in obscene speech by mentioning them outright.

In addition, Nuccoli also echoes the works of noncomic literature in his sonnets. For instance, he refers to classical literary sources when discussing the history of the Tiber River (sonnet 6.5). Importantly, he makes repeated reference to the courtly literary tradition of the Middle Ages. He mentions

King Arthur (sonnet 11A.8), and the knight Tristan (17.3). He also calls to mind one of Marie de France's *Lais* in which two lovers are compared to a chervil and a nut tree, two trees that die when separated (11A.9). His evocations of the chivalric past dovetail nicely with the more traditional, Occitanic expressions of affection that Nuccoli expresses for other men. He casts his homoerotic verse into the mold of the great courtly lovers of yore. According to Peter W. Sposato, the myths of chivalry exerted a strong influence on Italian culture of the late Middle Ages.[152] For example, throughout the thirteenth century, an increasing number of parents named their children not after Christian saints, but after the knights of the Round Table.[153] At times, Nuccoli positions himself as the heir to the chivalric culture of days long gone. Indeed, all of our poets do, to varying degrees.

Marino Ceccoli: Historical Resonances

Ceccoli shows strong similarities to Nuccoli, but his poetic corpus is more varied. He has more occasional sonnets than Nuccoli, and thus the topics he discusses range more widely. In one correspondence he consoles a man over the death of his wife (Ceccoli, sonnet 11), and there's another in which he comforts someone who failed to become a monk (sonnet 12). He also engages in a *tenzone* that addresses the theological question of free will (sonnets 22A, 22B, and 22C of Ceccoli's corpus). His lyric production contains a *tenzone* with the poet of the *dolce stil nuovo*, Cino da Pistoia (poems 10A and 10B of Ceccoli's corpus), who, it will be recalled, also addressed a sonnet to Meo dei Tolomei. In his sonnet, Cino portrays love as a powerful force that leads him to a sweet death (10A.5–11). Ceccoli replies by describing the destruction of the lover's mind through the metaphor of melting ice: "Just as melting ice drips out, / our mind dissolves when it contemplates fixedly / that accidental property / for which the soul produces / tears and laughter and other strange passions / that, for you, occurs beyond what is natural / and causes your reason to be submerged" (sonnet 10B.1–6). In his contribution to the exchange, Ceccoli displays his awareness of the amorous reasoning of the *dolce stil nuovo*, and he responds in kind. Elsewhere he expounds upon his own philosophizing about love, employing the vocabulary of scholasticism. He asks if love is a substance or an accident: "Something without potentiality seems to force / Nature if it should become a reality; /

otherwise, without matter, valor, and force / it shouldn't truly exist, lacking the efficient causes" (sonnet 20.5–8). He also composes a lengthy *canzone*, a multistanza poem, about the spiritual nature of loving (poem 25). Hence, he has absorbed the lessons of the other poets of the age, engaging in philosophical argumentation to explore the nature of love.

Ceccoli not only addresses immaterial questions but also, in several of his poems, focuses on life in Italy during the 1330s. He asks Ugolino da Fano about the woman who accompanied him to a festival (sonnets 23A and 23B of Ceccoli's corpus). In two sonnets, Ceccoli writes to a man named Tiberuccio, punning on his name by mentioning the Tiber River. In the first sonnet, he invites Tiberuccio to leave the Tiber valley, where he currently resides, and join the poet in Perugia proper (Ceccoli, sonnet 18). In the second, he offers Tiberuccio suggestions as to how to drive away the swarms of mosquitoes that infest the Tiber valley (sonnet 19); he can burn *canuta* plants or bring in the mosquitoes' natural predators, ant lions. In his sonnets, and in "If every single seed produced a bushel" (sonnet 4), Ceccoli expresses the superiority of city life (*urbanitas*) over life in the countryside (*rusticitas*), a commonplace contrast in the culture of the age.[154] In other words, Ceccoli repeatedly recalls the folk traditions, everyday practices, and prevalent opinions of the times.

Ceccoli also treats weightier topics in his poetry. In the first days of November 1333, heavy rains caused the Arno River to flood, damaging the cities along its course, including Perugia, Arezzo, Pistoia, and Prato. Worst hit was Florence, where the river burst its dikes and destroyed bridges and piers, killing more than 300 people.[155] Afterward, several writers described the disaster, including the chronicler Giovanni Villani and the poets Antonio Pucci and Adriano de' Rossi;[156] a scholarly debate also ensued about whether the flood was caused by natural causes or, rather, it was God's punishment.[157] Ceccoli also writes about the calamity (sonnet 16), seemingly participating in the cultural debate about its cause. Like other thinkers, he seemingly crafts a nuanced explanation that bridges the two positions, namely, that God employed natural causes to bring about the flood. Therefore, through several of his poems, Ceccoli offers a glimpse into everyday life in the Italian communes of the fourteenth century.

Closer to home, Marino composed three sonnets about the strife between Perugia and the lord of Arezzo, Pier Saccone Tarlati di Pietramala

(1261–1356).¹⁵⁸ On 8 June 1335, Perugia invaded Arezzo, but its army retreated to Cortona, after which the Aretine forces ravaged the Perugian countryside for three days. Later in the summer, however, Perugia retaliated, raiding Arezzo and doing great damage in turn. By September, Perugia took Città del Castello, a land traditionally possessed by the Pietramala family, led by the mercenary Neri della Faggiuola (1290–1355). By the end of October, Perugian forces were encamped outside the cathedral in Arezzo. The following February, the hostilities recommenced, Florence now aligned with Perugia, but by July 1336, Florence negotiated a separate peace with Arezzo, an act considered a betrayal by the Perugians. Ceccoli refers to these events in several sonnets. In a *tenzone* with Nuccoli and Gilio Lelli (sonnets 21A, 21 B, and 21C of Ceccoli's corpus), Ceccoli refers to the family crest of the Tarlati, gold nuggets on a field of blue, as crumbling, suggesting that they are falling from power. Nuccoli responds saying, on the contrary, that they might regain their position; it should be mentioned that Nuccoli also writes about the Tarlati crest in another sonnet in his corpus (sonnet 26). In a second *tenzone*, Ceccoli discusses the situation with someone named Ceccolo (sonnets 24A and 24B of Ceccoli's corpus), and in it he condemns Arezzo for its treachery. Ceccolo replies more optimistically, saying that Perugia will eventually be victorious. The political poems offer an insider's point of view on the war between Perugia and its neighbors as it unfolded. As a notary, Ceccoli was in a good position to form an opinion about the situations facing his commune during the 1330s.

The Poets' Position in Italian Literary History

The Fourteenth Century

All of our poets stayed informed of the literary movements of Italy. Meo dei Tolomei was fully engaged in the developments of Tuscan poetry; he and Angiolieri mutually influenced one another as writers, and both Dante and Cino da Pistoia corresponded with Meo during his lifetime. Decades later, Ceccoli exchanged sonnets with Cino da Pistoia, and some of Ceccoli's poems display the influence of the *dolce stil nuovo*. Later still, in 1369, the Florentine humanist Coluccio Salutati addressed Ceccoli as a man of eloquence, praising his direct style in Latin. Clearly, our poets drew inspiration from, and caught the eyes of, the great authors of their age.

Nuccoli, furthermore, exerted some influence on Italian literature after his death. His "Going down New Street and Wide Street" (sonnet 21) is a model of equivocal language, a common strategy when broaching taboo topics.[159] Ceccoli depicts a mock journey, wending circuitously from Paris through Ethiopia and then to Spain. He concludes his travels with a man named Lelli, probably the poet Gilio Lelli: "Going further down, I met Lelli in arms, / and I kissed the marble of the Holy Altar" (21.15–16). The double entendre of the final verses gives the impression that the mock journey was little more than a veiled depiction of a sexual encounter. Olle Ferm writes that linguistic incongruity is a staple of medieval comedies because it upends the representation of the world.[160] "Going down New Street and Wide Street" is probably the most notable example of ambiguous language in Nuccoli's lyric production, but it is not the only one. In fact, all of our poets employ similar linguistic strategies, to a greater or lesser degree, and they were not the last to do so. Other poets of the late trecento and early quattrocento used similarly subtle language.

The Fifteenth Century

At the turn of the fifteenth century, for example, Stefano Finiguerri, nicknamed il Za (d. ca. 1412), satirized the Florentine humanists as sodomites in such a manner.[161] In one of his poems, "La Buca di Montemorello," il Za describes the journey of its narrator to a cave in the side of one of the Florentine mountains, where he names the men who gather there: "I saw there the sodomite Corso Cei— / he who spent almost all his money— / and Minchia Amier, who always cries out, 'Alas!'" (1.262–64).[162] In another poem, "Il Gagno," il Za has a vision of being on an island where he sees a ship staffed with Florentine men; among the men on the ship, he claims to see one Giuliano Ciampelli (1.58), whom he later describes as Ciampellino: "Now you see someone who's pummeled—and I'm glad— / by Ciampellino because he doesn't know how to row: / his name is Bussotto and he gave me faint praise" (1.79–81).[163] Certainly, il Za's use of the name Ciampellino reinforces what we've said above about Ciampolino. Some scholars have posited the development of a homoerotic slang in the poetry of the trecento and quattrocento, and they list Nuccoli as one of the early adopters of it.[164] And though it can be difficult to determine if it rises to the level of a slang, Nuccoli's allusive language comes across as similar to that of the later writers.

Decades after Finiguerri, Domenico di Giovanni, nicknamed Burchiello (1404–49), dominated the poetry of Italy throughout the first half of the 1400s.[165] A Florentine barber by trade, Burchiello was a master of the comic style, and he may have been responsible for a reawakening of interest in comic poetry in the quattrocento.[166] He took inspiration from the tradition of comic literature, recollecting the lyrics of Rustico Filippi and Pieraccio Tedaldi;[167] indeed, he rewrote the sonnet by Cecco Angiolieri, "I'm so thin that I'm almost transparent," that Meo dei Tolomei also reworked (sonnets 1A, 1B, and 1C of Tolomei's corpus). Additionally, Nuccoli's "Going down New Street and Wide Street" has been cited by several critics as a precursor to Burchiello's poetics.[168] In a manner similar to that sonnet, Burchiello developed a distinctive style in which utter nonsense predominates.[169] He goes further, however, frequently employing onomatopoeic effects and the evocation of words to challenge the reader's interpretive expectations.[170] For as much as Burchiello destabilizes language, he never degenerates into complete incomprehensibility. Often he describes comic situations, such as the tavern, and many of his poems subtly describe sexual encounters.[171] In one sonnet, for instance, he depicts his sexual encounter with a friar, who exposed his erection to him while traveling to the baths:

> Going to the bath I caught up with a Minorite
> with his cloak so high above his knee
> that I could see his fierce skatapuck
> which was of the Major Order.
> It was hoodless because of the great heat
> and around its neck it wore a *mazzocchio*
> of fresh cheese and full of eye rheum,
> whence oozed its cold humor.
> A bell-clapper did not hammer so much
> as in the clothes in front and behind
> the naked bean of the great pod.

xlviii   Introduction

> I never saw a greater anti-fasting
> and his scrotum looked like a bagpipe's
> bellows, and its pipe resembled the stop.
>   Silently I followed him,
> and he, to avoid boredom during the voyage,
> continually spoke every language with his asshole.[172]

The sexual nature of Burchiello's encounter with the friar is unmistakable. The brother's penis is as large as a bell's clapper, he writes, which strikes against the inside of his robe, and his scrotum resembles a bagpipe. Burchiello then describes how he quietly went after the friar, presumably to have sex with him (v. 15). The friar, he concludes, was able to speak all languages with his anus during his journey (vv. 16–17), indicating his ability to seduce men of different nationalities. None of this discussion is intended to suggest a direct connection between Nuccoli's sonnet and Burchiello's, but only to highlight the general similarities in their poetic styles. Burchiello uses ambiguous language to describe a highly sexual situation in a manner similar to Nuccoli's. Like Nuccoli and il Za, Burchiello uses incongruous language to describe the sex acts and sexual organs. Thanks in part to Burchiello's importance in the quattrocento, however, same-sex desire became a commonplace in the literature of the period. Both Burchiello and il Za are important to the development of same-sex literature in Italy; neither of them appear in this book, however, because they are too distant from our poets in terms of their historical period, the early fifteenth century. Nevertheless, with his ambiguous sonnet, Nuccoli helped pave the way for the evolution of the homoerotic poetry of the late Middle Ages and early Renaissance.

This Book

This book consists of facing-page translations of the complete lyric productions of Meo dei Tolomei, Cecco Nuccoli, and Marino Ceccoli, and the four pseudo-Angiolieri sonnets. The lyric productions of Nuccoli and Ceccoli have never been translated, but much of Meo dei Tolomei's verse has been available to English readership in some fashion, but not under his own name. Two translations of Cecco Angiolieri's poetry were based upon the nineteenth-century assumptions about Chigiano L.VIII.305, and therefore they repeated the incorrect attribution of the twenty sonnets written by Meo. The first of these was by C. H. M. D. Scott, in Angiolieri, *The Sonnets of Cecco Angiolieri of Siena Done into English Doggerel* (1925), a private printing of thirty copies and therefore with a limited influence; that translation has recently been revised by Anthony Mortimer and republished.[173] The second translation, by Thomas Caldecott Chubb, exerted greater influence on English readership; it appears in Angiolieri, *The Sonnets of a Handsome and Well-Mannered Rogue Translated from Cecco Angiolieri of Siena*.[174] Perhaps more than any other translation, Chubb's introduced Angiolieri's poetry to English readership, and in the process unknowingly subsumed Meo's sonnets into it. Yet neither translation contains Meo's *caribetto*, nor do they reproduce the sonnets addressed to, and influenced by, him. With this book, English readership can experience Meo dei Tolomei as a distinct writer and see the full range of his poetics. In other words, this book represents the first time that the trope of homoeroticism in the poetry of the trecento has been rendered into English.

The first complete editions of Meo's work with the correct attributions were two important anthologies of comic poetry that both appeared in 1956: *Poeti giocosi del tempo di Dante*, edited by Mario Marti, and *Rimatori comico-realistici del '200 e '300*, edited by Maurizio Vitale.[175] Marti and Vitale based themselves on an earlier anthology edited by Aldo Francesco Massèra, *Sonetti burleschi e realistici dei primi due secoli*, which was published before Adele Todaro's ground-breaking studies. The anthologies by Massèra and Marti—but not that by Vitale—also contained the poetry of Nuccoli and Ceccoli. All three anthologies, moreover, incorporated the complete corpus of Angiolieri in some form, including the four homoerotic poems of debated attribution. The three anthologies are still acceptable to literary scholars as sources, but preferable are the edition of Meo's poetry by Anna Bruni Bettarini and the edition of the Perugian poets by Franco Mancini.[176] The most recent edition of Angiolieri is by Antonio Lanza, which also includes the four homoerotic sonnets.[177] The translations in this book are based on the works of Bettarini, Lanza, and Mancini, with alternate readings by Massèra, Marti, and/or Vitale placed in the footnotes when significant. The intention for doing so is to provide as much information as possible about the four poets so that scholars can see the ways that the poetry has been understood over the decades.

1 Introduction

A scholarly translation has a dual nature, and that is true in this book. A translation looks back to the past, citing the work of previous scholars, synthesizing their studies. This book was only made possible by the labor of the editors who transcribed the poems, and of the critics who made sense of them. At the same time, a translation looks forward to the future with the hope that other scholars can bring their own knowledge to bear on the literary texts, and that is also true in this instance. In recent years there has been a flurry of work on nonnormative sexuality as revealed in literature from the medieval and early modern periods, and many of those studies are published by individuals outside the field of Italian literature. When they include Italian works, they generally focus on great literature, such as the *Divine Comedy* or the *Decameron*, but the opinions expressed by Dante and Boccaccio about sodomy do not exhaust the range of possibilities throughout the Italian communes of the Middle Ages. It is my hope that, with these translations, some of those scholars will bring their insights to bear on these fascinating writers and their first-person statements. I believe that our poets balance out the severe moralizing of Dante and the disdain of Boccaccio, providing a more rounded picture of male same-sex desire in Italy during the fourteenth century.

PART 1

Siena

Poets of Chigiano L.VIII.305 and Related Manuscripts

CHAPTER ONE

Meo dei Tolomei

Poems by Meo dei Tolomei

Poems 1A, 1B, and 1C: Meo dei Tolomei's poem is a redaction of a sonnet by Cecco Angiolieri. Meo retains the first two lines from Angiolieri's lyric and changes the rest. Emilio Pasquini described the artistic practice of reworking other people's poetry as typical of fourteenth-century Italy.[1] In the original sonnet, for which two versions exist, Angiolieri adapts the comic motif of the complaint of poverty, a commonplace derived from the Latin

1A. Meo dei Tolomei

   I' son sì magro che quasi traluco
de la per[so]na, ma più de l'avere,
amico nè parente ho, che vedere
mi voglia, sol per ch'or non esco i· lluco;[3]
   e già del mi' poco i' me ne conduco,
ch'è viver di speranza c'ho d'avere,
e da[4] quel tempo avess'io de le pere,
ch'i' m[i]ei non me terranno così bruco!
   Esser ho ric[c]o, e 'l modo saper parmi:
mia madre, Ciampolino e 'l Zeppa tanto
per me guadagnan, che non ho ch'a starmi.
   Or mi rendessen del mi' pur arquanto!
Ché tutti i tre, en ben assot[t]igliarmi,
son Padre e Filio, e Spirito Santo.

Goliardic tradition. Angiolieri relates his impoverished conditions to his stereotypical actions as a lover, spending lavishly to woo the lady.

In his version, Meo also speaks about his economic hardships, but he blames them on the actions of his three enemies: his mother, Mino Zeppa, and Ciampolino.[2] In the fifteenth century, the poet Domenico di Giovanni, nicknamed Burchiello, will again rewrite Angiolieri's sonnet, transforming it into a statement about his own poverty.

1A. Meo dei Tolomei

     I'm so thin that I'm almost transparent[5]
in body, but more so in my belongings;
I have no friend or relative who wants
to see me, just because I now don't wear fine robes.
     And I conduct my life with my few funds,
because I live on the hope for money I will get;
and may I enjoy the fruits of that time
because my family won't keep me so bare then.
     I have what I need to be rich—the knowledge too:
but my mother, Ciampolino, and Zeppa
earn so much from me that I have nothing left.
     Now, if only they paid me some of it back!
Because all three of them, in thinning me out,
are the Father, and the Son, and the Holy Spirit.

1B. Cecco Angiolieri (ca. 1260–1312): Version 1

      I' son sì magro che quasi traluco,
de la persona no, ma più de l'avere;
ed abbo tanto più a dar che avere,
che m'è rimaso vie men d'un fistuco.
      Ed èmmi sì turato ogni mi' buco,
ch'i' ho po'che dar e vie men che tenere:
ben m'è ancora rimas'un podere,
che frutta l'anno il valer d'un sambuco!
      Ma non ci ha forza, ch'i' so' 'nnamorato;
ché s'i' avesse più òr che non è sale,
men me saria 'n poco temp'assommato.
      Or mi paresse almeno pur far male!
Ma com' più struggo, più son avvïato
di voler far di nuovo capitale.[6]

1B. Cecco Angiolieri (ca. 1260–1312): Version 1

      I'm so thin that I'm almost transparent
not in body, but more so in my belongings:
and I have to give up still more than I'll keep
so all I have of myself left is less than straw.
      And my every hole has been stopped up
because I have no more to give or hold,
but surely one farm is left to me
that each year bears one elderberry flower.
      But it does me no good because I'm in love—
for if I had as much gold as grains of salt
in short time I'd completely spend it.
      And it doesn't seem to be self-destructive:
the more I harm myself, the more I'm committed
to trying to make even more new capital.

1C. Cecco Angiolieri (ca. 1260–1312): Version 2

    I' son sì magro che quasi traluco
della persona, ma più dell'avere.
e' ho tanto più a dar ch'a rïavere
che 'l rimanente val men d'un fistuco;
    ed èmmi sì turato ogni mi' buco
ch'io non ho più che dar nè che tenere;
ma èmme ben rimaso un podere,
che frutta l'anno il valer d'un sambuco.
    Ma lassa andar ch'i' son ben avïato:
se io avesse tra man lo Sangradale,
en poco tempo l'avrei consumato.
    Ancor mi paresse a me pur far male!
quanto più struggo, più son avïato
di far di vecchio nuovo capitale.[7]

1C. Cecco Angiolieri (ca. 1260–1312): Version 2

      I'm so thin that I'm almost transparent
in body, but more so in my belongings,
and I have to give up still more than I'll get back
so all that remains is worth less than straw.

      And my every hole has been stopped up
because I have no more to give or hold;
but surely one farm is left to me
that each year bears one elderberry flower.

      But let it go, for I'm well on my way:
if I had the Holy Grail in hand,
in short time I'd consume it.

      And it doesn't seem to be self-destructive:
the more I harm myself, the more I'm committed
to trying to make new capital out of old.

Poem 2: Meo writes a sonnet consisting of insult, specifically of his own mother, who works tirelessly to defraud him of his inheritance.[8] She said something to him, which he describes ironically as pleasing, when she took some silver from him. He argues that she favors his brother, Mino Zeppa, whom she venerates to the same degree as a religious relic, the Holy Face of Lucca. The wooden crucifix in the Cathedral of San Martino, the Holy Face of Lucca, was the focus of a cult of veneration because of the legend that it was sculpted by Nicodemus after he assisted Joseph in the deposition of

    Mie madre disse l'altrier parol'una,
la qual mi piacque a dismisura molto:
che s'ella m'ha di mio argento tolto,
di farmene ragion tiell'una pruna.
    Ed io sì le rispuosi in una in una
—Perché m'avete sì 'ngiuliato e còlto[9]
che 'l date a quel che par lo Santo Volto
da Lucca, ciò è 'l Zeppa, che me luna?—
    Ché 'n ogni parte 'l veggo, e s'i' sapesse
loco trovare ove veder no ·l creda,
ciascuno 'l sa ch'io 'l farei, s'i' potesse.
    Ma far no ·l posso, più duro è che preda!
Potresti[10] dir che gli occhi mi traesse
come che poi vedrei men ch'el[l]a[11] preda.

Christ's body. The Holy Face of Lucca is also mentioned in Dante's *Inferno* (21.48). Meo asserts that the efforts of Mino and their mother serve to drive him crazy. He closes the sonnet by addressing his audience, who tells him to pluck out his eyes, evoking Matthew 18:9.

      The other day my mother said a word[12]
that I liked beyond all reasoning;
she took some of my silver away
and justified it as being merely a prune.
      And I responded to her, one for one,
"Why do you injure me and stab me so?
You'll give it to him who seems the Holy Face
of Lucca to you—Zeppa, that is, who drives me mad."
      For I see him everywhere, and if I knew
how to find a place where I wouldn't see him,
everyone knows I'd do it if I could.
      But I can't do it—it's worse than his thieving!
You could tell me to pluck out my eyes
since then I wouldn't see what she steals from me.

Poem 3: Meo's mother attempted to murder him when he was ill and unable to speak; he will reiterate that she tried to kill him in his sonnet 5. As he relates the event here, she tried to give him poison under the guise of administering medicine to him. He had lost the power of speech, but he understood her nefarious intents and refused her potion. He communicated to her through gestures, possibly alluding to the practices of deaf people during his age. Ironically, her attempt on his life cured him—he recovered his powers of

      Sì fortemente l'altrier fu' malato
ca tutt'avia perduto 'l favellare;
e mie madre, per farmi megliorare,
arrecom[m]'un velen sì temperato,
      ch'av[e]ria, non che me, m'attossicato
el mar, e disse:—Béi, non dubitare!—
Ed i' feci per cenni:—A ·mme non pare!—
Di non bere nel me' cor[e] fui fermato.
      Ed ella disse:—Odi, che pur ber[r]ai,
e questa prova perder ti faraggio!—
Allor de la paura terminai,
      e cominciai a dir:—Nessun mal aggio!—
Né bev[v]i da sua man né ber[r]ò mai,
né bevere' se ·mmi facesse saggio.

speech and confronted her. Much of the sonnet is in direct discourse, a technique common among comic poets of the time.[13] (Marti considers this sonnet to be of questionable attribution to Meo.)

      I was so fiercely sick the other day[14]
that I'd completely lost the power of speech;
and my mother, to make me better,
brought me a potion so tempered
      that it would have poisoned not only me
but the sea, and she said, "Drink, have no doubt!"
And I said, by way of gestures: "I don't think so!"
for I was firm in my heart not to drink.
      And she said, "Listen, you will drink,
and I will make you lose this contest!"
Because of my fear, I stopped
      and I began to speak, "I'm not sick!"
I didn't drink from her hand, nor will I ever,
nor would I ever drink it if I were wise.

Poem 4: Meo's mother uses her knowledge of medicine to bring about his demise. She recommends that he follow a diet inappropriate for his body's humorological complexion as a melancholic. In relating her advice, the poet mentions theriac, a compound believed to be antidote to many poisons; Tolomei will discuss theriac in sonnet 12, below, as will pseudo-Angiolieri in sonnet 3. According to the *Regimen Sanitatis Salerni*, peaches were to be

      Mie madre sì m'insegna medicina,
la qual non m'è, crudel[e]mente, sana:
ché mi dice ch'i' usi a la campana
da otto pèsche o diece la mattina,
      che ·mmi faran campar de la contina
e di febbre quartan'e di terzana;
molto mi loda l'anguille di chiana,
che 'l cap'è me' che ot[e]rïaca fina.
      Carne di bu'e cascio e cipolla
molto mi loda, quand'i' sento doglia,
e ch'i' ne faccia ben buona satolla;
      e se di questo non avessi voglia,
e stessi quasimente su la colla,
molto mi loda porri con le foglia.

avoided by people prone to melancholy, as were beef and cheese, and eels.[15] Were he to take her advice, the diet would slowly kill him. (Marti questions the attribution of this sonnet to Tolomei.)

       My mother teaches me such medicine,[16]
which, cruelly, isn't healthy for me;
because she tells me to eat at the tolling of the bell
from eight to ten peaches each morning,
       for they will save me from continuous fever,
and from quartan and from tertian fevers;[17]
she offers much for marsh eels
because their heads are better than fine theriac.
       She also praises beef,
and cheese with onions when I suffer pains,
and I should be full up with them.
       And if I had no desire for it,
and even if I were subjected to torture[18]
she'd praise leafy leeks highly to me.

Poem 5: Meo's mother tries again to murder him. He relates how she attempted to strangle him while he slept because he had requested his portion of the inheritance from Mino Zeppa. He compares her to Medea, who killed her own children to avenge herself against their father, Jason. Meo closes the sonnet by asserting that since he no longer speaks about his inheritance, she leaves him in peace.

  Su lo letto stava l'altra sera
e facea dritta vista di dormire,
ed i' vidi mia madr'a ·mme venire,
empiosamente, con malvagia cèra.
  E 'n sul letto mi salì molto fèra
e man mi pos'a la gola, al ver dire,
e solamente per farmi morire,
e se ciò non fosse ch'i' m'atai, mort'era.
  Sì che non fu [co]tanto ria Medea,
che le piacqu'al figliuol la morte dare,
che mie madre non sia tanto più rea;
  ch'a tradimento mi vols'affogare
perch'a Min dimanda' la parte mea;
là 'ndi' i' lel' queto, làssim'ella stare!

The other night I was lying in bed[19]
giving the appearance of being asleep,
and I saw my mother come up to me,
without pity, with an evil expression.

    And she climbed in the bed, most fiercely,
and put her hand on my throat, to tell the truth,
only because she wanted to kill me;
if I hadn't defended myself, I'd be dead!

    Medea—who was happy to murder
her own child—wasn't nearly as evil;
my mother is even more evil!

    She tried to choke me traitorously,
since I'd requested my portion from Mino.
Now that I'm silent, she leaves me alone.

Poem 6: Tolomei explores other facets of the poetics of vituperation, now insulting his brother. Here he discusses the cowardice of Mino Zeppa. At the sound of enemies' war cries, Mino Zeppa flees faster than Pier Fastello. According to legend, Piero, nicknamed Fastello, the founder of the Bandinelli family, participated in the First Crusade to the Holy Land (the eventual Kingdom of *Outre Mer*) in 1096. Piero Fastello was reputed to have returned

   El fuggir di Min Zeppa quando sente
i nimici si passa ogni volare,
e Pier Faste', che venne d'oltremare
in Sienna 'n una notte, fe' ·nniente
   a ·rrispetto di lui, che veramente
il su' fuggir si può dir millantare:
Die, dàgli tu 'l malanno, quando fare
non può 'l fuggir più temperatamente!
   Ché rimarrebbe tra ·lLodi e Pavia
e di ciò non vo dico che sia nulla[20]
ched e' facci'altro, ch'usato si sia,
   e' fuggiria per un fanciul di culla,
ond'i' per me non ci veggi'altra via
che d'andarmi a 'pic[c]are:[21]—Or chi ti crulla?—

from overseas to Siena in a single night. Mino Zeppa, conversely, would even run from a crying baby. But Meo sees no recourse from his brother's treachery except to commit suicide.

> Min Zeppa's fleeing, whenever he hears[22]
> his enemies, surpasses all other flight;
> and Pier Fastel, who came from *Outre Mer*
> to Siena in one night, achieved nothing
>   with respect to him—he truly can
> boast of his ability to flee!
> God, put a curse on him so he can
> no longer flee so quickly!
>   For he would arrive between Lodi and Pavia,
> and I'm not telling you it's nothing
> for him to act otherwise—he's used to it!
>   He would flee from a babe in a crib!
> I cannot see any other way for me
> than to hang myself—now say who it is that scares you.

Siena

Poem 7: Meo exposes Mino Zeppa's faults through a fictional dialogue with him. He reiterates Mino's cowardice, asking if the small size of his sword makes him run from his enemies; the discussion of his sword may be a backhanded slight on Mino's manhood. The dialogue sonnet was a comic form made famous by Cecco Angiolieri;[23] for another example of a dialogue sonnet by Tolomei, see poem 18.

   —Per cotanto ferruzzo, Zeppa, dimmi
se ti facesse fuggir ogne cria.—
—I' ti rispondo e dìcoti che sì ·mmi;
fu ben perfetta la risposta mia?—
   —Donqua ben posso dicer:—Lasso, chi ·mmi
tien?[24] Turbo, ch'al fuggir par' di carpia!
—Megli' è ch'i' fugga, che l'om dica:—Lì ·mmi
fu fatto per tardanza villania!—
   —Frate, or pur fugg' e non guardar chi sia
que' che ·tti caccia, ché 'n tal modo fìmmi-
se sì, che più contar no l[o] poria.—
   —Ben l'ho fatto,[25] ch'i' non te 'n serviria!
E non po[trà] mai dicer nessun:—Min mi[26]
fece partir un ichise di via.—

"Tell me, Zeppa, because of your small sword[27]
would any yelling at all make you flee?"
"I answer you that, yes, I would run:
Is my answer good enough for you?"

"So now I can say—no one is stopping me!—
that you run as fast as a dust whirlwind."
"It's better for me to flee than for everyone to say,
'he suffered villainy because of his slowness.'"

"Now flee, brother, and don't look at
whoever chases you off, because no matter how
he treated me, I wouldn't mention it."

"I spoke correctly, and I wouldn't assist you:
and no one will ever say, 'Mino
drove me X amount down the road!'"

Poem 8: Mino Zeppa is such a coward that he sues for peace even when he has suffered outrages; such behavior is shameful for a member of the nobility. Mino's shame is known to all because he carries the banner of the disgraced. Meo closes the sonnet with the backhanded comment that Mino Zeppa— his own brother—is the son of a whore. He asserts that his mother was a sodomite, having tired out all the pricks of the world. According to the *Grande Dizionario della Lingua Italiana*, the final verse of the sonnet contains one of the earliest uses of the word *cazzo* ("prick"), which at the time

    Par Die, Min Zeppa, or son giunte le tue,
or ti difendi, s'tu sai, d'esto motto:
che ti fu dato d'un matton biscotto
nel capo, che ·nne saria mort'un bue;
    e tu com'uom che no ·n volesti piue,
non ch'una pace n'hai fatta, ma otto,
or ti va 'mpicca, sozzo, pazzo cotto,
vitoperato più ch'anch'uom no fue.
    Ché s'tu temessi vergogna nïente,
tu anderesti con gli occhi chinati,
e non appariresti ma tra gente;
    tu porti 'l confalon degli sgraziati,[31]
figliuol di quel[l]a c'ha 'l cul sì rodente
che tut[t]i i cazzi del mondo ha s[tancati.]

was the only lexeme in the vernacular to denote the penis.[28] For this reason, the sonnet is an important document in the history of the Italian language. At the same time, however, the poem is a prime example of misogynistic insult, using a woman's sexuality to demean her.[29]

In this sonnet, Meo appears to echo a poem that Forese Donati had addressed to Dante, reiterating the accusation that cowardice renders someone unworthy as a nobleman.[30]

> By God, Min Zeppa, the battle is joined[32]
> and defend yourself from this statement, if you know how:
> for you were struck by a twice-baked brick
> in the head, such as would have killed an ox,
>
> and you, like a man who didn't want any more,
> sued for peace, not once, but eight times.
> Now go, hang yourself, you dirty crazy fool,
> who is more slandered than a man ever was!
>
> For if you feared any shame at all
> you would go about with your eyes lowered,
> and you wouldn't appear among the people.
>
> You carry the banner of the disgraced,
> son of the woman whose ass is so hungry
> that she has worn out all the pricks in the world.

24 *Siena*

Poem 9: Meo depicts his brother, Mino Zeppa, as a failed lover, and Meo finds him in the abject position of lying face down. Late at night Meo comes across his brother at Pina's doorstep, and he relates Mino's dialogue with the woman as he unsuccessfully tries to woo her with gifts. She dryly rejects him, refusing his money and claiming that it was the product of the notorious counterfeiter Capocchio. Capocchio was a famous alchemist and heretic whom Dante condemns to the *bolgia* of the falsifiers of metals in *Inferno*

       Boccon in terr'a piè l'uscio di Pina,
dipo le tre trovai Min Zeppa stare;
ed i' mi stett'e comincia' ascoltare,
e seria stato infine a la mattina,
       se tanto fosse durata la lena,
ché cominciat'ave', del favellare,
ché que' dicea di volervi entrare
e quella li rispos':—Or quest'è fina!
       —Almen piglia da me questi danari,
così com' e[lli] ti ca[g]l[ia] del mi' occhio:
sì ·nn'avra' già un paio di calzari.
       —Va pian, amor, un poco, ch'i' sconocchio:
s'e' fosser buon', tu li avresti più cari;
va' col malanno, e' fuor di Capocchio.—

(29.124–39, and 30.1–30). Dante portrays Capocchio as a charlatan who derided the "Crew of Spendthrifts" in Siena that wasted exorbitant amounts of money. Historical records demonstrate that Capocchio was burned at the stake in Siena on 15 August 1293.

       I found Min Zeppa face down[33]
on the ground at Pina's threshold after three o'clock,
and I stopped and began to listen.
I'd have stayed there until morning
       if my energy had lasted that long,
because he'd begun to speak.
He said he wanted to come in,
and she replied, "Now, this is nice!"
       "At least accept these coins from me
if it's important for you to catch my eye
and that way you'll have a nice pair of hose."
       "Go quietly, my love, a little more and I'd reject you;
if these coins were good, you'd value them more—
now, go on and be cursed! They were Capocchio's!"[34]

Poem 10: Meo depicts Mino Zeppa as a religious hypocrite. Mino makes a show of praying at church, not out of any sense of devotion but for concern of his social standing, seemingly echoing Matthew 6:5: "When you pray, do not be like the hypocrites, for they love to stand in the synagogues and on the street corners so that others might see them." Instead, Mino is as faithless as a Jew, Meo writes, echoing the medieval belief of the Jews as irrational and deliberately irreligious, knowledgeable about the truth of Christ but unwilling to accept it; in short, they are traitors.[35] Meo will protect himself by feigning insanity, poking himself in the eye with a club so that people will

        Quando 'l Zeppa entra 'n santo usa di dire:
—Die sì vi dea 'l buon dì, domine Deo!—
e sì ·ssi segna che quasi morire
fa ciascun' [om] che vede l'atto seo.
        E suo' peccati dice sì ch'udire
li pò ciascun, che non gli oda Id[d]eo,
e quand'e' se ne vien a dipartire,
cantando n'esc'e è omai giudeo.
        Nel su' segnar fa dritt' atti di pazza,
ché del dito si dà talor ne l'occhio,
e [ne][37] campa ch'alcun non l'amazza;
        forse ch'è ·rriguardato per Capocchio
o per ch'a Branca diè tal d'una mazza
che ben ve sta umà dicer:—Finocchio!—

believe him to be a madman. He would rather need to treat it later with fennel, which was believed to have medicinal properties for eye injuries.[36]

Meo refers again to Capocchio (see poem 9), and to Branca Doria, the traitor found in Dante's *Inferno* 33.134–47. Branca Doria was a politician from Genoa who was famous for having murdered his son-in-law Michele Zanche in 1275 during a feast in his home. In his poem, Meo seems to fear being burned at the stake like Capocchio or clubbed to death like Branca, which is why he pretends to be insane.

>   When Zeppa enters the church he always says,[38]
> "May God grant you a good day, my Lord God!"
> and he crosses himself so that everyone
> who sees his action almost dies from laughter.
>   And he confesses his sins so that
> everyone can hear him—but may God not hear him—
> and when it's time for him to leave
> he exits while singing and he's almost become a Jew.
>   And while crossing himself he does acts of insanity
> because sometimes he pokes himself in the eye,
> and for that reason he lives—no one kills him!
>   Maybe he's concerned by Capocchio
> or because he'll get such a clubbing from Branca,
> but for now it's better for him to call out, "Fennel!"

Poem 11: Not even Death can relieve Meo of Mino Zeppa's presence because the latter refuses to die. If Mino's head were cut off, it would reattach itself to his body, as in the miracle of Saint Uliva (*Uvil*), whose hands regrew after they were amputated.[39] If Mino drank poison, he would survive like John the Baptist;[40] and if Mino were thrown into the ocean, he would transform into the fairytale character Nicholas the Fish.[41] He also seems to refer to the Battle of Fossalta in 1249, when a Bolognese army reputedly catapulted a

    Se 'l capo di Min Zeppa fosse tagliato
come del giuoco d'Uvil n'averria,
ché 'l capo da lo 'mbusto partiria,
e puo' ritorniere' nel primo stato.
    E ·ssed e' fusse ancor manganeggiato,
vie men che minstrel mal n'av[e]ria;
e se venen prendesse li faria
ch'a san Giovan Batista lo beato.
    Ma no i n'avèn per la vertù di Deo,
ma la mort'è che ·ssi disdegna entrare
i ·lloco sì vilissimo e [sì] ·rreo;
    ché s'e' gittato fosse in alto mare,
legato spessament', al parer meo,
Niccola Pesce si poria chiamare.

live donkey into the city of Modena. In this sonnet, Meo echoes the poetics of Cecco Angiolieri, who repeatedly complains about his cruel father, depicting him as defying Death and therefore able to survive any act that would kill another man.[42]

If Min Zeppa's head were chopped off,[43]
it would turn out like the game of Uvil,
because his head would separate from his trunk
and then it would return to its first state.
    If he were shot from a catapult,
he'd suffer less than the donkey;
and if he took poison it would affect him
like it affected the blessed Saint John the Baptist.
    None of this happens because of God's grace
but because of Death, who disdains to enter
a place so very vile and evil.
    For if he were thrown into the high sea
bound most tightly, in my opinion,
he could be called Nicholas the Fish.

Poem 12: Nothing can warm Mino Zeppa to the point that he will act courageously—not the sun, which rises over India first, nor *vernaccino* wine, nor the medicinal compound theriac. Meo mentions theriac in sonnet 4, as does pseudo-Angiolieri in sonnet 3. Instead, he writes, Mino will put on airs of being as brave as a paladin of Charlemagne. But as soon as he hears other men's war cries of *lè lè*, he will be as crestfallen as the soldiers who were defeated at the castle of Radda, which was besieged in 1230.

   Se tutta l'otrïaca d'oltre mmare,
e quant'ha in Genova [di] vernaccino
fosser raunate nel corpo di Mino,
il qual si solea far Zeppa chiamare,
  no 'l potrìen tanto di spera scaldare,
ch'e' non prendesse d'Indïa 'l cammino,
e ·llevala ch'e par un paladino,
pur ch'egli udisse:—Lè lè!—[om] gridare.
  Quell'è 'l sollazzo, ch'e' ·ssi tien valente!
Ma ·mme non mettare[bbe] quell'a bada,
sed i' non sia di mia donna dolente;
  ch'i' l'ho per un de' cattivi da Rada;
se 'l conoscesse com'i' tutta gente,
gridando li and[e]reb[b]er dietro:—Dà, dà!—

If all the theriac from overseas[44]
and all the *vernaccino* of Genoa
were collected in the body of Mino—
the man who's usually called Zeppa—
      they couldn't heat him like the sphere
that starts its path over India;
and he arises and seems to be a paladin
even when he hears *lè lè* shouted out.
      That's his game, for he considers himself valiant,
but he'll never make me feel fearful—
so too may my lady not cause me pain!
      I think of him like the captives from Radda;[45]
if everyone knew him as I do,
they'd all run after him shouting, "Go! Go!!"

Poem 13: This sonnet marks the first of five poems dedicated to criticizing Ciampolino, an ex-lover who frequents the taverns. In all of them, "Ciampolino" establishes the A-rhyme. In this poem, Ciampolino steals Meo's money, and the poet foresees Ciampolino's eventual financial ruin caused by dicing and eating fine foods. Thus, Meo evokes the ideology of the tavern in this poem, presenting it as a type of anti-church that housed all sorts of sinful behaviors, such as gambling, drinking, and sex.[46] By listing off three pleasurable activities, Meo echoes a verse by Cecco Angiolieri, in which he proclaims that only three things delight his heart: "Women, the tavern and a game of dice" (v. 4);[47] Tolomei adapts it to partridges, gambling, and "the masculine." According to Danielle Collegari, partridges were a delicacy that only the highest members of society could afford; they were also believed to heat the body, inspiring lust in those who consumed them.[48] Thus, in this poem, Meo suggests that he too can be a wastrel like Ciampolino, eat-

      Da ·tte parto 'l mie cor[e], Ciampolino,
e se ·nno' fum[m]o giamma' dritt'amici,
or[a] sarem mortalmente nemici,
perché del mie mi nieghi più che Mino.
      E quando te 'l dimando, 'n tuo latino
sì usi spesso:—Non so che ·tti dici!—
Sie certo ch'i' sapre' mangiar pernici
e giucar, e voler lo mascolino,
      sì ·ccome tu, ma aggio abbandonate
queste tre cose, perch'om non potesse
dir:—Quegli è giunto in gran[de] povertate!—
      Or tu ·sse' 'l bon garzon, chi ·tti credesse!
Così ·tti dia Iddio vit'e santate;
e tu hai ben a dir:—Cristo 'l volesse!—

ing costly foods that spur him to sexual acts with other men. Nonetheless, he writes, he would rather act frugally.

This sonnet provides perhaps the clearest indication that the relationship between Meo and Ciampolino was sexual. The phrase "desire the masculine" (*voler lo mascolino*) (v. 8) is a clear reference to Meo's sexual attraction to other men. At the time, "mascolino" occasionally denoted the penis itself, and that is a possible interpretation in this poem; it also may have been a means to refer to a male lover.[49] The poet may also employ willfully enigmatic language when he depicts his relationship with Ciampolino as being "fast friends" (*dritt'amici*) (v. 2). The adjective "diritto" meant "loyal," but also "erect" or "rigid."[50] When combined with the statements later in the poem, the ambiguous language becomes highlighted.

> I cut my heart off from you, Ciampolino,[51]
> and if we were ever fast friends,
> now we will become mortal enemies
> because you deny me what's mine worse than Mino does.
> And when I ask you for it, in your language,
> you often say: "I don't know what you're saying!"
> Be assured that I'd know how to eat partridges,
> and gamble, and desire the masculine
> just like you do; but I've given up
> all three of these things, so no one could say,
> "He's come to great poverty from them!"
> You're such a good lad (to those who believe you).
> Thus, may God grant you long life and health.
> You may well say, "Christ wanted it to be so!"

Poem 14: Meo portrays Ciampolino as impoverished, using the metaphor of candles: there was a green strip at the base of candles, which indicated that they needed to be replaced. In this instance, he asserts that Ciampolino no longer has any excess cash. Again, Meo evokes the concept of the tavern, such as seen in poem 13. He writes that Ciampolino is exhausting his goods by gambling, and he anticipates Ciampolino's eventual end in debtors'

       Sì 'sse' condott'al verde, Ciampolino,
che già del candellier hai ars'un poco;
a mal tuo grado rimarrai del gioco,
poi t'han condotto sì i dadi del mino.
       E de' tuo' fatti fu' bene 'ndivino,
ch'assai ti dissi:—Non toccar lo foco!—
Ma mie parole 'n te non eb[b]er loco,
e 'l tu' non fu del senno di Merlino.
       Ma perched i' ti sent'alquanto grosso,
dispònar voglio 'l motto che ttu sai;
del candellier[e] no mmi son mal mosso:
       ché sopra la persona debito hai;
e 'sse non se' gittato prim'al fosso
che maggio venga, 'n pregion mor[i]rai.

prison or buried anonymously as a pauper. He also contrasts Ciampolino's foolishness to the legendary figure of Merlin, who was reputed to possess great wisdom.

   You've arrived at the green, Ciampolino,[52]
of the candle that you've burned a little,
but despite yourself you'll stay out of the game
since the dice have brought you so low.
   And I foresaw clearly your current state,
because I often said, "Don't play with fire!"
But my words didn't find fertile ground,
and your wisdom didn't match Merlin's.
   But since I know you to be dense,
I want to explain the proverb that you know—
I haven't moved on from that candlestick;
   for you've brought this debt upon your very self,
and if you're not tossed in the ditches
before May comes, you'll be dying in prison.[53]

Poem 15: Meo portrays Ciampolino as a coward, using terms reminiscent of his poems about Mino Zeppa. Like the poet's brother, Ciampolino is a coward. Meo depicts him fleeing from an enemy, Tese (Contese), who approaches the Tolomei house that was near the church of San Pellegrino.

    Se ·ttu se' pro' e forte, Ciampolino,
ora m'aveggio che bisogno n'hai,
ch'i' veggio venir Tes', e tu 'l vedrai,
se tu pon' mente ver' san Pellegrino.
    E seco men'un che par un mastino:
oramai, Ciampolin, come farai?
Dimmi se di bon cor combatterai,
o ti farà' 'pelar borgognino.
    Ché ·sse ·ttu fuggi, se' vitoperato,
ma se combatti ben, di bon coraggio,
tu dìe pensar che ·nne sarai lodato.
    Ma già ti veggio cambiar nel visaggio,
perciò credo che 'l fuggir ti sie 'n grato,
o a ·llevarla quando tu ha' 'l vantaggio.

　　　　　If you are proud and strong, Ciampolino,[54]
now I see that you need to be so,
because I see Tese coming, and you'll see him too
if you turn your gaze toward San Pellegrino.

　　　　　And he brings someone who seems a mastiff:
now, Ciampolino, what will you do?
Tell me if, with a good heart, you'll fight,
or if you'll be called a low coward.[55]

　　　　　Because if you flee, you'll be derided,
but if, with a good heart, you fight,
you should think that you'd be praised.

　　　　　But already I see the change in your face:
hence, I believe that you'll prefer fleeing,
or running when you have the advantage.

Poem 16: All three of Meo's enemies are united against him. Ciampolino was unfaithful to Meo, and he has taken Meo's money as nefariously as Mino Zeppa did. Indeed, like Meo's mother, Ciampolino used to discuss murdering him and stealing his money; fortunately, Ciampolino could not scare anyone. By saying that Ciampolino was unable to keep his hands on his belt, he may again be alluding to the sexual nature of their relationship, or he might be suggesting Ciampolino's avarice, because the purse was typically

        Mia madre m'ha 'ngannat'e Ciampolino
non s'ha tenute le man a ccentura,
ch'e' mi soleva dir com' gran ventura
si contirìe morir me' assessino.
        E cert'e' non farebb'a un taupino
in mie servigi, una picciol paura,
ma di to[g]liar lo mie ben s'asicura:
e di ciò non [nè] parlò Santo Agostino.
        Ch'e' me ne renda sol un vil denaio,
ché mie madre ha saputo ben sì fare,
che Mino colm'ed io vòti ho lo staio;
        e ch'i' sie su' figliuolo a me non pare,
ma figliastr', e ch'i' batt'acqu'a mortaio
dice, se ['n] quel di Min credo fruccare.

hung from the belt. The last five verses of the sonnet deal with his mother's treachery.

       My mother tricked me, and Ciampolino[56]
didn't keep hold of his belt:
for he used to tell me what great luck
it would be to have me assassinated.
       And, in my favor, he wouldn't cause
even a little fear in a weakling in my service—
but he ensures that he'll take all that's mine.
Saint Augustine never spoke about this!
       He should return just one thin coin to me!
Because my mother knew how to do it
so that Mino's bushel's full and mine's empty.
       And it doesn't seem like I'm even her son
but stepson; I should pound water in a mortar,[57]
she says, if I think I'll use what's Mino's.

Poem 17: When they were together, Meo had transformed himself into the mirror image of Ciampolino, because he believed they were united in love; Ciampolino, however, had another opinion about them altogether. Meo describes his passion for Ciampolino in terms reminiscent of *fin'amor*, positioning himself as subservient to his beloved. Instead, Meo says, Ciampolino believed they were entirely separate from one another, seemingly alluding to his infidelity. As in sonnets 13 and 14, he evokes the ideology of the tavern in this sonnet, warning everyone not to trust a man who gambles. Meo struc-

        Io feci di me stesso un Ciampolino,
credendomi da lui esser amato,
ed eravam, di du' un dal meo lato,
e dal su' Pier e Giovanni e Martino.

        E se giamma' egli m'eb[b]e 'n dimìno,
or è da me di lunga da mercato,
per che di lu' i' mi trovo 'ngannato;
né ·ss'i' vedesse far de l'acqua vino,

        no ·mmi fiderei i ·llu' d'un bagattino,
e pur di quell ch'i' mi vi son fidato,
già non ne manda sì bianca 'l mulino;

        ché ·lla m'ha tolt'a tort'ed a peccato,
usando la maniera di Caino:
or ti va' ·ffida in uom ch'ag[g]ia giocato.

tures this sonnet so that the A-rhyme and C-rhyme are identical (e.g., "Ciampolino," v. 1; "bagattino," v. 9).

      I made myself into a Ciampolino[58]
believing that I was loved by him,
and we were, though two, one for my part,
and in his mind, "Piero," "Giovanni," and "Martino."
      And if he ever had me in his power,
he's now far from having business with me
because I now find myself tricked by him.
Nor, if I saw him turn water to wine
      would I trust him with even a penny:
and yet what I've already entrusted to him
didn't make the mill any whiter for me.[59]
      Because he's wrongly and sinfully taken
what's mine by using the methods of Cain—
now go, and trust a man who has gambled!

Poem 18: Meo presents himself as a failed lover of a woman in this dialogue sonnet. He tries to woo Ghinuccia with jewels, but she rebuffs him because of his previous inaction; he did nothing when her mother struck her in his presence. This sonnet portrays the inversion between the genders that love brings about, making the man subservient to the woman. For another example of a dialogue sonnet, see poem 7, and for another example of Meo's self-representation as a failed lover, see poem 21.

—Le gioi' ch'i' t'ho recate da Venezia
prendi, Ghinuccia, puo' ch'aprir non vuo'mi.—
—Sappi, Meo, che da me a tte ha screza,
sì che tu non vedrai come tu suo'mi.—
 —Omè, amor, tu par' pur una speza;
fistol viemmi, quando tu per dirlo puo'mi.—
—S'tu mmi facessi reina di Greza,
non m'av[e]resti co m'avesti: tuo'mi!—
 —Anzi ch'i' parta dal tu' uscio mic[c]hi,
se 'l perché non mi dici, morto tièmmi,
e dimandata sarai:—Chi 'l fedì, [c]chi?—
 —[Per]ché mie madre in tuo presenza dièmmi
e non m'atasti, onde se tt'impicchi,
poco vi do, quando di ciò sovviemmi.—

"These jewels that I brought back from Venice—[60]
take them, Ghinuccia, since you don't want to open up to me."
"You know you'll get an argument from me, Meo,
and you won't see me as you usually do."

"Oh my, love, you're so spicy to me!
I may get a fistula simply hearing you speak that way."
"If you made me even the queen of Greece,
you wouldn't have me like you did—get away from me!"

"Before I leave from your doorstep,
if you don't tell me why, consider me dead;
then you'll be asked, 'Who wounded him? Who?'"

"Because my mother hit me in your presence,
and you didn't help me; so, if you hang yourself,
I'll care little when I remember it."

44 *Siena*

Poem 19: This *caribetto*, a multistanza poem intended as a song for dancing, constitutes a *summa* of all of Mino Zeppa's faults:[61] he is a coward, who presents himself as brave up until the moment he faces his enemies; he is a thief,

Caribetto: Meo di Scemone, fratel di Messer Min Zeppa

I.   A ·nnulla guisa me posso soffrire
ch'eo non comenze a ·ddire
de Min Zeppa zo che ·mme 'n par sentire:
come se crede en gran presio venire
per lo so[lo] scremire;
enn-una se dà al fogire
quando vede apparere
li nemici, de[62] retro non se mira.
        E per sé 'nn-otto fai sì grande bradire
ch' ogn'om mett'al morire,
ma sol besogno ha voglia de dormire;
ma quando sa che gli convegna gire
e ·lloco da ferire,
s'ell'avesse en sé l'ardire
com'ell'ha en sé rapire,
de la soa vita prenderia no ira,

II.   anti conforto, ché morto seria
cert'e scamper non porrea;
ma s'ell'avesse en sé de vegoria,
enn-alcona battaglia remar[r]ia,
altr'a Deo non cheria;
ma la soa gran codardia
lui fai partir empria
che neson se departa, tanto 'l tira
        fogendo che par una sagettia,
così tosto, e più, vai via.
Or dunqua como ne verrò a la mia,
che de soa morte tardi se morrea?

who tries to appropriate Meo's inheritance; he gambles in the tavern, losing to the point of poverty. Each stanza follows a different rhyme scheme and meter.

19. Caribetto: Meo di Simone, brother of Messer Min Zeppa

I.   In no way can I endure
not beginning to say
what I feel about Min Zeppa:
how he believes he'll come to great praise
only by shielding himself—
and in an instant he takes to fleeing
when he sees his enemies
appear, and he doesn't even look back.
        And by himself later[68] he cries out
that he'll kill every man,
but he only has need and desire of sleep.
But when he learns that he needs to go
to where he can do battle,
if he'd had any courage,
like he does about robbing,
he wouldn't feel mad about saving his own life

II.   but rather comfort, because he'd have died—
surely he wouldn't have survived;
and if he had any vigor,
he would refrain from any battle.
He'd ask God for nothing else.
But his great cowardice
makes him flee sooner
than anyone else's flight. It pulls him so
        that, fleeing, he appears quick as an arrow.
He runs away so quickly, and more.
Now, how could I come to my point,
because he will arrive too late at his death?

Megli'è che me [ne] stia
e più pensèr non mi dea
de quel che non varria:
ma far nol posso, ché 'l cor me sospira

III.   de la voglia
ch'egli remanesse
e ·lloco che 'l fogir no gli valesse;
però no ·l voglio fare,[63]
ch'anti me ·nne voglio dare
fazza Deo zo ch'a ·llui pare,
ch'io starò
firmo là unqua 'l vedrò
e za per lui no me departirò.
     E la doglia[64]
crederia crescesse
sed eo per lui de loco me movesse,
ma no lo voglio fare,
ch'anti 'l vo' tanto regalare;
poi derò
de lui zo ch'io saverò:
e degli atti e dei fatt' econterò.

IV.   Del corsetto
si fai taülazzo,
e guanti porta spesso sotto brazzo,
e di piè fai corona,
e sì forte s'abbandona
ch'ad ogn'om par terz' o nona;
così stai
di gran passi che on dai:
neson [ne] campa degli atti che fai.
     Caribitto,
giamai più non fazzo
de quil cattivo, che ·nne scrivo e 'ngrazzo,[65]

It would be better for me stay,
and not to think about it anymore
because he's not worth it;
but I can't do it, because my heart is sighing

III.   from the desire
for him to stay
in a place where fleeing doesn't serve him.
But I don't want to do it,
rather I'd refrain from it;
may God do what He will,
for I will stay
fixedly wherever I see him
and I won't leave because of him.
      And I would think
my pain would grow
if I left from that place because of him,
but I don't want to do so,
rather I'd want to note it
and donate it to myself;
and then I'll relate
what I know about him:
and I'll recount his actions and deeds.

IV.   He's turned his shield
into a gambling table,
and he often carries his gloves beneath his arm.
And he's crowned his feet,
and he strongly allows himself
to appear as a bell that sounds terces and nones.
Thus he remains
and he doesn't take great footsteps.
No one survives because of the deeds he does.
      Caribetto,
I'll never again write
or speak ill of that bad man;

e giamai cosa bona
de così fatta persona
non si porrea dir nesona.
Così fai,
dir ve vo' degli atti c'ha,
or ve derò de qui ch'ogn'om non sa.

V.   Ca guarda de pónte
mette mantenente,
prestamente—co la mente
de bona scremita;
poi fai colpi da tagliar la lanza,
e di stoc[c]o mette
e sì svaria i tratti
che non ne viddi mai de così fatti,
né vedrò tutti miei dì.
         Co· le gambe gionte
salta mantenente
che fra gente—caunoscente
col bradir s'aita;
colpi a mano renversa non so' en Franza,
e giamai non stette
firmo en soli fatti;
s'ell' odesse [omo] dire: "Gatti, Gatti!"
fugerebbe certo sì.

VI.   De quil ladro dico
ch'al figliol furarebbe,
traderebbe,—sì farebbe;
ver' è ch'eo me beffo,
ma consiglio ad ogn'om che se guarde,
ch'ogne male farebbe
[co]tant' [egli] è reo:
or como 'l pò soffrir Domenedeo
ne la soa malvascetà.

and no one could ever say
anything positive
about such a man.
He behaves so:
I want to tell you of his deeds,
and now I'll talk of something that no one else knows.

V.   He puts himself
in the point position
right away, with a mind
to take the defensive
he strikes to break the lance
and thrusts with the pike,
and he so varies his blows
that I've never seen any like them
nor will I again in all my days.
        With his legs together
he jumps right away
and among knowledgeable people—
he helps himself by yelling;
his backhanded blows aren't found in all France;
and he never stayed
fixed in his actions,
for if he heard someone say, "Cats! Cats!"
he'd certainly flee.

VI.   And I speak of that thief
who'd rob his own son;
he'd betray him—yes, he would.
It's true that I'm teasing, but I advise
everyone to be on their guard
because every sin he commits is quite evil.
Now, how could Lord God suffer him
in all his maliciousness?

50 *Siena*

        S'e' fosse al tempo antico
chi darebbe,—e chi trarrebbe
e chi lo sagettarebbe,
d'u ·maglion nocesse;
ma ben vezzo ch'ogn'om lo reguarde.
. . . . [-ebbe][66]
sì volesse Deo,
del suou fego 'l pagasse, al voler meo,
de la soa malvascetà.

VII.   Ma ill' è sì cattivissimo
che credo che la gente lo desdegna
de dargli, o de fargli 'ncrescimento,
ma no me 'n contento,
megli' è per un cento
serebbe a me, ch'ogni sou mal m'è bene.
        El ment' ha sì longissimo
qualunqua [omo] l[o] vede se ·nne segna
e prendenne sì grande smarrimento
che de pian convento
perde 'l suou talento:
'nanti vorrebbe soffrir forte pe[ne].

VIII.   El naso ha sì acutissimo
che pare una lesna di trag[ole],
ma' ch'i[n]e[67] tragole non pò gir più sù.
        Se moresse 'l trestissimo,
morrebbe una volta lu diavole,
megli'è ch'e' mora mill'e mille più.

IX.   Néd amore,
né sentore,
tradetore,
calatore,
d'ogni er[r]ore
porta en core,

If these were the ancient times,
someone would have given it to him, someone would have betrayed him,
and someone would have shot him
and damaged his chainmail;
but I see now that everyone esteems him.
. . . .
May it please God,
if I had my way, he'd pay
for his maliciousness!

VII.   For he is so evil
that I think people disdain
to give it to him, or to cause him remorse;
but I'm not happy.
It would be one hundred times better to me,
for his every ill is good for me.
         His chin is so very long
that whoever sees him crosses himself;
and they feel such dismay
that by plain necessity
they lose their appetite.
They'd rather suffer harsh pains.

VIII.   His nose is so pointy[69]
that it seems a javelin,
except that javelins don't go up so high.
         If he died most sadly,
that devil would die but one time;
it would be better for him to die a thousand times, and a thousand more.

IX.   Neither love
nor feeling
that traitor—
that faker
of every error—
carries in his heart;

non ha se ·nnon de dir palore:
pur parlando
con altri sta 'n gota
e spessamente si fa una rota,
e zamaï de paone,
un sì fatto pazzarone,
e' tènse savio 'l garzone.
E doisé,
che non sa 'l secol, do' se',
e' dice ch[ed] ogn'om gli par de fé.

X.   Non tardando
Và ·llui e dinota,
deh, carobetto, ch'eo fazza 'na nota.
Se per reprensïone,
di zo lassarò
e no ne derò
zo ch'eo saverò,
lass'a te,—doimé:
fagli le fiche e dì: —Min Zeppa, tè!'—,
fagli[le] tosto, s'él te 'n cal di me.

he only becomes pallid when he speaks,
for his speech
with others catches in his throat,
and he often wheels about
just like a peacock,
such a crazy man
he considers himself a wise youth!
And, listen,
this world doesn't know, listen!
It's said that to everyone he seems a man of faith.

X.   Oh caribetto, go to him
without delay
and tell him that I'm writing a note.
If, with reprehension,
I abandon such work
and I don't tell
what I know,
I allow you, alas!
to give him the figs[70] and to say: "Min Zeppa, take them!"
Do it right away, if you care about me.

Meo dei Tolomei: Poems of Debated Attribution

Poem 20: Meo crafts a self-portrait, first emphasizing his melancholy, and then relating it to his penchant for falling in love with women who don't return his affection. The poem, with its emphasis on melancholy and passion, recalls similar verses by Cecco Angiolieri,[71] but the reference to Mino Zeppa indicates authorship by Meo dei Tolomei. The poet claims that he always falls in love with people who know as much about passion as Mino Zeppa

        Caro mi costa la malinconia,
ché per fuggirla, son renduto a fare
l'arte disgraziata de l'usurare,
la qual consuma la persona mia.
        E ancor ci ha una maggior ricadia
che sempre mi convene innamorare
di tal che tanto s'intende d'amare,
quanto Min Zeppa de la storlomia.
        Ch'i' n'aggio amate—parecchie parecchie,
ch'assa' più fredde d'amor l'ho trovate,
che s'elle fosser di cent'anni vecchie.
        Ed or n'amo una di bellezz'e etate
che ben mi sian tagliate—ambo l'orecchie,
s'ella potesse far pepe di state.[72]

knows about astronomy, which is to say nothing at all. She is as cold as an elderly woman, and he would do anything for her to grow black pepper in summer, that is, to heat up her physical complexion.

       Melancholy costs me dearly[73]
because, to escape it, I have turned to do
that disgraceful art of usury,
which consumes my entire person.
       And then there's a far greater torment—
for I always find myself falling in love
with someone who knows as much about loving
as Min Zeppa knows about astronomy.
       For I have loved many, so many women,
and I've found them all to be colder about love
than if they were one hundred years old.
       And now I love one of such beauty and age:
may both my ears be lopped off
if she would grow peppers in summer.

Poem 21: Meo depicts himself as wooing a woman in a manner similar to poem 18. In this case, however, he successfully wins the woman over with his money. The poet presents love not as an emotional bond, but as a financial transaction between the man and woman. In this case, she concedes when he shows her his purse, and at the end, it is empty.

    L'altrier sì mi ferio una tal ticca,
ch'andar mi fece a madonna di corsa;
andava e ritornava com'un'orsa
che va arrabbiando e ·lluogo no si ficca.
   Quando mi vide credett'esser ricca,
disse:—Non avrestù cavelle in borsa?—
Rispuosi:—No.—Quella mi disse:—Attorsa,
e ·llevala pur tosto, o tu ·tt'impicca!—
   Mostrav'aspra come cuoio di riccio:
e' le feci una mostra di moneta;
quella mi disse:—Avesti caporiccio?—
   Quasi beffava e stava mansüeta
che·ll'avari' tenuta un fil di liccio;
ma pur ne venni con la borsa queta.

The other day I was stricken by such an urge[74]
that made me run to my lady;
I came and went like a she-bear,
which goes about raving and cannot find its den.
    When she saw me, she believed herself to be rich
and said: "Don't you have anything in your purse?"
I responded: "No." She said to me: "Turn around,
and get out of here quickly, or go hang yourself!"
    She showed herself to be as prickly as hedgehog skin:
I made a show of my coins.
She said: "Were you joking?"
    She almost snorted and was mild,
and I could have held her with a thread of silk,
but I came away with my purse totally quiet.

Poem 22: This sonnet taps into a long cultural tradition describing generosity as a noble trait. In the Italian communes, people debated about the nature of nobility, ranging from Aristotle's criteria of ancient possessions and virtue, to more recent opinions, such as those found in Dante's *Convivio*.[75] In this sonnet, the author sententiously expounds upon *largesse*, the most exalted attribute of medieval nobility. He explains that to delay a gift debases it, and regret only demeans the donor.

       Non è donar larghezz', al mi' parvente,
né non è detto largo alcun per dare;
ma quelli che 'n donare è canoscente
con cor allegro senz'alcun tardare,
       è da chiamare largo degnamente,
ché 'l don si vende per troppo indugiare.
Chi dona e pente in tutto n'è perdente
e se medesmo offende per donare.
       Per te lo dico, amico che lo intende,
ché non dimori 'n troppo tardamento,
ché 'l doppio val lo don che non s'attende.
       E chi promette e 'n poco tempo scende,
lo su' servir ha messo 'n perdimento,
e già non dona, ma con noia vende.[76]

   Giving isn't necessarily *largesse*, it seems,
nor is anyone called generous by giving;
but rather, those who are knowledgeable in giving
with joyous hearts and without delay
   are correctly called generous.
Because a gift, if delayed greatly, is sold[77]
Whoever gives and then rues it loses all,
and he offends himself through giving.
   For you I tell you this, my understanding friend,
so that you won't delay too much,
that a gift is worth double if it's not late.
   And whoever promises and then soon refuses
has turned his service into loss,
and doesn't really give, but sells with annoyance.

Poems 23A and 23B: It appears that Meo dei Tolomei reacted to a sonnet by Guido Cavalcanti (ca. 1250–1300). Cavalcanti, I mentioned in the introduction, was derided by Lupo degli Uberti for his alleged sexual interests. In this sonnet, Cavalcanti employs the trope of *vituperium in vetulam*, the insult and abuse of a stereotyped old woman.[78] Cavalcanti asks his addressee, Manetto, to contemplate her hideousness, which contrasts sharply to her fine clothes and to the lovely gentlewomen who accompany her.[79] Cavalcanti concludes that no pain or anguish is so strong that they wouldn't be driven out of a man's heart by the laughter her ugliness will inspire.[80] Thus, Manetto's laughter at her misshapenness will cure his lovesickness.

Meo's poem is extremely similar to Cavalcanti's, with parallel expressions and the same A-rhyme (-UZZA). Furthermore, Meo uses a B-rhyme

23A. Guido Cavalcanti (ca. 1250–1300)

    Guata, Manetto, quella scrignatuzza,
e pon' ben mente com'è divisata
e com'è drittamente sfigurata
e quel che pare quand'ella s'agruzza!
    Or, s'ella fosse vestita d'un'uzza
con cappellin' e di vel soggolata
ed apparisse di dìe accompagnata
d'alcuna bella donna gentiluzza,
    tu non avresti niquità sì forte
né saresti angoscioso sì d'amore
né sì involto di malinconia,
    che tu non fossi a rischio de la morte
di tanto rider che farebbe 'l core:
o tu morresti, o fuggiresti via.[82]

that is consonant with the original A-rhyme (-IZZA). Meo encourages the addressee, Ciampolo, to observe the old woman's hideous state, which will be contrasted further by her attempts to straighten herself. Like Cavalcanti, Meo concludes that the woman's ugliness will cure Ciampolo of any amatory feelings he might have in his heart. Scholars are divided about the attribution of the sonnet. However, the addressee of the poem, Ciampolo, may be the same individual insulted by Meo in other sonnets, Ciampolino; if so, then Meo's advice to cure him from loving women may be considered from the light of their sexual relationship. Cavalcanti's poem is itself based on other examples of insult and of *vituperium in vetulam*, thereby forming a chain of influence that leads to Meo dei Tolomei.[81]

23A. Guido Cavalcanti (ca. 1250–1300)

    Look, Manetto, at that little hunchback
and set your mind on how she's dressed,
and how she's so thoroughly misshapen,
and what she seems to be when she withdraws.
    Now if she were clothed in a cape
with a hat, or veiled with a wimple,
and if she appeared in daylight accompanied
by some beautiful, noble ladies
    you wouldn't feel a wrath so strong,
nor would you be so tormented in love,
nor so encompassed by melancholy
    that you wouldn't be at risk of death
for all the laughing your heart would do:
either you'd die or you'd run away.

23B. Meo dei Tolomei[83]

    Deh guata, Ciampol, ben questa vecchiuzza
com'ell'è ben diversamente viz[z]a,
e quel, che par, quand'un poco si riz[z]a,
e come coralmente viene 'n puzza;
    e com'a punto sembra una bertuzza
del viso e de le spalle e di fattezza,
e, quando la miriam, come s'adizza
e travolge e digrigna la boccuzza.
    Ché non dovresti sì forte sentire
d'ira, d'angoscia, d'affanno o d'amore,
che non dovessi molto rallegrarti,
    veggendo lei che ·ffa a maravigliarti
sì, che per poco non ti fa perire
gli spiriti amorosi ne lo core.

23B. Meo dei Tolomei

      Now look well, Ciampol, at this little old woman,[84]
how she is most strangely withered,
and how she seems when she straightens a little,
and how she causes a stink in your heart,
      and how she seems exactly like a Barbary ape
in her face, in her shoulders, and in her form,
and how, when we stare at her, she gets angry,
and grimaces and twists up her tiny mouth.
      Because you shouldn't feel strongly
any wrath, or angst, or struggles of love
that you shouldn't rejoice greatly
      seeing her, for she'll inspire such wonder
that it will nearly cause the death
of the amorous spirits within your heart.

Poetry Addressed to Meo dei Tolomei

Poem 24: In this sonnet, Dante Alighieri personified the poem itself as if a messenger. He asks it to behave courteously toward its recipient. It appears that the sonnet was an introduction to the other poems that accompanied it (vv. 12–14).

A general scholarly consensus exists that Dante probably intended Meo dei Tolomei as the addressee of this sonnet.[85] A *marginalium* accompanying

Dante: A Meuccio

     Sonetto, se Meuccio t'è mostrato,
così tosto ·l saluta come ·l vedi,
e va' correndo e gittaliti a' piedi
sì·cche tu paie bene acostumato.
     E quando sè con lui un poco stato
anche ·l risalutrai, non ti ricredi;
e posci' a l'ambasciata tua procedi,
ma fa' che 'l tragghe prima da un lato
     e di': "Meuccio, que' che·tt·am'assai
de le sue gioie più care ti manda
per acontarsi al tu' coraggio bono."
     Ma fa' che prenda per lo primo dono
questi tuo' frati, e a·llor sì comanda
che stean co·llui e qua non tornin mai.[86]

Dante's sonnet in the manuscript Chigiano L VIII 305 reads, "meuccio tolo. da siena" (f. 60r). Although composed in a later hand, the *marginalium* seemingly possesses some authority among the editors of Dante's lyrics.

24. Dante: To Meuccio

    Sonnet, if Meuccio is shown to you,
as soon as you see him you should greet him,
and run to him and throw yourself at his feet,
so that you'll appear well-mannered.
    And when you've been with him a little while,
greet him again—don't be hesitant!
And then proceed to your entreaty,
but first be sure to take him to one side,
    and say, "Meuccio, he who loves you greatly
sends you one of his most precious jewels
to become friendly to your good heart."
    But make it so he takes as his first gift
these brothers of yours, and command them
to stay with him, and never to return here.

66 *Siena*

Poem 25: Cino da Pistoia presents himself as a traditional medieval lover; he is in thrall to the beloved lady who treats him with disdain. Scholarship generally accepts that Cino's addressee for this sonnet may have been Meo dei Tolomei.[87] Cino will also engage in a *tenzone* with Marino Ceccoli (see sonnets 10A and 10B of Ceccoli's corpus).

Cino da Pistoia: A Meuccio[88]

  Meuccio, i' feci una vista d'amante
ad una fante—ch'è piacente in cera,
e 'ncontenente lo suo cor, ched era
come di cera—si fece diamante:
  ed ancor più, ché 'n ogni su' sembiante
passa avante—d'orgoglio ogn'altra fera:
aguila o falcone o cosa altera
a sua manera—non è simigliante.
  Per che si può veder nel mio distino
ch'ognuna d'umiltà ver' me si spoglia,
alza ed orgoglia—quant'io più m'inchino:
  e sì tosto mi dà di capolino,
com'io fo mostra d'una coral voglia;
per che m'è doglia—ch'i' testè non fino.

25. Cino da Pistoia: To Meuccio

      Meuccio, I cast the glance of a lover
toward a maiden whose face is pleasing,
and immediately, her heart, which was
soft like wax, became a hard diamond;
      and even more, for she surpasses
in pride every other wild beast with her looks—
eagle, falcon, or other haughty thing
is not like her in her manners.
      For that, one can see my destiny:
she strips herself of humility toward me,
and raises up in pride as much as I bow to her,
      and quickly she looks down her nose at me
when I demonstrate my heart's yearning,
so I'm in pain that doesn't end quickly.

Siena

POETRY INFLUENCED BY MEO DEI TOLOMEI

Poem 26: Cecco Angiolieri depicts himself as someone who cannot exist unless he is in love; in so doing, he compares himself to other sinful individuals, such as sodomites and heretics. Angiolieri lists a number of people about whom almost nothing is known: Moco di Pietro Tolomei (ca. 1285–1306), Mino di Peppo Accoridore Petroni, Tano, and Migo. By enumerating a group of individuals to be vituperated, it may be that Angiolieri took inspiration from the sonnet derisive of Niccola Muscia by Iacomo dei Tolomei,

Cecco Angiolieri[89]

  Io poterei star senz'amore
come la soddomia tòllar a Moco,
o come Ciampolin gavazzatore
potesse vivar tollendoli 'l gioco,
  o come Min di Pepo Accorridore
s'ardisse di toccar Tan pur un poco,
o come Migo, ch'è tutto d'errore,
ch'e' non morisse di caldo di fuoco.
  Però mi facci Amor ciò che li piace,
ch'i' sarò sempre su' servo fedele
e sofferrò ciò che mi farà 'n pace;
  e sed e' fosse amaro più che fele,
con l'umiltà ch'è vertù si verace,
il farò dolce come cannamele.

nicknamed il Graffione, mentioned in the introduction; if so, there are no specific textual links between this sonnet and Iacomo dei Tolomei, however.

In his list of people, Angiolieri describes Ciampolino in a manner consistent with Meo dei Tolomei's poetry, namely, as a gambler (vv. 3–4). Thus, he too evokes the concept of the tavern, such as seen in Meo's sonnets 13, 14, and 17.

26. Cecco Angiolieri (ca. 1260–1312)

  I could so live without love
just like you could take sodomy from Moco,[90]
or like Ciampolin the gambler
could live if you took his game from him,
  or like Min di Pepo Accorridore[91]
might hazard to strike Tano[92] even a little,
or like Migo,[93] who is full of heresy,
wouldn't die by feeling the flames' heat.
  But Love should do with me what he will,
for I will always be his faithful servant,
and I'll suffer in peace whatever he does;
  and if it were more bitter than bile
with humility, which is such a true virtue,
I'll make it sweeter than sugarcane.

CHAPTER TWO

Pseudo-Cecco Angiolieri

Poem 1: In this dialogue sonnet, the poet addresses his audience, asking if they have seen a man (*cotal*) whose face displays the three telltale colors of being in love. In so doing, he evokes the traditional concept of *fin'amor*, where love is treated as a feudal service to the beloved. When the audience responds that the man seemed no longer to be in love with the poet, he claims that he will lie down and cry, anticipating that he will be dead within

   —Udite udite, dico a voi, signori,
e fate motto, voi che siete amanti:
avreste voi veduto, tra cotanti,
cotal c'ha 'l volto di tre be' colori?
   Di ros'e bianch'e vermigli' è di fuori;
or lo mi dite, ch'i' vi son davanti,
sed elli inver' di me fé tai sembianti
ched i' potessi aver que' suo colori.—
   —Noi non crediam che li potessi avere,
però ched e' non fece ta' sembianti
che fosse ver' di te umilïato.—
   —Sed e' nol fece, i' mi pongo a giacere
e comincio a far ta' sospiri e pianti
che 'n quattro dì cred'esser sotterrato.—

four days.[1] Like Meo's brother, Mino Zeppa (Tolomei's sonnets 9 and 18), the poet lies down in a position of amorous submission, raising the question of who serves whom. By describing himself as currently in love in this sonnet, the poet seemingly anticipates several poems by Cecco Nuccoli (e.g., 1, 2, 8, 20).

"Listen, listen—I am speaking to you, sirs—
and speak, you who are lovers:
Would you have seen, among so many,
one man who has three lovely colors on his face?
    He is pink, and white, and red on the outside;[2]
now tell me as I stand before you,
if he acted in any way toward me
that I might have his three colors?"
    "We do not believe that you will have them,[3]
because he did not give the appearance
that he was in any way subject to you."
    "If he did not, then I lay myself down
and will begin to heave sighs and tears
so that in four days I will be dead and buried."

Poem 2: In this sonnet, the poet swears that he will never again love a man who does not return his affection. In discussing his emotions, he uses the tropes of troubadouric love poetry, depicting his adoration as a service (vv. 6, 11) and asserting himself to be faithful (v. 6). He also describes the beloved man as cruel, evoking another commonplace of amorous poetry. Because of his pains, the poet hopes that the other man's rejection will eventually cause

     I' so' non fermo in su questa oppenione
di non amar, a le sante guagnele,
uomo che sia inver' di me crudele,
non abbiendo egli alcuna cagione;
     ma questo dico, sanza riprensione,
di non servirti; né sarò fedele,
poi che di dolce mi vòi render fèle:
fàilti tu, ma non ne hai ragione.
     Da ch'i' conosco la tua sconoscenza,
che, ricredente, tu contra me fai,
vogli' arrestare di te mai servire.
     Per la qual cosa i' crederei 'nsanire
stu non n'avessi gran [de] penitenza,
con essa avendo grandissimi guai.

him to soften and take pity upon him. The phrasing of the *incipit* verse of this sonnet will be echoed by Cucco di Messer Gualfredduccio Baglioni in his *tenzone* with Cecco Nuccoli (poems 13A and 13B).

    I'm not firm in this opinion,
by the Holy Gospels, not to love
a man who acts cruelly toward me
without having any cause at all,
    but I say this, without any reprehension:
I will not serve you, nor will I be faithful,
since you wish to turn my sweetness into bile—
you are doing it, but you have no reason to.
    I now know about your rejection
because, changing your mind, you act against me,
and wish to stop me from serving you.
    Because of that, I think that I would lose my mind
if you did not feel great regret
and having with it immense pains.

Poem 3: The first of two sonnets about the amorous cruelty of a man, Corzo or Corso. In this one, the poet writes about how much he is in love with Corzo, discussing his passion with the traditional language of lovesickness. The poet asserts that he cannot cure his affection with either theriac or centaurea, both of which were treatments for poisoning; he later emphasizes that

      Un Corzo di Corzan m'ha sì trafitto
che non mi val cecèrbita pigliare,
né dolci medicine né amare,
né otrïaca che vegna d'Egitto.
      E ciò che Galïen ci lasciò scritto
aggio provato per voler campare:
tutto m'è gocciol' [una] d'acqua in mare,
tanto m'ha 'l su' velen nel mie cor fitto.
      Là 'nd'i' son quasi al tutto disperato,
[da] poi ch'e' non mi val null'argomento:
a questo porto Amor m'ha arrivato.
      ché son quell'uom che più vivo sgomento
che si' nel mondo o che mai fosse nato:
chi me n'ha colpa di terra sia spento.

not even enemas can help him. The presence of medicinal substances like these recalls several poems by Meo dei Tolomei (e.g., sonnets 3, 4, and 12).

      A Corzo from Corzan has so transfixed me[4]
that it isn't worth it for me to take centaurea,[5]
nor medicines bitter or sweet,
nor theriac that comes from Egypt.
      And I have tried everything
that Galen left written because I want to live;
it is all just a drop of water in the sea,
so much poison has he put in my veins.
      Thus, I despair almost completely,
and there is no use in me having an enema;[6]
Love has brought me to this port.
      Consequently, I'm the most anguished man alive
in the world, or who has ever been born,
may he whose fault it is be extinguished from the earth!

Poem 4: In the second sonnet about Corso (or Corzo), the poet addresses another unnamed person. He curses the addressee to fall in love with Corso, and, as in the previous sonnet, he describes lovesickness in language reminiscent of being poisoned. As in that instance, references to poisoning recollect similar statements in the poetry by Meo dei Tolomei (e.g., sonnets 3 and 4). In this sonnet, the poet compares himself to animals—an ox and a bear—

       In tale che d'amor vi passi 'l core
abattervi possiate voi, ser Corso,
e sì vi pregi vie men ch'un vil torso,
e come tòsco li siate in amore;
       e facciavi mugghiare a tutte l'ore
del giorno come mugghia bue od orso,
e, come l'ebbro bee a sorso a sorso
il vin, vi facci ber foco e martòre.
       E se non fosse ch'i' non son lasciato,
sì mal direi, e vie più fieramente,
al vostro gaio compagno e avenente
       che di bellezze avanza ogni uom nato;
ma sì mi stringe l'amor infiammato
che verso lui ho sparto per la mente.

and to a drunkard, and through these metaphors, he stresses his loss of rationality as a lover; in so doing, he draws connections to other comic sonnets by Angiolieri.[7]

      May you run into the man for whom[8]
love pierces your heart, ser Corso,
and may he consider you less than a meager stalk,
and, like poison, may you be in love.
      He will make you roar at all hours
of the day like an ox or bear roars;
and, just as the drunkard gulps mouthfuls
of wine, he will make you drink fire and pain.
      And were it not that it hasn't abandoned me,
I would speak ill, and even more fiercely,
to your joyful and handsome companion
      whose looks surpass every man ever born;
but I am restrained so much by the burning love
that I have cast toward him in my mind.

PART 2

Perugia

Poets of the Vatican Barberiniano Latin 4036 Manuscript

CHAPTER THREE

CECCO NUCCOLI

Poem 1: In this poem and numerous others that follow, Nuccoli writes about passion using language typical of courtly love (e.g., sonnets 2, 4, 6, 8, 9, 16, 22, 23, 24, and 25). Here, Nuccoli writes a traditional complaint about the cruelty of his beloved, in this instance a man he calls "lord" (*signore*). Marino Ceccoli also calls his beloved a "lord" (e.g., poems 6, 7, and 8), indicating the strong connection between the two poets; one may have influenced the other, or both may have taken inspiration from Occitanic love poetry, in which the poet referred to his beloved as "my lord" (*midons*).[1] In this sonnet,

Ser Cecchus Nuccholi de Perussio

    Po' che nel dolce aspetto abandonai
e legai l'alma nei vostre costume,
o signor, de mia vita guida e lume,
prima ch'io mòra, vederov' io mai?
    Io me partie da voi e 'l cor lassai,
onde conven che sempre io me consume;
e ben ch'io sparga de lagreme fiume,
pianger non posso che me paia assai.
    Non serà mai—piager che mi contente
né ch'ai dogliose spirte done pace,
fin ch'io non veggio voi, signor verace.
    Ma questa angoscia che così me sface,
signore, or ve recorda il cor servente,
che, poi ch'è vostro, non v'esca de mente.

Nuccoli explains that he suffers a great deal, and he sheds a river of tears. The beloved man, in contrast, treats him cruelly, and does not take pity on Nuccoli's pains. In another poem, he discusses the origin of the Tiber (sonnet 6), perhaps forming a connection between the two sonnets.

Ser Cecco Nuccoli of Perugia

     Ever since I lost my soul in your sweet face,[2]
and I bound it up in your behaviors,
oh, my lord, guide and light of my life,
will I ever see you before I die?
     I departed from you and left my heart
where it is always necessary that I be destroyed,
and even though I shed a river of tears,
I can't cry so much that it seems like too much crying.
     You'll never find it pleasing to make me happy
nor to grant peace to my pained spirits
by gazing upon you again, my true lord.
     But may this anguish, which so undoes me,
lord, now remind you of my faithful heart:
since it belongs to you, may you never forget about it.

Poem 2: Using the language of *fin'amor*, Nuccoli begs forgiveness from his "lord" (*signore*). The subservient lover who repents for disobedience is a commonplace of medieval poetry that originated in the Occitan tradition of the twelfth century.[3] In this poem, Nuccoli calls for mercy, a traditional trope of love poetry, and he adds that the beloved man can punish him severely if necessary. He would accept even being killed, he writes, if first the other

Ser Cecchus Nuc[c]holi

Pecchavi, Deus, miserere mei!
De, dolce Signor mio, or mi perdona!
e pensa che, se ogne opera fussa bona,
luoco de misericordia non serei.
      Se non mi receve, e io te vegno ai pièi,
molto serà crudel la tua persona;
però che pièta mai no abandona
chi dice: "Mercé cheggio, ch'io mal fei!"
      Ma perché[4] meglio perdonar mi posse,
dove e quando tu vòl, tutto m'alide,
flagella la mia carne e i nerbe e gl'osse.
      E se di questo saciar non ti vede,
e non t'appaghe de cotal' percosse,
perdonaraime prima, e puoi m'ancide.

man would forgive him. Marino Ceccoli writes a similar sonnet, "Oh, see now that I myself will come" (sonnet 7), in which he begs forgiveness of his "lord," again illustrating the strong connection between the two poets.

Ser Cecco Nuccoli

> *I've sinned, God, have mercy on me!*
Ah, my sweet lord, pardon me now,
and consider how, if every act were good,
there would be no place for mercy.
>> If you don't receive me, and let me approach your feet,
your appearance will be quite cruel,
because Pity never abandons whoever says,
"I beg for mercy for I've done wrong!"
>> But so that you can better pardon me
wherever and whenever you like, strike me all over,
flagellate my flesh, nerves, and bones.
>> And if from this, I don't see you satisfied,
and if you aren't fulfilled from this beating,
pardon me first, and then have me killed.

Poems 3A and 3B: A poetic correspondence with Gilio Lelli. In the opening sonnet, Nuccoli mentions that he lost a colt while gambling, and he complains about how his father chastises him for the loss. He had wagered the colt during a game of *minoretto* (a card game) and he promises never again to gamble on *zara* (a dicing game). He has lost his mantle and is dressed only in his doublet (a garment that was worn beneath the robes), hoping not to remain hidden under the roof, that is, in the attic, composing sad poetry. In this sonnet, Nuccoli reiterates comic commonplaces about poverty, the loss of clothes by gambling, and the lament about cruel fathers who do not sup-

3A. Ser Cecchus

      Nel tempo[5] santo non vidd'io mai petra
nuda escoperta, com'è el mio farsetto,
e porto una gonella senza occhietto,
che, chi la mira, ben par cosa tetra.

      Ma s'io avesse i denar de la poletra
la qual vendei e misi a minoretto,
io più nascosto non staria so 'l tetto
a far sonette ne' dolente metra.

      E mille fiade êl giorno mi coruccio
collo mio padre, che no vòl vestirme:
"V'à la puledra?" e questo è 'l mio riproccio.

      Ond'io m'acorgo che non val più dirme
ched ei mi vesta; ch'esso s'è disposto
di non mettere in me un denaio di costo,

      perch'el mi fe' un farsetto, e io gli promise
de non giucar né a tavol né ad azara,
dov'ò perduta la poletra cara.

port their sons' extravagance; for examples of these motifs, see the corpus of Cecco Angiolieri. Here, Nuccoli composes *sonetti caudati*, seventeen-line sonnets to which a third tercet has been added, and Lelli will do likewise in his response.

Lelli replies using the very same rhymes as Nuccoli (*per le rime*). Lelli writes that sometimes the best son is the prodigal son who returns, and the best geometer comes from the poor neighborhood of Malborghetto. Nonetheless, Lelli continues, Nuccoli's father is correct to castigate him for his gambling.

3A. Ser Cecco

      I never saw, in the holy temple, a rock[6]
as nude and uncovered as is my doublet;
and I wear a tunic without eyelets,
which, to whoever sees it, seems a glum thing.
      But if I have the money for the colt
that I sold and bet on *minoretto*,
I wouldn't stay hidden under the roof
writing sonnets in a doleful meter.
      I get angry a thousand times a day
with my father, who doesn't want to clothe me.
"Do you have the colt?"—this is the reproach I get!
      Hence, I realize that it's not worth it to say
he should buy me clothes: he's so disposed
not to take on another coin's expense!
      Because he had a doublet made and I promised
not to play the tables, nor at *zara*
where I lost the dear colt.

3B. Responsio Gillij Lelli

     Talor se tène alcun sommo geumetra,
ch' egl'è pur di collor de Malborghetto;
e tal se tiene el figliuol benedetto,
che da la vera sentenza s'aretra.
     S'io miro bene aglie specchiate vetra,
non se' per pace del padre dilletto;
ché s'el te bisognasse un calciaretto
sonarà sempre simigliante cetra.
     Né mai per te discioglierà tascoccio,
ancie spesso dirà: "Co' puoi desdirme
ch'a la puledra non fusse mal soccio?
     Giucàstela? Briga de casa uscirme."
E tu fa' guerra, e l'acordo 'l proposto;
entanto, se tu puoi, vende del mosto.
     Se non farai così, vederai rise!
Ch'al tuo farsetto—glie faràì ripara
solaio o tetto,—se non vai po' bara.

3B. Response by Gilio Lelli

   Sometimes the man reputed to be the best geometer
comes even from the people of Malborghetto,
and some believe that the blessed son
is the one who turns away from the correct path.[7]

   If I look well into the mirrored glass,
you're not the happiness of your father's peace,
because if you needed a pair of leggings,
he would always play a similar zither.[8]

   Nor will he ever loosen his purse strings,
but instead he'll say, "How can you deny
that you weren't a bad owner of the colt?

   You gambled it! You're trouble in my house—leave!"
And you wage war, and the provost[9] will make peace,
and then, if you can, sell the dregs of the wine.

   If you don't do that, you'll see laughter
about your doublet—you'll need to repair
to your attic or roof—if you don't stop gambling.

Poem 4: Another traditional complaint about love. Nuccoli feels the urge to look upon his beloved, and when the other person is far away from him, he suffers. He describes the beloved's beauty in terms of luminosity, again a commonplace in the amorous poetry of medieval Italy. The poet adds a couplet to the sonnet that functions as an *envoi*, telling the sonnet to travel to the person he loves.

Ser Cecchus Nuc[c]holi

    Voi che portate de mia vita luce
nel viso chiaro col piacevele aspetto,
e non vedete me, vostro soggetto,
ch'Amor per voi a la morte conduce;
    poi che 'l toccar da me fugg'e desduce
e del parlarvi sòfero 'l diffetto,
de, non siat' aspre a mostrarm' el cospetto,
che raggio di salute al cuor traluce.
    Per lo qual amirar sì spesso vegno,
e, voi celandol, divento tereno
e sempre 'l tristo spirito più vien meno.
    Vergogna nel venir no à, né freno,
ben ch'altre parle o me dimostre in segno
(m'è pur magior la pena ch'io sostegno).
    Dinancie a sua figura tu sie messo,
sonetto mio, vicario di me stesso.

Ser Cecco Nuccoli

>You who bring light to my life[10]
in your bright face with its pleasing aspect:
you don't see me, your subject,
whom Love, for you, drives toward death.
>>Since he leads you to flee from my embraces,
I'll suffer my inability to speak to you.
Ah, don't be harsh to me by not showing yourself,
for you radiate well-being and it glows in my heart.
>>For that reason I come so often to see you,
and when you hide your face, I turn to earth,
and my sad spirit always fails me even more.
>>I have no shame in coming to see you, nor any restraint—
even though others talk about me or point me out;
the pain I suffer is still greater than any of that.
>>My sonnet, my stand-in,
may you be sent before his person.

Poem 5: The context of this sonnet is not entirely clear, and it may have been part of a *tenzone*. In it, Nuccoli offers advice to a friend, Nicolò, to be careful about what he says. He warns Nicolò about the many enemies he has made in this way. This poem appears to highlight the dangers of the poetics of invective, the use of insult in the comic literature of the age. Nuccoli employs the phonology of comic poetry, employing consonantal clusters in the rhym-

C. Ser Cecchus predictus

    Nicolò, io vero amico te consiglio
che tu ti guardi inanti che ·tti atacche,
perché l'onor de toi vertute affiacche
e cange l'ordo nero e 'l bel vermiglio.
    Empara di tacer e farai meglio,
e guarda che chi t'ode non te fiacche;
ceco se', se non vede quante bracche
cercante de pigliar, però ti sveglio.
    Parlano molti, che tacer non sanno,
dannandosi colle lor sceme bocche,
che spesse fiade recevono 'l malanno.
    Or fa' che quisto vizio non ti tocche;
molte recevon, di lor tacer, danno:
or pensa ogiemai, inanti che scocche.

ing position (A: -IGLIO; B: -ACCHE; C: -ANNO; D: -OCCHE);[11] the B- and D-rhymes are also consonant of each other.

Song [Sonnet] of the aforementioned Ser Cecco

    Nicolò, as a true friend I advise you
to look ahead before you attack
because you weaken your virtue's honor
and change the black lines and the nice vermillion.[12]
    Learn to stay quiet, and you'll do better,
and you'll see that whoever hears you doesn't blame you;
you're blind if you don't see how many hounds
seek to catch you—this is why I'm rousing you.
    Many people say they don't know how to be quiet,
harming themselves with their silly mouths
that many times bring about misfortunes.
    Now make it so that this vice doesn't touch you;
many others are harmed by their silence;
so think before you shoot off your mouth.

Poem 6: Nuccoli complains about loving a flawed man, but he hopes that, over time, the beloved will transform into a more virtuous individual. Nuccoli uses a discussion of rivers to depict love's power to elevate someone, possibly connecting this poem to the river of tears in sonnet 1. Here, Nuccoli builds upon the legend that the Tiber River had originally been named the Albula, but it was renamed after the King Tiberinus drowned in it during a battle. It now runs as clear as the Ticino, he writes, and flows directly to the sea.

Massèra proposed the interpretation that Nuccoli was punning on the similarity between the first syllable of the Tiber River (*Te*vere) and the first

C. Ser Cecchus

      Non moriêr tanti mai di calde febbre,
dal giorno in qua ch'el primo fanciul nacque,
quant'io ò pentîon', ched el mi piacque
la scurità di quel ch'è amar co' lebbre.
      E ·cco' l'Alpino trasmutato in Tebbre
fu per fortuna de le soperchie acque,
così io sono, poi che ·lloco giacque
ove assaggiai del ben del dolce Tebbre;
      ché corre sempre chiar come Tesino
questo fiume real sovr'ogne fiume:
infino al mar non perde il suo camino.
      Risplende in esso un sì lucente lume
che chi lui mira di coraggio fino
può dir ch'Amor lui regge in bel costume.
      Sì ch'io ò lasciata l'aiera de le Chiane
e vòi la Teverina per mio stallo;
cambiando il viso, adoro un chiar cristallo.

syllable of the beloved man *Tre*baldino in this sonnet. Massèra's interpretation would put the sonnet in line with Nuccoli's poem 8, below, where he places the recipient's name in an acrostic. However, it seems more likely that Nuccoli is writing here about Tiberutium de Montemellino, the addressee of two sonnets by Marino Ceccoli (sonnets 18 and 19); the name "Tiberutium" directly evokes the Tiber River. In other words, it may be about Nuccoli's attraction to another individual entirely. If this is the case, then it is also further evidence of the mutual influence between Nuccoli and Ceccoli. This is another *sonetto caudato*, a seventeen-line sonnet to which an additional tercet has been added.

Song [Sonnet] by Ser Cecco

    So many haven't died from hot fevers
since the day the first child was born
as I have regrets, for I enjoyed the darkness
about loving someone who has many flaws.[13]
    But just as the Albula was transformed into Tiber
by the fortune of overabundant waters,
so too I, when I lay in that place
where I tasted the sweetness of the Tiber.
    For it runs as clear as Ticino,
this royal river, above all other rivers;
it never loses its course until it reaches the sea.
    A light shines on it so bright
that whoever with a fine heart looks upon it
can say that Love reigns in it with fine manners.
    So that I have left the clear air of the Chiana valley,
and you've left the Tiber valley[14] for my location;
swapping them, I adore a crystalline brightness.

Sonnets 7A and 7B: A *tenzone* between Nuccoli and someone identified as Girardello about mistreatment of a hawk, Monna Raggia.[15] In the opening sonnet, Nuccoli rails against someone who mistreated Monna Raggia and pulled off her tail. He then asserts that he would physically attack the person who plotted the assault, which he describes with the metaphor of the merchant who brings grain to the mill to be ground, that is, someone prepared to do business. For him to even be around such a person would be a punishment to him, he says, bringing further shame upon him. When imagining his vendetta, Nuccoli uses an expression like one found in the poetry of Cecco Angiolieri, further indicating the influence of Angiolieri on him.[16] Given that Nuccoli uses metaphors of hawks or hawking to discuss sexual

7A. Ser Cecchus

    S'io potesse saper chi fu 'l villano
che prese tanto ardir, per quel ch'io oda,
ch'a monna Raggia mia trasse la coda,
fariel grattar con ambendue le mano;
        sì ch'elli avrebbe lavorato invano
(se del mio dir sentenzia si disnoda;
ond'io ne porterebbe vera loda)
s'el mercenaio arpuse in l'arca grano.
        Ben so ch'ell'è vendetta corporale,
se no ch'en farla pigioràra l'onta
chi se ponesse col brutto animale.
        Ben che darei a tal derrata gionta
e farebbei giustar sì fatto sale
che derie monna Raggia: "Io so' mo sconta!"
        Sì fatta doglia porta monna Raggia,
che, per la coda, sua bellezza cala,
che non si cura di coltel de l'ala.

matters in other sonnets (e.g., sonnets 10, 11C, and 14A), it is possible that Monna Raggia exemplifies his penis.

In his response, Girardello informs Nuccoli that the person who harmed Monna Raggia has already been punished. He asserts that the Arthurian knight Tristan would not have exacted a harsher penalty on the perpetrator. Thus, he tells Nuccoli not to pursue further vengeance because Monna Raggia is healthy and able to fly. However, Girardello is not entirely clear in his sonnet, with several statements that appear to contradict his overall message. Girardello responds using the same rhymes as Nuccoli (*per le rime*), and both writers compose seventeen-verse *sonetti caudati*.

7A. Ser Cecco

If I could find out who the villain was
who, from what I hear, dared so much
that he pulled the tail off my Monna Raggia,
I'd scratch him with both of my hands!
    Thus, the merchant who brought his grain to the mill
would have done his business in vain
(if the truth of my statements is understood
so that I'd get high praise for it).
    I know well that it is corporal punishment
just to be with such an ugly animal—
merely by doing it, the shame worsens!
    I would give him such a repayment
and make him taste such saltiness
that Monna Raggia would say, "I've been repaid!"
    Monna Raggia bears such pains
that, because of her tail, her beauty has been reduced
that she doesn't even care about the knife that cut her wing.

7B. C. Responsio Girardelli

      Ben me rincrebbe perch'io foi lontano
da monna Raggia, ch'arviene a dar loda;
e però, miser Cecco, el cor ve 'n goda
che vendetta fu fatta a mano a mano;
      ma se si ravistasse il buon Tristano
non avrè' fatta vendetta più soda!
Se ciò non è, io prego che m'ennoda
colui che cadde dal cenno sovrano.
      Ma ben vi dico c'a cotanto male
non si satisfarei, ché sua bontà,
che porta monna Raggia, è 'n le suoe ale;
      ché del volare ell'è cotanto pronta
ch'ella non prenderebbe due cicale;
e questo è vero, per quel che si conta.
      Nei suoi sembianti si mostra sì saggia
che mai non si vorrè' partir di sala;
però cacciate via la cosa mala.

7B. Song [Sonnet] Response by Girardello

     I so regretted that I was distant
from Monna Raggia, whom you are now praising;
and so, my Messer Cecco, my heart now rejoices
that vengeance was done bit by bit.
     But if good Tristan were alive again,
he wouldn't have exacted a harsher revenge!
If that isn't so, I beg him who fell
at the sovereign's hand[17] to hate me.
     But I tell you clearly that I wouldn't have repaid
such a bad action, because the goodness
that Monna Raggia bears is in her wings,
     for she is so ready to fly
that she wouldn't catch two cicadas,[18]
and this, according to what I've said, is true.
     She shows herself to be so wise in appearance
that she'd never want to leave her rooms—
so drive away that cruelty from you!

Poem 8: A poem about Nuccoli's love for Trebaldino, which has lasted for three years at this point and has caused him great suffering. Again, the poet echoes commonplaces of the *fin'amor* tradition in this sonnet, for instance, describing Trebaldino's beauty through the metaphor of brightness. Massèra noted that the first syllable of each line forms acrostics indicating its recipient (Trebaldino Manfredino), the poet (Ser Cecco), and Trebaldino's mother (Rabeluccia, shortened to Luccia). No attempt was made to retain the acros-

C. Ser Cecchus

      TRE anni e più fa mo ch'Amor mi prese,
ma 'n ben so' certo che mai non mi lassa;
BALlenò uno splendor c'ogn'altro passa,
*fre*dd'era il tempo, di callor m'acese,
      DI morte in vita mia alma sospese.
*Di*telme, donque, Amor se mai s'abassa.
NOn vede tu ch'io sto co' pesce i ·nassa,
no po' fugir da lui né far defesa?
      SERvir ce puoi, Amore, e togler doglie!
*Ra*mo fiorito, che stai in sul Monte,
CEllatamente fa che tu ne coglie;
*be*n puoi saper qual nome io porto in fronte:
COlui, che già dinanze fe' menzione:
Luccia ferito al figliuol pon cagione.

tics in the translation. In this sonnet, Nuccoli refers to the beloved Trebaldino as a "flowering branch" (*ramo fiorito*), a designation that will recur in other sonnets about him (e.g., sonnet 9).

Song [Sonnet] by Ser Cecco

  Three years and more now since Love claimed me,
and I'm certain that he'll never abandon me;
a bright light flashed, which surpasses all others;
the weather was cold, but it heated me up.
  My soul hung between life and death—
tell me, therefore, if my love will ever diminish.
Don't you see that I'm like a fish in a trap,
nor can I flee from him, nor make my defense.
  You can make use of me, Love, and reduce my pains!
Flowering branch, who are atop the mountain,
hidden so you can act to seize me.
  You know which name is imprinted on my forehead—
he, whom I discussed before:
Luccia, correct your son, who too has been wounded.

Poem 9: A love poem to Trebaldino, whom Nuccoli calls "flowering branch," as he did in sonnet 8. He describes the pain he feels on any day he does not see Trebaldino, again imitating an *incipit* verse of a poem by Angiolieri.[19] He expounds on the metaphor of Trebaldino as a tree, asking to spend the afternoon in his shade. Nuccoli reiterates his amorous pains in this sonnet, fearing that he might die from his suffering if he is not allowed to see him. Interestingly, he portrays gazing upon Trebaldino as "Love's sweet fruit" (*suo*

Idem Ser Cecchus

  Ramo fiorito, êl dì ch'io non ti veggio,
mio lieto cor di doglia si traffigge
e la mia smarrita mente se reffigge
con quel signore Amor, cui sempre chieggio.
  Ond'io ne prego voi, prima ch'io peggio
stia, ch'io vegna so la tua merigge;
se non, la morte dal corpo defigge
l'alma, che nel mio cor per voi posseggio.
  Donque vi piaccia per Dio, signor caro,
di farme grazia prima ch'io sia morto,
ch'io no n'espero mai altro conforto
  se no 'l suo dolce frutto (per me amaro!);
ma se per lui mia vita non riparo,
girò nell'atro mondo da te scorto.
  Sì·mme prendeste, Amor, con novo ingegno
ch'io sempremai so' stato vostro segno.

dolce frutto), possibly echoing Brunetto Latini's description of Dante in hell's circle of the sodomites as a "sweet fig" (*dolce fico*) (*Inferno* 15.66). In this instance, Nuccoli composed a sixteen-verse *sonetto caudato*, adding a couplet to the sonnet.

The Same Ser Cecco

     Flowering branch, the day I don't see you,
my happy heart is run through with pain,
and my bewildered mind takes refuge
with that lord, Love, whom I always beseech.
     Hence, I pray to you, before I worsen,
to let me pass the afternoon beneath your shadow;
if not, may Death separate from my body
my soul, which lives in my heart only for you.
     Therefore, may you, my dear lord, find it pleasing
by God, to do me this grace before I die,
because I can't hope for any other comfort
     than Love's sweet fruit (now bitter for me).
If I don't defend my life on his account,
I'll be sent by you to the Other World.
     Love, you've snared me with a new trap
for I always have been your target.

Poem 10: A complaint about Trebaldino's mother, Rabeluccia (Luccia), addressed to another person, who is Nuccoli's friend. Nuccoli compares his anger at her to the fits of rage of Pope Boniface VIII (d. 1303). Luccia prevents the poet from seeing her son, and she tries to drive Nuccoli off. It is a commonplace in comic literature to rail against the woman who impedes the lover's advances, a trope related to *vituperium in vetulam*.[20] In this poem, Nuccoli compares Luccia to Medea and suggests her wantonness, evoking Meo dei Tolomei's invectives against his own mother (e.g., poem 5). He then blames Luccia for "killing his hawk," a metaphor for the loss of sexual interest. It is possible that this metaphor relates to the identity of Monna Raggia

C. Ser Cecchus

    Rabbia mi morde el cor con magiur izza
che quella che conquise Bonifazio
(benigno aspetto d'un desso ch'io sazio
sì del bel cor ch'emmaginando frizza!);
    Luccia, la landra, che per me se drizza
sovra 'l suo figlio a far diverso strazio,
dicendo sempre: "Io non ti darò spazio,
ladro, che tu mai parle a quel ch'atizza."
    Così è questa crudel de pietà nuda,
più che no fu al suo tempo Medea,
ch'el mio sparvier à uciso ne la muda.
    Ma ella coi van' penscier se fa una dea,
ma la natura 'l dà ch'el gioven facia,
enella sua età, cosa che i piaccia.
    S'el mio ci è morto, non è cosa nova,
che quel de Giovanel ne fe' già prova.

in Nuccoli's poems 7A and 7B, as not only a bird but also as Nuccoli's phallus. Nonetheless, he concludes here, even if his hawk has died, that of another man, Giovannel, faces a similar challenge. This sonnet resembles Meo dei Tolomei's invective against the old woman (23B); its A-rhyme is identical to Tolomei's B-rhyme (-IZZA) and both sonnets describe an elderly woman who pretends to be young, and who impedes the interaction of the poets and their lovers. For a fuller discussion of the phonology of comic poetry, see Meo dei Tolomei's poem 23A.

Song [Sonnet] by Ser Cecco

    Rage bites my heart with greater fury
than that which conquered Boniface:
you, with the benevolent face, who satisfies me
with your lovely heart that makes me burn just to imagine it.
    Luccia, that slut, moves above
her son to cause me a new type of torture,
always telling me: "I won't make room
for you to speak, thief, with the man who makes you burn."
    This cruel woman is so devoid of pity—
more so even than Medea in her time—
that she's killed my hawk in its molting nest.
    But in her vain thoughts she considers herself a goddess,
for her nature makes the man, young in age,
do whatever she wants him to do.
    So it's nothing strange that my hawk has died;
Giovannel's has already been put to the test.[21]

108   *Perugia*

Poems 11A, 11B, and 11C: A poetic correspondence between Gilio Lelli, Trebaldino, and Cecco Nuccoli. In the opening sonnet, Gilio chastises Nuccoli for loving Trebaldino, saying that Trebaldino withholds his heart from Nuccoli. He underscores the reference to *fin'amor* by evoking the grandeur of King Arthur. Gilio then compares Nuccoli to a chervil, which Mancini explains via reference to the *lai* of the same name by Marie de France (ca. 1160–1215); in the *lai*, two lovers are compared to a chervil and a nut tree, two plants that grow together but both die when separated. Gilio concludes by saying that Nuccoli should abandon Trebaldino and take him for a lover instead.

Trebaldino responds to Gilio, proclaiming his love for Nuccoli and continuing the plant metaphor of the first sonnet. He too is under Love's lordship, but he mentions that his life is more dishonest than that of any woman; not only does he evoke the commonplace misogyny of the time, but he also

11A. C. Gillius Lelli Trebaldino in personam Ugholinj

   O tu, che l'amorosa fiamma prove,
la qual nel tuo bel dir si manifesta,
com'è che tu non ài la voglia presta
et a servir Amor non ti retrove?
   Ché chi dal dir l'effetto suo remove,
non sente amor, ma vanità di testa;
e vòi' che sappi ch'è magiore inchesta
che quella dove—Artus fe' cose nove.
   Tu credi ad un che ti pasce di vento,
che non può aver per sé pur de lo scoglio,
e lascie quel che ti può far contento.
   Ma tu vuole esser un tuo cirafoglio,
dicendo, poi ch'avesse êl gioco vénto:
"Questo mi tolgo e de megl'non ti voglio."
   Se tu 'nno 'l fai, te 'n puoi lavar li mano.
Che vai tu più cercando, s'i' dico: "Ecco,
io servo te se tu serve ser Cecco"?

suggests a gender inversion as regards his relationship to Nuccoli. Nuccoli concludes the exchange, writing in the voice of another person, Ugolino. He tells Gilio that he has lived beneath him, and that he will come to him at any time. Nuccoli imbues his sonnet with suggestive language, including saying that he resides beneath Gilio's clothing, and then telling Gilio to "suck on my beak"; the beak as a euphemism for the penis was not uncommon, and it may relate to his use of metaphors of hawks and hawking in other sonnets (e.g., Nuccoli's sonnets 7A, 7B, 10, and 14A).[22] Furthermore, Trebaldino also implies fellatio in his poem ("kiss his goodness," v. 17). Nuccoli and Trebaldino are unusual in this regard because fellatio was a subject matter unusual in medieval culture.[23] Nevertheless, in their poetry they appear to echo Meo dei Tolomei's insinuation of the penis ("desire the masculine," v. 8) in his sonnet 13.

11A. Song [Sonnet] by Gillio Lelli to Trebaldino in the person of Ugolino

   Oh, you who feel the amorous flame
that is made manifest in your lovely speech,
how is it that you don't feel ready
to find yourself serving Love anew?
   Because whoever puts distance between words and deeds
doesn't feel love, but has an empty head:
Do you want me to think it's a greater quest
than the one on which Arthur did great deeds?
   You believe that man who feeds you on air
because you can't have even the smallest part of him,
and he omits the one piece of himself that could make you happy.
   But you want to be his chervil,
saying after you've won the game:
"I take him from you, and I don't want any better for you."
   If you don't do it, then wash your hands of me.
What are you still searching for, because I'm saying,
"I'll serve you, if you'll serve Ser Cecco"

11B. Responsio Trebaldini

  Egli è ben ver che sotto Amor mi trove
e provo spesso in me com'è molesta
la vita degli amante, e che lor pésta;
ma se provato ài, fa' che riprove.

  Sì io servo ad Amore; e saper fòve
ch'io non so' al mondo so l'altrui podesta,
onde par la mia vita disonesta
più ched è inn·onne donna (De mi jove!).

  Ma tu dice sì spesso io mi pento
d'aver detto del sì che s'io mi spoglio
d'ogni mia volontade e più non sento

  te en me sì come sentir soglio,
e d'engannare altrui non n'ò talento;
ma tu, che dice "Voglio"—e poi "Disvoglio."

  Al mio signor ser Cecco,—tutto sano,
libero glie me do, e verde e secco,
poi che se dice ch'io del suo ben lecco.

11B. Response by Trebaldino

      It's true that you find me beneath Love,
and I often feel in myself how difficult
is the life of lovers, and how he batters them.
But if you've tried it, then he leads you to try anew.
      But I serve Love, and I know how
not to be under anyone else's lordship in the world,
so my life seems more dishonest
than that of any woman (so may God help me!).
      But you so often say that I will repent
of having said yes; that I so strip myself
of any will, and I feel nothing for you
      in myself, as I usually feel;
and I have no desire to trick anyone
except you, who say, "I want" and then "I don't want."
      I freely give myself to my lord Ser Cecco,
wholly, healthy, green, and dry,
then it will be said that I kiss his goodness.

11C. Responsio Ser Cecchi in personam Ugholini

    El tuo bel dir ligiadro ver' me piove
sì spesso ch'ei conven ch'io prenda in presta
de le tuoi dolce rime e faccia festa
teco, bel frate, puoi c'a ciò ti move;
    ond'io ti prego che me diche dove
tu vuol ch'io vegna, o da terza o da sesta,
ché mill'anni me par ch'io so tua vesta
dimore quanto vòl, non penso altrove;
    però ti prego che tu non sie lento
a far quel che v'è scritto in questo foglio,
da po che io servirte non pavento.
    Ma io del tempo perduto mi doglio,
perch'io non t'ò servito volte cento,
po' che tu grane sempre dov'io gioglio.
    Vostro mi fo en monte e 'n coste e 'n piano;
da poi che col bel dir teco m'atecco,
dimme ove vegna e sucheràim' el becco.

11C. Response by Ser Cecco in the person of Ugolino

     Your beautiful speech rains toward me
so often that I need to borrow
your sweet rhymes, and I rejoice
with you, lovely friar, since you're moved to say them.
     Hence, I beg you to tell me where
you want me to come at the third or sixth hour,
for it seems to me a thousand years since I've resided
beneath your garments, and I think of nowhere else.
     But I beg you not to be slow
to do what's written on this piece of paper
since I'm not hesitant to serve you.
     But I regret the time I've already lost
because I haven't served you one hundred times,
since you always flower where I rejoice.
     I'll make myself yours on the mountain, coast or plain;
since I attach myself to your lovely words,
tell me where to come, and suck on my beak.[24]

Poems 12A and 12B: The first exchange between Cecco Nuccoli and Cucco di Messer Gualfreduccio di Baglioni. Cucco was the brother of Uccio, a monk who participated in the conspiracy that resulted in the murder of Oddo degli Oddi on 1 December 1331; Nuccoli may allude to these political intrigues in his poem 25.

In the opening sonnet of this *tenzone*, Nuccoli says that he is in limbo and he prays to God that he will be able to sustain the pains of love, thereby

12A. Cucchus d. Gualfredutj Ser Ceccho

> Io sto nel limbo e spero di vedere
> la gloria de Colui ch'è somma luce,
> la qual da morte a vita me conduce,
> tenendo me sogetto al suo volere.
>
> E ciò 'spetando, non sento martire,
> sperando sempre udir la dolce voce,
> la qual lo spirto mio tutor riduce
> a benigno signor sempre ubedire.
>
> Però lui prego che troppo non tardi
> al servo suo mostrar quilla chiarezza
> ch'escampe 'l cor dagli amorosi dardi.
>
> Ché 'n verità niuna magiur fortezza
> dar si porria al cor per sostenere
> li grave colpe, che li fan patère.

winning over his beloved. Nuccoli replies by asserting that Cucco is in hell, calling to mind Christ's harrowing of limbo, and noting that he did not lead Cucco out to heaven. Therefore, Nuccoli states, Cucco should hope for no divine assistance. Rather, Nuccoli concludes, Cucco should employ *largesse* to win over the person of his desires. Interestingly, in the second verse of the sonnet, Nuccoli echoes the opening line of Dante's *Paradiso* ("La gloria di Colui").

12A. Lord Cucco Gualfreduccio to Ser Cecco

 I'm staying in limbo and hope to see
the glory of Him who is the highest light,
who'll lead me from death to life,
keeping me as a subject to His will.
 And awaiting this, I don't feel any pains
while always hoping to hear His voice,
He whose voice still reduces me
to obey this benign lord.
 However, I beg Him not to show
that brightness to His servant too late,
because it saves one's heart from amorous darts.
 For in truth, He couldn't give
greater strength to the heart to sustain
the grave blows that make it suffer.

12B. C. Responsio Ser Cecchi ad Chuccum

    Tu se' nel loco, se bien ti rimire,
che gloria in ben per te mai non traluce;
né mai la giù non scende el Sommo Duce,
poi ch'Abraàm ne trasse e gli altre sire.
    Ma se tu crede rinascere e morire,
cotest'è un van pensier che sempr' enduce,
né mai a perfezion nessun s'aduce
a uscir di fuor, ma averòn doppie sospire.
    Ma ei par ch'en tua matèra nel mondo arde
l'alma col cor sol per l'altrui bellezza,
rubato pur dagli amorose darde.
    Ma, se mi crede, usa magiur largezza
poi che téste novelle son pur vere;
proverbio antico: *Iddio si fe' li sère.*
    Non piacquer mai sonette a tai persone,
ma, se i t'acoste, dònai del bolgione.

12B. Song [Sonnet] Response by Ser Cecco to Cucco

    If you look around yourself, you're in the place
where glory of your well-being doesn't shine;
nor has the Highest Leader descended there
ever since He brought out Abraham and the other lords.
    But if you believe you'll be reborn and die again,
it is a vain thought you'll always hold.
Nor has anyone ever since been led to come out
to perfection—they will heave double sighs.
    In this matter, it seems that your soul will burn
in this world for that person's beauty, along with your heart
that was stolen by the amorous darts.
    But if you believe me, you should employ greater *largesse*
because this news is still true:
the ancient proverb, *God made the nobles.*
    Such people never liked sonnets,
so if he approaches you, shoot a crossbow bolt at him.[25]

Poems 13A and 13B: The continuation of the exchange between Cucco di Messer Gualfreduccio Baglioni and Cecco Nuccoli (poems 12A and 12B). Cucco replies that he is not in hell; nonetheless, he will take Nuccoli's advice and use money to win over his love. He asks Nuccoli not to include other matters in his poetry, because Cucco cryptically claims that he does not come from Arles; it is not clear what Cucco means, but perhaps he suggests that he is not highly educated. The *incipit* verse of Cucco's sonnet recollects

13A. Responsio Chucchi Ser Ceccho

  Io so' êlla mia oppinion più fermo,
ser Cecco, ch'en la tua non ragionaste;
però che di speranza mi privaste,
come s'io fusse mortalmente infermo.
  Ma in verità ti dico, e sì t'afermo,
ch'en quilla parte, dove mi trovaste,
scise el verace lume, che rimast'è,
e ferì 'l cor che non glie valse schermo.
  Però ti prego che quando tu parli
che tu non esche fuor di la matera;
ben vòi' che sappi ch'io non so' da Arli.
  Ch'io giuro a ·dDio ch'a seguir la bandera
sarei più presto con mille fiorini
ch'un altro non siria di bagatini.
  Ma poi ch'entendi ad esser camarlinga,
servirte conven d'altro ca de linga.

the second homoerotic sonnet attributable to Cecco Angiolieri ("I'm not firm in this opinion"). In his response, Nuccoli asserts again that Cucco is in hell and notes that any suggestion that he will exit from it violates Christian teachings.

13A. Response by Cucco to Ser Cecco

      I am more firm in my opinion,
Ser Cecco, than the one you expressed in yours,
since you've deprived me of any hope
as if I were mortally ill.
      But in truth, I tell you and affirm:
in that place where you found me
the True Light descended, He remained,
and He wounded my heart, which needed no defense.
      However, I beg you, when you speak,
not to stray from the material—
you know well that I'm not from Arles.
      Because I swear to God that in following His banner
I'll be faster with one thousand florins
than another man would be with pennies.
      But since you intend to be his chamberlain
you'll need to use something other than your tongue.

13B. Responsio Ser Cecchi Cuccho

    Saper ti fo ch'el mio detto rifermo,
da poi che li miei rime mal notaste;
come Iddio fe' li sère tu 'l provaste,
s'io traggo ben l'effetto del tuo sermo.

    E vòi che sappi ch'io non mi disfermo,
ché mai non uscierai, se là giù intraste;
però ti prego che più no 'l constraste,
ch'en sul Dicreto el disse Quel da l'ermo

    che 'l Signor sommo saria in briga a trarli
fuor di tal luoco, e questa è cosa vera;
ond'io ti prego che più non ci sparli,

    ché converrà che tua opinion pèra;
io vincitor ne remarrò a la fine
e girò in sella, e tu t'aterrai a crine.

    Ben so che l'ài mainèr, ma se ramenga
ch'altre glie dà denari e no i berlenga.

13B. Response by Ser Cecco to Cucco

    I'll have you know that I confirm my statement
since you've understood my rhymes poorly;
you've experienced how God makes nobles,
if I've understood well what you've said.
    And I want you to know that I won't waver:
for you'll never come out if you entered down there;
I beg you not to argue because the man
from the hermitage said so in his Decretals.[26]
    Because the Highest Lord would be in trouble
if He brought them out of that place, and this is true:
hence, I beg that you no longer speak ill of it to us.
    For it's necessary for your opinion to die,
and I'll be the victor in the end,
and I'll ride in the saddle while you run alongside the mane.[27]
    I know that you have manners, but when he wanders,
others give him money, and not just idle speech.

Poems 14A and 14B: Another exchange between Cucco di Messer Gualfreduccio Baglioni and Cecco Nuccoli. In 14A, Nuccoli reiterates the incipit verse of 13B; in this sonnet, he boasts of the pleasurable life he leads while residing in Perugia with Bartoluccio of the Montemelino family. He does not eat local fish that swim past the bridge, but rather he enjoys other meals that Bartoluccio pays for.[28] He employs ambiguous language throughout this sonnet, as he will again in sonnets 21, 28A, and 28B. On one level, the poet indicates that he stops at Bartoluccio's home (*ucelarte*: literally, "a bird's roost") where he eats and drinks with gusto; on the other, he insinuates that he per-

14A. C. Ser Cecchus Chuccho

      Saper ti fo, Cucco, ch'io mi godo
e traggo vita chiara in alto monte,
e sto con Bartuluccio, chiara fonte,
che cortesia spande in ogne modo.

      E se anguille o ténche o lucci o pesce sodo
si trova in Prosa, già non vène al Ponte,
ch'el signor nostro spende più che conte
che sia in crestentà, per quel ch'io odo.

      E ode dilletto, ch'i'ò per confortarme:
ch'andand'io po'[29] mangiare a l'ucelarte
e lasciammo[30] a la porta le greve arme

      et ogni gitto fo poi le sucherte;
et tu al Teber vai avisando i cupi,
et io l'ingogliert fo come fan lupi.

      Les is gut nich nengert:[31]
egli è 'l mio buon signor, di cui i' ò fame,
che spende e spande come fronde in rame.

forms fellatio (*sucherte*: literally, "sucking"; *ingogliert*: literally, "swallowing"). Additionally, this is another example of Nuccoli using avian metaphors to discuss sexual acts and organs (e.g., sonnets 7A, 7B, 10, 11C). He also writes part of one verse in German, making further sexual insinuations because of its similarities to Italian lexicon.

Cucco does not catch the reference, however, telling Nuccoli that he does not understand German. Nonetheless, he too alludes to the activity of hawking, perhaps connecting to the sonnets about hawking found in Nuccoli's corpus.

14A. Song [Sonnet] by Ser Cecco to Cucco

>I'll have you know, Cucco, that I rejoice
and I lead a bright life on the mountain,
and I stay with Bartuluccio, the bright source
who spreads courtesy in every way.
>If eels or tenches or pikes or mullets
are found in Perugia, they don't come past the bridge,
for our lord spends more than any count
found in Christendom, from what I hear.
>Now hear the pleasantry I use to console myself:
when I go to the bird's roost to eat,
I now leave my heavy arms at the door,
>and with every hunt I slurp down
and swallow as does the wolf;
and you, by the Tiber, go about alerting sullen men.
>*By God, I'm hungry:*[32]
he, for whom I hunger, is my good lord
who spends, and opens[33] like a leaf on a branch.

14B. Responsio Chucchi Ser Ceccho

  Se tu gode, ser Cecco, come conte,
e trai sì chiara vita, io ti llodo;
e so' ben certo, se non erri al modo,
che tu ài ogne ben come tu pronte.

  Ma se vivanda avess' quant'à Visconte,
de ciò non curo; ma se 'l forte nodo
se desugliesse, per lo tuo arlodo
buia deventeria la chiara fonte.

  Ma puoi che t'è piaciuto contarmi
el gran dilletto che, po' mangiar, m'acerte;
ond'io te dico che per quel che parmi

  che guardi bene a lo scender dell'erte
et ancor meglio al saltar de le rupe;
e se lo 'ngogli, fa che non l'alupi.

  Io non entendo el tuo parlar tedesco,
ma credo, quando vai a l'ucelerte,
che dirieto a lui tu facce le minverte.

14B. Response by Cucco to Ser Cecco

      If you rejoice, Ser Cecco, as you relate,
and you lead a bright life, I praise you,
and I'm certain, if you don't err in the way
you write, that you have all goodness.
      But even if you had as much food as a Viscount,
I don't care about that; but if the tough knot
were untied, despite your praises,
your bright source would become dark.
      But then it pleased you to tell me
about the delights you assure me you eat;
so I tell you that, from what it seems,
      you should watch out not to go down the slope,
or, even better, you should leap over that cliff;
and if you eat it, you shouldn't become a wolf.
      I don't understand your German speech,
But I believe, when you go out hawking,
you'll do some somersaults behind him.[34]

Poems 15A and 15B: A continuation of the exchange between Cecco Nuccoli and Cucco di Messer Gualfreduccio Baglioni begun with poems 14A and 14B. Nuccoli attempts to explain himself to Cucco, claiming that his beloved is as beautiful as Absalom, the biblical figure noted for his physical attractiveness—that man is so comely that he makes both men and women fall in love with him. Cucco replies by accusing Nuccoli of speaking foolishly and warning him that he might fail. Cucco refers to the "Song of Gianni," a

15A. Ser Cecchus Chuccho

  Amico, s'tu me fai mutar lenguaggio,
risposta ti faro, e paràti buia,
di la 'mpromessa ch'i'ò ad le 'lleluia
sì ch'el conven ch'io faccia il dolce saggio.
  E a più cautela la pòllizza n'aggio
scritta di sua mano; or pur m'ingiuia
come ti piace, ch'io faro co' fuia
lupa ch'à i lupachin, che fugge oltraggio.
  E parme ciascun giorno ben mill'anni
che varchi i dì santi e vegna el tempo
ch'io veggia lui vestito i novi panni.
  Or se ne vada ormai chi gir se 'n pò,
che chi lui mira dice ch'è Asalonne,
inamorar ben fa uomin' e donne.
  Et io mi godo, come che tu crede,
ch'aponer non si puote a mia pollizza;
ma, nel contraro, molte n'àn grand'izza.

narrative that circulated in Perugia about a man who tried to earn enough money to live comfortably, but he failed miserably. Cucco also makes reference to Ciuccio di Simonelli of the Boccoli family, who was famous for his failures in life.

15A. Ser Cecco to Cucco

    Friend, if you make me change languages,
I'll give you an answer—and it'll seem dark—
about the promise that I have about a "halleluia!"
so that I'll need to act like a sweet sage.
    And with greater caution I have
my happiness written in his hand; yet injure me
as you like, because I'll become the sly she-wolf
with her cubs, who flees from danger.
    And every day seems like a thousand years to me,
may the holy days pass and the time come
that I'll see him wearing his new clothes.
    Whoever can leave should go away now
because whoever sees him says he's Absalom—
he makes men and women fall hard in love.
    And I rejoice, as you say, because
no one can oppose this happiness I have;
but on the contrary, many get angry about it.

15B. Responsio Chucchi Ser Ceccho

      Poi che disdice, non se' di lignaggio
et ogni tuo parlar par che sia fuia,
onde curo di te men che di luia
ch'esce del fuoco e non fa alcun dannaggio.

      Et anco il tuo parlar par men che saggio,
ché prima dice che l'aveste i ·ngiuia
e poi de la 'mpromessa fai tal giuia
come s'a noi avesse fatt'omaggio.

      Però ti dico che te stesso inganni,
ché tale impromessione aspette a tempo;
non ti racorda la canzon di Gianni?

      Io credo, dico prima e non d'empo',
la nova vesta averà quel Giasonne
che conquistò 'l Monte cacciando donne.

      Se di ciò gode, tu fai come rede,
che de piciola cosa tutto frizza
poi nel contrario tosto si dirizza.

      La tua pollizza—serà de quel' de Ciuccio
di Simonello e non de Bartuluccio.

15B. Response by Cucco to Ser Cecco

     Though you disagree, you don't have the lineage,
and all your speech appears to be furious,[35]
so I care less about you than about a spark
that comes out of the fire and does no harm.
     And yet, your speech seems less than wise,
for first you said that you'd been injured,
and then you speak of the joy of a promise,
as if you'd made a gift to us.
     So I tell you that you're fooling yourself
because you'll be awaiting that promise for some time:
Don't you remember the Song of Gianni?
     I believe, I say, that sooner and not later,
that Jason, who conquered the hill
by chasing women,[36] will have those new clothes.
     If you rejoice in that, you'll act like the heir
who shivers over every small thing
but then turns away to its opposite.
     Your happiness lies with Ciuccio
di Simonello, and not with Bartuluccio.

Poem 16: Nuccoli writes about his lover's callousness, reminding the sonnet's addressee that God does not reward cruel people. In this instance, however, Nuccoli rejoices because the lover's harsh treatment has caused him to fall out of love. The direct discourse in the sixth verse appears inspired by a statement from Cecco Angiolieri's poetry.[37]

Ser Cecchus

    Ogni pensier ch'i'ò 'n te se dispera,
poi che con crudeltà te se' compliso;
Eddio a tal gente non dà paradiso
ancie i descaccia (e questa è cosa vera).
    Se ben racordi il salutar di sera,
me rispondeste: "Or va, che tu sie uciso!"
Sempre col fin de tuoe parole un riso
t'uscia 'ndi bocca con alegra cera.
    Ond'io, mirando a voi, foi sì contento
che no m'increber le villan parole
(mi rischiaraste come l'aier el vento
    fa, se da nuvoli è coverto el sole);
sì ch'io di tal disio ognor mi pento
poi ch'ascaran se' fatto e 'l cor m'invole.
    Ma quel signore Amor, ch'a amar mi trasse,
non vuol ch'io retro ritorne coi passe.

Ser Cecco

     Every thought that I have about you despairs
since you are pleased with all cruelty;
and God doesn't grant paradise to such people,
but He drives them off, and this is the truth.
     If you remember well that evening's greeting,
you responded to me: "Go, and may you be killed!"
And at the end of your words a laugh
left from the mouth on your happy face.
     And thus, while looking at you, I was so happy
that your villainous words didn't hurt me;
but you enlightened me, like the wind does
     the sky, when the sun is covered in clouds;
such that, now I repent that I felt so much desire
because you attack me and steal my heart.
     But that lord, Love, who pulled me into loving
doesn't want me to return even by one small step.

Poem 17: Nuccoli complains about an ex-lover while suffering exile from his native city in this sixteen-verse *sonetto caudato*. Nuccoli resides in the countryside with the frogs and crickets, while his former lover can enjoy Perugia, which he personifies as a Lady; Marino Ceccoli will also allegorize Perugia as a Lady (sonnet 14). As elsewhere, Nuccoli contrasts urban life to the rustic. He is so unhappy in the countryside that he would even take up jousting against the Arthurian knight Tristan to return home. In contrast, while Nuccoli's addressee is in Perugia proper he can enjoy the tavern, dice, and "Ciamprolino" (vv. 12–14), an apparent reference to Meo dei Tolomei's adversary;[38]

C. Ser Ceccus

      El mi rincresce sì lo star di fuore
dai mura de Colei c'ogni ben mostra
ch'io con Tristan ne prindiria la giostra
sol per veder gl'ochiucce ner co' more
      di quel furel che m'à 'nvolato el core
e tiénlosi in presion dentro ai suoi chiostra;
ond'io so' certo ch'a me molto costra
prima ch'io de pregion ne 'l cave fore.
      El gran dilletto ch'io abbo in contado
sì è d'odir cantar rane e saleppe
e le lucerte correr per le greppe.
      E tu in Prosa e 'l ciamprolino e 'l dado
a la taverna colle borse zeppe
et io in essa m'artrovo di rado.
      Molto divisa l'esser mio dal vostro:
saluta 'l ciamprolin c'usa col nostro.

Nuccoli also evokes Tolomei's poem 13 more generally in this sonnet. This poem constitutes reliable proof of Meo's influence on Nuccoli. Furthermore, Nuccoli's statement echoes one made by Angiolieri, who asserted that only three things gladdened his heart: women, the tavern, and dice.[39] Thus, with this sonnet, Nuccoli demonstrates his knowledge of the comic poetry of Siena.

Song [Sonnet] by Ser Cecco

  It so annoys me to stay outside
of the walls of the Lady who displays all goodness
that I would take up jousting with Tristan
just to see the tiny eyes as dark as blackberries
  of that little thief who stole my heart
and keeps it imprisoned in his cloister;
hence I am certain that it will cost me greatly
before I can draw it out of that prison.
  The great pleasure that I have in the countryside
is hearing frogs and crickets sing
and seeing lizards run through the thickets.
  You're in Perugia, with Ciamprolino and the dice
in the tavern with bursting purses,
and I find myself there only rarely.
  My essence is so different from yours;
greet Ciamprolin for me, who has dealings with both of us.

Poem 18: Nuccoli writes to someone named Giovanni, who resides outside the city, and he depicts the countryside in negative terms, discussing the peasants, their physical labor, and their poor foods. In so doing he reiterates the cultural commonplace of contrasting life in the city (*urbanitas*) to that in the countryside (*rusticitas*).[40] Ceccoli, too, criticizes *rusticitas* in his sonnet "If every single seed produced a bushel." In this poem, Nuccoli asserts that the recipient has become a veritable farmer while living in the countryside. Nuccoli then informs him that two men, a father and son, have been pun-

C. Ser Cecchus

    Fatto ti se', Giovagne, contadino
e mane e sere mange coi bevolche
e fai zappare e metter forme e solche,
e bee aceto adaquato per fin vino,
    e frasche vai mozzando col falcino,
con trista compagnia ti leve e colche;
onde ti prego che più non ti folche
a ritornare al tuo dolce camino.
    Saper ti fo novella men che bona:
el padre e 'l figlio stettero a gran rischio
ch'envellenate fuor dal badalischio.
    L'uno è scampato (e de ciò si ragiona),
ma sempre portar nel viso un cischio;
per l'altro s'oderan que' che triste sona.
    Vanne, sonetto, davante a Giovanni,
e di' che Francischin de biso à panni.

ished. He does not explain their crime, but he describes their motive as similar to being poisoned by the mythical basilisk. He closes the poem by attaching a two-line *envoi*, telling the sonnet to go to Giovanni and inform him that someone named Franceschino now wears grey, presumably because he has joined a monastery. The sonnet also uses a phrase similar to the *incipit* verses of poems 13D and 14A ("Saper ti fo," v. 9); Nuccoli will use the same formula as the *incipit* in poem 25.

Song [Sonnet] by Ser Cecco

  Giovanni, you've made yourself into a farmer,
and morning and evening you eat with the peasants,
and you have furrows hoed, and rows built up,
and you drink watered-down vinegar as fine wine,
  and you go chopping down branches with a sickle,
and you arise and lie down with miserable company—
hence, I beg you not to delay any longer
your return along the sweet road.
  I bring you news that is less than good:
the father and son were at great risk,
because they were poisoned by the basilisk.
  One of them has survived and is talking about it,
but he'll always bear a scar on his face;
for the other, sad bells are tolling.
  Now go, sonnet, before Giovanni,
and tell him that Franceschin wears grey clothing.

Poems 19A and 19B: A poetic correspondence between Cecco Nuccoli and Cola di Messer Alessandri, about whom nothing is known. Cola initiates the *tenzone* by bringing up the situation in Spoleto, where he resides, noting that the city has cast out its common women (i.e., prostitutes), so all the men are now engaging in sodomy with one another. Cola describes the men as the heretical Patarines,[41] capitalizing on the association between heresy and sodomy. He closes the poem by asking Nuccoli to send frottolas

19A. Cola d. Alesandri Ser Cec[c]ho

    Amico, sappie l'uso di Spolete
e la qual vita ine si può trare
e do' convience castità servare
e l'arte frequenter d'i sodomite.
    Femine comune ne sono sbandite
né nulla vi si trova per denare;
son tutte patarini, al ver parlare,
e 'naturate sodome condite.
    Sòncie di belle, al ver, ma del vagheggio
curano men che brïaca del fuso,
ché 'naturate son in sì mal uso.
    Però amico vero io te richeggio,
ché tu ce mandi alcuna frotolletta,
che noi non periam sì de nighetta.

(*frotolletta*), a poetic form that often dealt with nonsensical topics;[42] the frottola may have been the predecessor to the ambiguous language employed by these poets. Nuccoli's response is fragmentary. He mentions how Spoleto was already punished when it was besieged by the Perugian forces led by Oddo degli Oddi in 1322–24, to whom Nuccoli alludes in sonnet 25.[43]

19A. Cola degli Alessandri to Ser Cecco

    Friend, you should know the custom of Spoleto
and the type of life that you can lead here;
and where you need to preserve your chastity,
and where you can practice the sodomitic arts.
    The common women have been cast out,
and not one of them can be found for money;
to tell the truth, they've all become Patarines,
and habituated as unnatural sodomites.
    In truth, there are some beautiful ones, but they care
less for beauty than drunk women care for the spindle—
they've become accustomed to such evil ways.
    But, I ask you, my true friend,
to send some frottolas to us
so that we don't die of neglect.

19B. Ser Cec[c]hus Responsio

    Se bien racorde, già ne fuor punite
glie spolletin del lor mal loperare,
ché fuor quase condutti a consumare,
mangiando l'erbe a guisa di romite.
    E puòiti ben recorder d'i rostite
e degl'altre a cui conven dimenticare,
puoi fe' ·dDio l'aire e la terra tremare
con terramoti e stronanti bonite.

19B. Ser Cecco's Response

    If you recall well, the Spoletans
were well punished for their evil actions;
they were almost driven to starvation,
eating grasses in the manner of hermits.
    And you can remember well the burnings,
and the other acts that are best forgotten,
and then God made the air and earth tremble
with earthquakes and terrifying thunderclaps.

Poem 20: Nuccoli complains about the lover he calls "lord" (*signore*). The poet suffers because of the cruelty and inconstancy of the other man, but he can alleviate Nuccoli's suffering by administering his medicine. Thus, he depicts his passion in the stereotyped language of lovesickness. By mentioning medicine, Nuccoli may be subtly evoking the Meo dei Tolomei's invec-

C. Ser Cecchus

    Le toi promesse me vegnon sì in ordo
colle tuoi volte, che n'ài più che golpe,
né no mi poss'[44] scudar dai mortai colpe
ch'amor mi trà perch'io di te fu' ingordo.
    Ond'io ti prego, e questo ti ricordo,
che tu almen facce sì che tu ti scolpe,
ch'io sento l'alma che lascia le polpe
fredde per doglia, ond'io le man mi mordo.
    Però ti prego, signor, che socurghe
con la tua medicina e vin 'ne a capo,
poi che tal mal conven per te si purghe.
    Se non ch'en quisto mondo più non capo
e già mi renderia a morte vinto,
se n'ò[45] 'l tuo viso, ch'i'ò nel mio cor pinto.
    Vanne, sonetto, tosto e rieca 'l pasto,
prima ch'io sia da morte al tutto guasto.

tives against his mother (sonnets 3 and 4). This is another sixteen-verse *sonetto caudato*, a sonnet to which a couplet has been appended.

Song [Sonnet] by Ser Cecco

    Your promises come to me in a long row,[46]
along with your turn-abouts, of which you surpass the fox,
nor can I shield myself from the mortal blows
that love hurls at me because I was so greedy for you.
    So I beg you—and I'll remind you of this—
that you at least excuse yourself
because I feel my soul leaving my cold flesh
from the pain for which I bite my own hands.
    However, I beg you, lord, to rescue me
with your medicine and bring it to a head
since it is necessary that you purge my sickness.
    If not, then I'll no longer have a place in this world
and I would have already surrendered to death,
were it not for your face, which I've painted in my heart.
    Go quickly, sonnet, and bring me the response
before I have been completely ruined by death.

142 *Perugia*

Poem 21: A sonnet that depicts a mock journey from Paris through Ethiopia and eventually to Spain using ambiguous language, as in Nuccoli's sonnets 14B, 28A, and 28B. Here, Nuccoli composes a facetious quest in the manner of other comic texts, such as the anonymous *Detto del Gatto Lupesco* or the sermon by Fra' Cipolla in Boccaccio's *Decameron* 6.10. In this instance, it is hard to ignore the double entendre in the final verse where he kissed the marble of the Holy Altar, suggesting that the entire sonnet consists of a veiled description of a sexual encounter.[47] Thus, the entire poem may be composed

C. Ser Cecchus predictus

    Andando per Via Nova e per Via Maggio,
già per Thiopia mi trovai in Parige;
salse nel mondo ch'à le gran pendige,
con Guiglielmin di Flanda fec'el saggio.
    Poscia tornai ov'è 'l gran baronaggio
(io dico in Francia, ove son cose lige),
Giotto mi folse ed empì mia valige;
poi mmi partie e presi mio viaggio.
    Enver Galizia prese 'l mio camino;
poco più oltre mi fu minacciato
e dimandomme s'io avea del fiorino.
    Ond'io ristetti et avisai 'l mercato,
e mia risposta fu ch'io malandrino,
sì ch'ei da me se partì corucciato.
    Andando giù trovai Lellio 'n armo
e di la santa altar basciai lo marmo.

of metaphors for sexual acts (e.g., "Going down New Street," "I rose up in the world," "Giotto . . . filled my luggage," "Going down further") or the sexual organs (e.g., "steep slopes," "William of Flanders," "the great Barony"). Nuccoli may have inspired subsequent writers, such as Stefano Finiguerri, nicknamed il Za, and Domenico di Giovanni, nicknamed Burchiello, who also employed incongruous language.

Song [Sonnet] by the aforementioned Ser Cecco

    Going down New Street and Wide Street,
just from Ethiopia, I found myself in Paris;
I rose up in the world that has steep slopes
and I became wise with William of Flanders.[48]
    Then I returned to the great Barony
(I mean in France, where there is fealty),
Giotto[49] shined upon me and filled my luggage,
then I departed and continued my travels.
    And I took the road toward Galicia,
but a little bit beyond it I was threatened—
and he asked if I had any florins.
    So I stopped and I alerted the market
and my response was that that I too was a brigand,
so he departed from me, quite enraged.
    Going further down, I met Lelli[50] in arms,
and I kissed the marble of the Holy Altar.

Poem 22: A complaint about the lover's disregard for the poet. Because of his misfortunes, Nuccoli is losing his courage, and as it disappears his ability to express himself is waning. He fears that ultimately he will die from his pain. The *incipit* verse of the sonnet recollects that of Guido Cavalcanti's poem "I fear that my misfortune may have led" ("Io temo che la mia disaventura").

Ser Cecchus predictus

 Io veggio ben la mia desaventura,
che per temenza perdo el mio desire;
e veggio ben che om ch'è senza ardire
suo pregio no acquista per paura.
 Uom ch'à coraggio puote aver ventura,
e bene è matto chi perde per dire
co' ch'el crede per poter fornire,
umillïando sempre la natura.
 La gran temenza mi toglie ardimento
de dire a voi quello ch'io porto in core;
tal ò paura di non far falimento
 ch'io non vi dico s'io vi porto amore;
ch'io sono in fuoco et in grande tormento
e son già quase morto del dolore.

Aforementioned Ser Cecco

      I clearly see my misfortune
because, for fear, I lose my desire,
and I clearly see that a man without daring
doesn't acquire what he's worth, out of fear.
      A man with courage may have fortune,
but he's mad if he loses it by only hearing people talk,
just like he who believes he can acquire it
by only humbling his own nature.
      My great fear takes away my bravery
to tell you what I bear toward you in my heart.
So great is my fear of failure!
      For I don't tell you that I feel love for you;
I am in flames and great suffering
and I've almost died from my pain.

Poem 23: Nuccoli apparently replies to a message from his "lord" (*signore*), and he uses the opportunity to complain about his amorous pains. In spite of them, he will persist in loving the other man, and in the process he uses biblical language that a temple of love will be rebuilt in him (John 2:19). This is a *sonetto caudato*, a sixteen-verse sonnet to which a couplet has been attached.

C. Ser Cecchus

   Signor, tanto me piacquer tuoi salute
ch'io mille grazie ne rendei al messo;
e ben mostre nel dir che sol se' esso
colui ch'avanze sovr' ogne vertute.
   Ma i giorni e l'ore e notte ch'i'ò perdute
dògliome 'n molto e biasemo me stesso
e pato mille morte via più spesso
che quei che stanno fra l'ardente lute.
   Ma ell'è sola una spem che ci persevra
l'alma nel corpo, immaginando forse
ch'Amor di su' opinion tria mort'e levra.
   Né io mai per tal camin passòce 'n forse
né lascirò l'andar, tanto so' empio
(inprima s'arfarebbe per me il Tempio!).
   Sonetto fatto in riso e pianto e lutto,
a chi te legge non ti scovrir tutto.

Song [Sonnet] by Ser Cecco

  Lord, I found your greetings so pleasing
that I gave a thousand thanks to the messenger,
and with your words you show yourself to be
what you are—the one who surpasses every virtue.
  But I feel pain about the days, hours, and nights
that I've lost, and I chastise myself for them,
and I suffer more than a thousand deaths for them—
more even than those who are cast into burning flames.
  But there is only one hope that keeps
my soul in my body, imagining perhaps
that Love selects or frees many, by his judgment.
  Nor do I ever walk that path in doubt,
nor will I stop walking it, I'm so stubborn—
the Temple would sooner be rebuilt for me.
  Sonnet crafted in laughter, tears, and grief,
don't reveal everything to whoever happens to read you.

Poem 24: Another poem in the style of typical courtly love. In it, Nuccoli expresses his love for the letter *T* because it is the start of the name Trebaldino. He again positions himself as subservient to his beloved, comparing himself to both a child and to a servant. He reiterates the complaint that Trebaldino treats him cruelly, such that Nuccoli might die from his amorous pains.

Ser Cecchus pro Trebaldino

    Io son del .*T*. sì forte innamorato,
perché principio de ligiadro nome
(sònne più vago ch'el fanciul d'i pome);
tra letter' e vocal ch'io l'ò chiosato,
    e, per più onor, de perle fegurato,
per piagere a colui di cui io fòme
suo servidor del quel ch'io posso, come
colui ch'aspetta d'esser meritato.
    Solo una grazia t'adomando, Amore:
fa ch'io non pera sotto 'l tuo pennello,
però che vi siria gran disinore
    sed io morisse d'un picciol quadrello;
da puoi che tu m'ài messo in tanto errore,
fa ch'io non mora nel tempo che gello.

Ser Cecco about Trebaldino

  I am so strongly in love with *T*
because it's the beginning of the lovely name;
I'm more pleased with it than a child by an apple;
among the letters and vowels I've glossed it,
  and, for greater honor, decorated it with pearls,
to be pleasing to him to whom I make myself
a servant in all I can do, just as
he deserves to be recompensed.
  I only ask for one grace from you, Love:
make it so that I don't die under your banner
because it would cause you such dishonor
  if I died from such a small arrow;
since you have placed me in such error,
make it so that I don't die in the time of iciness.

150 *Perugia*

Poem 25: A poem about the pain Nuccoli feels being far from the "lord" (*signore*). The exact context of the sonnet is unclear, but the beloved man appears to have been involved in some sort of political strife. He had temporarily taken refuge in a cloister where he engaged with Nuccoli, but then he was driven off. Nuccoli says that he made his way to the Palazzo degli Oddi, in Perugia, in the neighborhood of Porta Santa Susanna, and called on God to curse someone he calls "the cleric"; the latter may be a reference to Uccio di Messer Gualfreduccio Baglioni, who was involved in a conspiracy against

Ser Cecchus

    Questo saper ti fo, signor mio caro,
che mentr'io viverò, sì serò vostro,
sì gran conforto mi deste nel chiostro,
quando i vostre occhie verso me miraro.
    Male[52] beccaste quel dolore amaro,
el qual saper ti fo senza dimostro;
ma per lo star, dico, d'un patrenostro
loco staesti e puoi t'aleceraro.
    Vostra partita mi fe' tanta noia
cch'io star di sotto con gli altre non podde
ma anda'mi a ripossare in su la loia;
    fe' me ad un sentiere e vidde casa gli Odde
e dissi: "O dDio, tu m par ben bellerco,
s'a mala morte no ucide quel chierco!"

Oddo degli Oddi, whom he murdered on 1 December 1331.⁵¹ The poet structures the sonnet so that it repeatedly makes reference to monastic language. Again, Nuccoli uses the same phrase in the *incipit* verse as that seen in sonnets 13D and 14A ("saper ti fo").

Ser Cecco

  I'll have you know this, my dear lord,
that while I live, I'll belong to you,
because you gave me such great comfort in the cloister
when your eyes turned toward me.
  You never swallowed that bitter pain
that I'll make known to you without showing it.
And for the time it took, I say, for a Paternoster
you remained, but then they drove you away.
  Your departure caused me such discomfort
that I wasn't able to stay down below with the others,
but I went to the loggia to rest myself.
  I took the path and I saw the house of the Oddi
and said: "O God, you'll appear to wage war on me
if you don't kill that cleric with a harsh death!"

Poem 26: The first of two sonnets in which Nuccoli writes about political intrigues facing Perugia in the 1330s. In 1328, the Holy Roman emperor Henry of Luxemburg invested Pier Saccone Tarlati of Pietramala as the lord of Arezzo, and in the following decade he engaged in a series of violent encounters with Perugia and with Florence. In 1332, Ranieri (Neri) della Faggiuola, the second son of the Ghibelline leader Uguccione, became involved in the conflicts against Pier Saccone Tarlati in response to losing a castle to the Tarlati over the years.[53] In 1335 and 1336, Perugia and its allies, Florence and Siena, waged war against Pier Saccone, and after some setbacks its army entered Arezzo and encamped at the cathedral on 12 November 1335; the

C. Idem Ser Cecchus

    O tu che pigni in due parete azuro
e vàice mettendo òr senza mordente,
e l'una fàite in vista sì lucente
ch'en l'altra sì doventa buio escuro;
    e già non pense nel tempo futuro
né co' al Signor despiace ei fraudolente
né ancor non guardi ch'i deria la gente,
vedendose in palese quisto furo.
    Ma sappi ch'io non so' sordo né muto
ch'io non conosca le parole false
che, nella vista, mi parver sì salse,
    odendo dimandar sì gran trebuto.
Chi partir crede quel del suo fratello,
el suo veggia partir collo coltello.

following summer, Florence too invaded Arezzo.[54] In March 1337, Pier Saccone Tarlati sold the lordship of Arezzo to Florence for the sum of 42,800 florins and the back pay of his troops.

In the first sonnet, Nuccoli addresses an unnamed artist, who is painting the crest of the Tarlati family of Pietramala, which consisted of gold nuggets on a field of blue. He warns that God will punish the Tarlati in the near future. This sonnet in particular shows links to the *tenzone* between Ceccoli, Nuccoli, and Gilio Lelli (sonnets 21A, 21B, and 21C in Ceccoli's corpus); similarly, Ceccoli will engage in a *tenzone* with one Ceccolo about the topic (sonnets 24A and 24 B in Ceccoli's corpus).

Song [Sonnet] by Ser Cecco

    O you who paint blue on two walls
and go about putting up gold without adhesive,
and you make one be so bright to see
and the other seems so dark and shaded,
    and you don't already think of some future time,
about how fraudulence so displeases the Lord,
nor do you see how the people talk
seeing this thievery so apparent.
    But know that I'm neither so deaf nor dumb
that I don't recognize false words,
which on their face seemed so bitter to me,
    hearing such recompense be requested.
May whoever believes he can rob from his brother
see his own items stolen at knifepoint.

Poem 27: Like the previous poem, this is about the political strife between Perugia and the Tarlati, lords of Arezzo. This time, Nuccoli composes it as a seventeen-verse *sonetto caudato*, a sonnet to which he adds an additional tercet. In it, Nuccoli describes the dejected state of the Tarlati now that they have received God's punishment.

Ser Cecchus

      Mostransi chiaro per divin giudizio
già quei da Pietramala condannate,
ei quai dell'alta rota son chinnate
e giù desposte d'ogne loro offizio.
      Sì gran peccato di superbia e vizio
sofrir non podde el redentor Pate:
Luciferro angelo e gli altre chiamate
private fuor d'ogne ben e letizio.
      Poi che sentenz'a tal' sia manifesta,
o qual conforto in ciò possa valere,
che non convegna d'inchinar lor testa;
      ma, per trattato di pace volere,
credevan su montare a far gran festa
e nel lor primo stato remanere,
      non rivocò ma' Iddio suo concistorio:
però che ·l'infinita sua giustizia
fraudo nol' si può far né già malizia.

Ser Cecco

       By divine judgment the people of Pietramala
already seem clearly condemned,
and they have been bent over by the high wheel[55]
and deposed from all their offices.
       The Redeemer Father could not endure
such a great sin and vice as pride;
the angel Lucifer and the other select
were deprived of every good pleasure.
       From the moment it is decreed, may it be manifest
and in this way may they be worthy of the discomfort
to go about with their heads bent down.
       But by wanting a peace treaty
they believed they could arise and rejoice
and regain their prior state.
       God never revoked His edicts
because His infinite justice
cannot abide any fraud or malice.

Poems 28A and 28B: Two poems that share the same rhymes and may consist of a poetic exchange; if so, the ascription of both to Nuccoli is probably incorrect. In the first, the poet, possibly addressing himself, describes Trebaldino's sexual infidelity, using comic language that recollects that of Meo dei Tolomei. Like Meo before him, Nuccoli focuses on the other man's nose, probably as a euphemism for the penis (see Meo dei Tolomei's poem 19, stanza VIII). A snake struck his nose, he writes, and he walked away wiping

28A

   Ser Cecco, vole udire un novo incialmo?
Quando, doppo colui, bevve a quel nappo
Trebaldin tuo, un serpe i diè di grappo
in su nel naso, per magiore spalmo;
   puoi ci sputò e disse un cotal salmo.
Alor dis'egli: "S'io da questa scappo
en simel caso già mai non rincappo,
se tu mi desi di fiorini un palmo."
   Toccando se n'andava così 'l naso,
pensandos' en se stesso averlo mozzo,
guardando ancor s'el sangue era rimaso.
   Alor diss'io: "Quest'è ben atto sozzo!
né io non vorria veder sì fatto caso;
empria me gitarebbe giù in un pozzo."

off his blood. The poet concludes that he would prefer to drown himself. In the second sonnet, the poet asserts his attraction for a woman who lives on a mountain, and he too closes the poem by asserting that the pain of love makes him want to drown himself. Both lyrics contain ambiguous language that is reminiscent of that seen in Nuccoli's sonnets 14B and 21.

28A

     Ser Cecco, do you want to hear about an odd curse?
When, after another man, your Trebaldino,
drank from that goblet, a snake struck him
on the nose and smeared him further;
     then he spat and recited a type of psalm.
Then he said, "If I flee from this
I'll never again be in a similar situation
even if you gave me a fistful of florins."
     He went away touching his nose just so,
thinking to himself that he'd cut it off
and looking still if any blood remained.
     Then I said, "This is a filthy act!
Nor would I want to see a case like this—
I'd rather throw myself down a well!"

28B

    La verde fronda ch'io porto sul palmo
sì me ricovre quel ch'io in acqua zappo;
né 'n tal vagheggio non cadde mal trappo,
ma per iscusa fo questo rimpalmo.
    Donna ligiadra, per lo cui amor scalmo
sì mia persona ch'io dicer non sappo
(e vestì cotal donna novo drappo),
dimora al Monte là cu' io[56] spesso calmo,
    ed àmmi d'alegrezza sì 'l cor raso;
ira e melenconia porto in gozzo
quand'io non veggio el Monte de Parnaso,
    et ogne mal mi dà 'ncontro di cozzo;
ma sempre Amor ver' me destende el paso
ond'i' anegar vorebbe entro 'n un lozzo.

28B

      The green frond that I hold in my palm
recompenses me so for hoeing the water;[57]
nor did my loving fall into that evil trap
but, as a penance, I make this pact:
      a beautiful lady, for whose love I so
disquiet my body that I can't describe it
(and that woman wore a new cloak)
lives on the mountain where I often go calmly;
      she has so deprived my heart of joy
that I feel rage and melancholy in my throat
when I can't see Mount Parnassus.
      Every ill strikes against me,
but Love always advances my footsteps
so I'd like to drown myself in a pond.

CHAPTER FOUR

Marino Ceccoli

Works by Marino Ceccoli

Poem 1: Ceccoli appropriates the Occitanic language of *fin'amor* in this sonnet, as he does in several others (e.g., sonnets 2, 3, 6, 7, 8 and 9). In this sonnet, he communicates the traditional complaint about the pains of love, this time for "that man" (*tal*); this appellation might indicate a connection to the first sonnet attributable to Cecco Angiolieri ("Listen, listen—I am speaking to you, sirs") where the poet refers to his beloved similarly (*cotale*). Ceccoli describes the pain of love as surpassing all other suffering, and his heart is

Ser Marinus Ceccholi de Perussio

        Oi me, ch'el dolce tempo tutor vassene!
Et Amor, mentre con parole spassame,
e così a poco a poco morir lassame!
Né già mia via più defender sassene;
        aitar me può tal che da longe fassene,
che m'à ferito sì c'oltr'oltra passame;
e già dal core ogne vertude cassame,
ma pur senza pietà da canto stassene.
        Tutti glie spirite[1] mei "mercé!" li cridano
et io, piangendo, ancor grazia demandoglie
che gl'occhie suoi alquanto almen me ridano.
        E forsa camparia così guardandoglie,
perché ch'a lor piacer tutto me guidano,
tanta vaghezza vien fra lor voltandoglie.

losing all its strength. As in the amorous poetry of Guido Cavalcanti, he personifies the bodily spirits that animate his organs ("spirite," v. 8), who call out for mercy; he will also do so in other poems (sonnets 3 and 6).

Throughout this sonnet Ceccoli uses *endecasillabi sdruccioli*, twelve-syllable hendecasyllable verses, with the A- and B-rhymes assonant to one another (e.g., "vàssene," v. 1; "spassame," v. 2).

Ser Marino Ceccoli of Perugia

      Alas, for the time always moves on sweetly,
and while Love, with his words, diverts me
he allows me to die bit by bit!
Nor does he know how to defend my life anymore.
      That man, who lives far away, can help me,
for he has so wounded me that the pain surpasses all,
and all strength has fallen from my heart;
but still he stands aside, without any pity.
      All of my spirits cry out "mercy!" to him,
and I, weeping, still request the grace
that his eyes should smile a bit toward me even a little.
      And perhaps by looking at them I'd survive,
because they completely guide me by their whims,
since so much beauty comes out when he turns them.

Poem 2: Ceccoli imitates the commonplaces of courtly love, as in the previous sonnet. Here, he describes himself as subservient to his beloved, and he elaborates on the cruelty of the other person. It is not clear who the recipient of this sonnet was, whether "that man" in poem 1 or someone else entirely. Marino writes a traditional amorous lament, telling the beloved that he is

Ser Marinus Ceccholi

     Morto so' già per te, e tu non cure,
védeme venir meno, e tu te 'n ride;
Amor, dentro, per te tutto m'alide,
e tu, fugendo, più ver' me t'endure!
     De, non sai tu che dolce el cor me fure?
De, che te giovarà se tu m'ocide?
Que[2] ne serai de meglio, se pur stride
mia vita, che se vede a tal condure?
     Ond'io m'ò posto in cor de ciò far cusa
(se caso deverà che per te mòra),
come talvolt'a chio ofende s'usa.
     Lamentaròme al Signor nostro ancora,
e converraten gire a far tua scusa,
perché sì concio m'averai alora.

dying from passion and accusing him of having stolen his heart. After he passes away, he asserts, Ceccoli will beg God to forgive the other person for his disdain.

Ser Marino Ceccoli

     I'm now dead because of you, and you don't care;
you see me grow weak, and you laugh about it;
Love, within me, strikes me all over,
and you allow it by fleeing from me.
     Ah, don't you know that you sweetly steal my heart?
Ah, how will it benefit you if you kill me?
How will you be better off if my life screams
when it sees you lead it to such an end?
     Hence, I've resolved in my heart to do something
(in case it should happen that I die)
like those who've been offended sometimes do:
     I will lament to our Lord then,
and you will need to beg His forgiveness,
for you'll have left me so battered.

Poem 3: Another complaint about the pains of love similar to poems 1 and 2. Ceccoli describes love as removing thoughts of all else from his mind, and he hopes that his beloved will take pity upon him; if not, Ceccoli's soul will exit his body. As before, Ceccoli personifies the bodily spirits that animate his organs, as seen in the poetics of Guido Cavalcanti.

Ser Marinus Ceccholi

   Amor me trà de mente ogn'altra cosa,
for che de te pensar, dolce mia vita;
et ò nel cor sì tua vertù sentita,
ch'a te "mercé!" cridar già mai non posa.
   De, fa che tua beltà venga pietosa
ver' quel che sempre te dimanda aita,
prima che l'alma sia del corpo uscita,
che va per te, come tu sai, pensosa.
   Prego che 'l face! Or fa', anema mia;
fàl, prègotene, fàl, ché, se tu 'l fai,
giovartene porrà quando che sia.
   Ché m'ài furato 'l core e tolto m'ài
ogne mio spirito, sì ch'io non porria
già viver senza te, ch'a te me trai.

Ser Marino Ceccoli

      Love pulls every other thing from my mind
except thoughts of you, my sweetness, my life,
and I've felt your power in my heart,
so it won't stop crying out to you for mercy.
      Ah, make it so that your beauty takes pity
toward me, who always requests your help,
before my soul should leave my body
and, because of you, will wander about deep in thought.
      I pray that you'll do it! Now go, love of my soul—
do it, I pray, do it! For if you do it
you'll find it of benefit, whenever that might be.
      You've stolen my heart and have taken
my every spirit, such that already I can't
live without you, because you draw me to yourself.

168 *Perugia*

Poem 4: About a man who left the city for the countryside. The contrast between city life (*urbanitas*) and country life (*rusticitas*) was a literary commonplace in the literature of the thirteenth and fourteenth centuries, illustrating the increasing influence of the Italian communes; Ceccoli will take up this topic again in sonnet 19, and both may have links to Cecco Nuccoli's sonnet

Ser Marinus cuidam iuveni dum esset in comitatu

      Se ciascun àcen facesse un canteo,
et ogne paglia avesse mille spighe,
vegnir deverian men le tuoe fatighe,
se tutto 'l careggiasse a capesteo;
      e quel' che prima le somente fèo,
mettendo per le prata lunghe righe,
affannate non fuor da sì gran brighe
né mai de te più trasser tempo reo.
      Ciaschedun dé' fugire a le merigge,
quando 'l calor del sol la terra fende!
E tu più fermo in esso ognor te figge
      e fuor con glie villan' solazzo prende,
currendo per le piagge e per le rive,
e le cicaglie cante per l'olive.

"Giovanni, you've made yourself into a farmer." Ceccoli criticizes the recipient of the poem for staying among the peasants and the cicadas instead of returning to the city of Perugia.

Ser Marino to a certain young man while he was in the county

  If every single seed produced a bushel,
and every blade of straw a thousand corns,
your efforts should then be less
than if you carried it all to be threshed.
  And the people who first sowed seeds,
putting long rows in the fields,
did not suffer the pains that you feel,
nor did they have worse weather than you do.
  Everyone should flee the southern lands
when heat of the sun strikes the earth,
but you still remained fixed there, even now,
  and you take solace with the peasants
running through the fields and on the river banks;
and the cicadas sing among the olive trees.

Poems 5A, 5B, and 5C: A *tenzone* between Ser Marino Ceccoli and Lord Ugolino of Fano. Ugolino initiates the exchange by bringing up the public accusation that Ceccoli was a sodomite. Ugolino allegorizes sin as a she-wolf who has feasted on human blood since the Fall, blaming her for the murder of the biblical figure Abel. Ugolino concludes by hoping that Ceccoli will allow God to remove any sin from his heart.

Ceccoli responds twice to Ugolino, first in an epistle composed in Latin, then in a sonnet. In the epistle, Ceccoli replies to Ugolino by calling him "fa-

5A. [d. Ugolino de Fano] C. d. Ugolinus ser Marino quando dictus ser Marinus fuit increpatus de vitio sodomie excusans quod de predictis non erat culpabilis[3]

    L'antica lupa, che mai non remase
bever lo sangue de l'umane polpe
dal tempo ch'el' progenitor' per colpe
si fuor privati de le beate case,
    non tanto mai sua orràgene spase,
prendendo forma de bramosa golpe,
quanto che mo, per dar magiure colpe
sì che la carità nascosta stase.
    E fo tanto famellica sua vita
che comenciò con glie prime frateglie
bever lo sangue de quel giusto Habelle.
    Et a me cerca de togliere aita
da te, germano per amor destretto,
en cui servire[4] io trovo ogne delletto.
    Io prego Quello che Verità sé disse
che la demostre, s'è nel vostro core;
che ne remova, se ce fusse, errore.

ther." He proclaims his innocence and criticizes the people who have brought forward the charges against him. He is pained by the accusation, and he will comfort himself by singing about love for another person. In his sonnet, he prays that God will help him to endure the tribulations he faces. Both poems of the exchange are seventeen-verse *sonetti caudati*, sonnets to which the poets attach an additional tercet.

5A. Song [Sonnet] by Lord Ugolino to Marino when said Ser Marino was accused of the vice of sodomy, excusing himself that he was not guilty of the aforementioned

> The ancient she-wolf, who never refrained
from drinking the blood of human flesh
since the time when our ancestors
were deprived of their blessed residence for sin,
> > has never shown its origins as obviously,
taking the form of the hungry fox,
as much as now, to inspire greater vices,
so that charity is hidden from us.
> > > And her life was so hungry
that with the first brothers she began
drinking the blood of that righteous Abel.
> > > > And she strives to deny my help
from you, my brother, whom I love closely
and whom I serve with all delight.
> > > > > I pray to Him who called Himself the Truth
that He should make Himself apparent, if He's in your heart,
and He should remove any sin, if it's there.

5B. Responsio Ser Marini per epistulam primo deinde per sonictum inferius scriptum

Heu, quia de numero dapnatorum factus sum ab hijs qui vias meas non congnoverunt; sinplici sinplitiumque credulitati comissus, omnibus allijs quam meis benivolus; et qui debuerunt allere nechaverunt. Virtus enim pro vitio posita michi fuit, quorum anellitu tristitiam canere iubeor, nam forsam iras meas aliena passio satiabit. Vobiscum deploro, pater, prius quam cum illo deplorem, qui me sine se plorare fecit. Suspirabitque quamdiu hora veniet virtusque perichuli plorativa. Iniuria enim acerbior quam mors est, quoniam quilibet morti nascitur, non tamen iniurie; quo claudo literulam ne videar verbis suplere facta, que servius cor impulsant.

5B. Response by Ser Marino first in an epistle, then written in the sonnet below

Alas, I have been situated among the number of the damned by those who don't know my ways. I am committed to the simple idea of the simple people—that everyone is benevolent to me—and yet, the people who I needed to comfort me have died. My virtue was now substituted with vice, and I have been compelled to sing about my sad circumstance because my passion for another person will perhaps calm my rages. I lament with you, father, before I lament with him who made me weep in his absence. And my virtue will sigh until the sad time of danger comes. The pain I now feel is more bitter than death, because everything that is born will come to death but not necessarily to suffering. With this thought I close this short letter, lest I seem to have coupled my words to actions that have struck my lowly heart.

5C. Responsio ser Marini ad d. Ugolinum

    O voi, che 'mmaculate—per la via
d'Amore andate—per divina legge,
da parte de Colui che tutto regge
sia ver' me la vostra mente pia.
    Io son colui, che per fortuna ria
eletto fui tra le profane gregge,
condutto da vertù—de fregge orregge
en parte ove salute se desvia;
     pregate per me, prego, el Re dei venti,
che me conduca a seguir vostra barca,
sì che gemino segno non diventi.
    Tutor vedete che non sia sì carca
che forza de vertù—non ce spaventi,
prima ch'ei veli drizze la grand'arca.
    Messer Gulin, tutte seran felice,
se quel verace Amor, che regge 'l cielo,
non devenisse en noi saturno gelo.

5C. Response by Ser Marino to Lord Ugolino

    Oh, you who are sinless and walk
down the street of Love through Divine Law
on behalf of He who rules all,
may your mind be pious toward me.
    I am the one who, because of ill fortune,
was selected by the group of the profane,
led by the powers of the cold winds from those parts
where a person goes astray from salvation.
    Pray for me, I beg you, to the King of the Winds
that He should lead me to follow your ship
so that I don't become a double target.
    Now you see that my great ark isn't so laden
that the force of the winds don't cause fear
before its sails can be raised.
    Messer Ugolino, everyone will be happy
if that True Love that reigns in Heaven
doesn't become for us a saturnine frigidity.

Poem 6: Ceccoli imitates the language of courtly love in this poem. He complains about the cruel treatment he suffers at the hands of his beloved, a man he characterizes as "lord" (*signore*) in this poem and the following two. The "lord" holds Ceccoli in sway, having even the power of life and death over him. Nuccoli also addresses a beloved man as "lord" (e.g., sonnets 1, 2, and 20), suggesting a connection between the two poets, but they both may take inspiration from the Occitanic trope of calling their beloved "my lord" (*midons*). In this instance, the "lord" chases Ceccoli off, and he is dying slowly,

Ser Marinus Ceccholi

    Poi che senza pietà da te m'escacce,
almen me dí', signor, che via io tenga,
ch'io non so du' me stia né du' me 'n venga,
e volontier morria suglie toi bracce;
    e s'ucider me déi, prego che spacce,
ch'è mèi' me morir vaccio ch'io sostenga,
vivendo, morte, et infra me desvenga
a poco a poco, pur co' fònno[5] i giacce.
    S'io so' senza mercé da tu fugito,
e con glie desperate a star me mande
fuor de speranza do' trovare aito,
    famme esta grazia che de me demande
alcuna volta poi ch'io sirò gito,
sì che deserto al tutto no m'armande.

like ice melting away; the latter statement anticipates a similar depiction in his exchange with Cino da Pistoia (poem 10B). Ceccoli concludes by asking the "lord" to ask about him after he has passed away, a statement similar to that of poem 2.

Ser Marino Ceccoli

     Since you chase me off without pity,
at least tell me, lord, what road I should take,
for I don't know where I am or where I should go,
and I'd willingly die in your arms;
     and if you must kill me, I pray you do so quickly,
for it is better for me to die soon than to go on
living; Death should not come to me
bit by bit, like the way ice melts.
     If I flee from you without any of your mercy,
you send me to be with the desperate
without hope—where will I find help?
     Do me the grace of asking about me
once in a while after I have gone off,
so that you will not send me away utterly bereft.

Poem 7: Another example of Ceccoli's use of traditional amorous language. In this sonnet, he reiterates the cruel treatment of the poet at the hands of the beloved man he calls the "lord" (*signore*), as in poem 6. Like before, he is subservient to the "lord," who has complete power over him. Here, Ceccoli asserts that he will throw himself at the other man's feet, confess his sins, and beg for mercy. This sonnet resembles poem 2 by Nuccoli, a confession of sins

Ser Marinus Ceccholi

  Or[6] pur vegghˈio chˈiˈ me verrò iˈ stesso
e gitteròme steso ai vostre pièie,
e tanto piangerò ei peccata mieie,
fin chˈel dellitto mio sirà remesso.
  Daglˈocchie caderòn lagreme spesso,
che nˈanderònno al core a sei a seie,
dicendo: "Tristo, ognˈom te deverèie,
alapidar per quel che tu ài commesso!"
  Et io dirò: "Mercé, per Dio, mia colpa!
Non mˈocidete, ben chˈio seria degno
che no me remanesse osso né polpa."
  Forse chˈalora el mio signor benegno
udendo el servo suo, che sì se scolpa,
alquanto mˈaverà meno a desdegno.

to try to win over the man he also calls "lord." Here, Ceccoli claims that he will endure any punishment that the "lord" decides to mete out in the hopes that he will earn back his favor.

Ser Marino Ceccoli

  Oh, see now that I myself will come[7]
and I'll throw myself prone at your feet
and I'll weep so much about my faults
until I pay remission for my crime.
  Tears will fall thick from my eyes
and they will go to my heart, six by six,[8]
saying, "Miserable me, everyone should
stone you for what you have done."
  And I'll say, "Mercy, by God! *Mea culpa*!
Don't kill me even though I deserve
that neither my bones nor flesh should remain."
  Perhaps then my benevolent lord,
hearing his servant so reproach himself,
will hold me in less disdain.

Poem 8: A sonnet about the beloved man that Ceccoli calls the "lord" (*signore*) similar to the previous two. Again, Ceccoli imitates the poetics of Occitanic *fin'amor*, directly addressing the god of love, whom he depicts as an archer. He decries the beloved's cruelty in love, and claims that he can no longer endure the wounds he receives. He also recollects the poetry of Guido Cavalcanti, describing the vital spirits fleeing his body. His heart may never

Ser Marinus Ceccholi

      Signore, io so' remasto ormai sì vénto
ch'io non potrò sofrir più tuoie ferute,
e abandonato m'àn sí le vertute
ch'el corpo è daglie spirte mezo spento.
      Nel miser core un mortal colpo sento
tal che desfida de trovar salute;
le toi bataglie sì crudel' son sute
che tratto m'àn fuor d'ogne entendemento.
      Molt'anni fa, ch'io so' piangendo gito
sotto tua ombra, et ora giongo al ponto
ch'a morte me conduce sì ferito,
      perché tu m'ài con tua saietta gionto
et già non m'è valuto esser fugito
tanto che dai tuoi stral' non sia rigionto.
      Sonetto, chi del tuo fattor dimanda,
diglie che tu 'l vedeste
en su la morte, quando te parteste.

be healed, he writes, and he fears that he is heading to his death. He concludes the sonnet with a third tercet, which functions as an *envoi*; in it, he tells the sonnet to inform any readers that he is about to die.

Ser Marino Ceccoli

     My lord, I now remain so distraught[9]
that I can no longer endure your wounds;
and my strength has so abandoned me
that my body has lost half its spirits.
     I feel such a blow in my miserable heart
that it despairs of ever attaining well-being;
your battles with me have been so cruel
that they've taken from me all understanding.
     It has been many years that I've gone weeping
beneath your shadow, and now I've reached the point
that it drives me, wounded, toward death.
     For you have struck me with your arrow,
and it has not been worth it for me to flee
such that I haven't been struck by your bolts.
     Sonnet, tell whoever asks about your maker
that you saw him on the verge
of death when you left him.

182 *Perugia*

Poem 9: The description of the god of love, who arrives in the figure of Venus during the springtime and thus he causes the earth to flower anew. In so doing, Ceccoli reiterates a medieval commonplace in portraying Venus in a diametrically opposed fashion: either as the goddess of lust and sexuality or as the embodiment of natural laws that cause the earth to flourish.[10] Ceccoli seems to present Venus as the latter in this sonnet. The emphasis on flower-

Dulcis oratio amoris aparentis in tempore veris. Marinus

    Quando i fiorette fra le foglie tenere
ridon e spandon tutte en color varie,
per lo vigor che zeffirro da l'arie
spira, perché più dolce umor s'egenere,
    Amor descende en figura de Venere,
nel ciel serrando glie spirte contrarie,
e cerca el verde, non con ale ycarie
ch'al liquido volar devener cenere.
    Ogne creato el gran valore annunzia
de tal Signor, che già venir sensibele
ciascuno ucel con suoe note pronunzia.
    El mondo alora vèn tutto resibele,
ch'a la vertude elemental renunzia;
e 'l sole, a seguir lui, se fa possibile.

ing in this sonnet, furthermore, seems to echo Nuccoli's epithet for Trebaldino, "flowering branch."

Sweet oration of Love who appears in Springtime. Marino.

     When the little flowers among the tender leaves
laugh and open in all the various colors
due to the force that zephyr, from all the airs,
blows, so that sweeter humors are generated,
     Love descends in the figure of Venus,
blocking the sky's opposing spirits,
and she seeks greenery with wings unlike Icarus's
that turned to ash in their smooth flight.
     Everything in creation proclaims the great valor
of such a Lord, to whom all birds utter
and bring forth to the senses their songs.
     The world then becomes wholly joyful
and it reveals anew the elemental virtue;
and the sun would follow him if it were possible.

Poems 10A and 10B: An exchange with the stilnovistic poet Cino da Pistoia about the paradoxical state of being a lover. We saw in chapter 1 that Cino also apparently addressed a sonnet to Meo dei Tolomei. In this sonnet, Cino mentions his desire to gaze upon the eyes that cause him pain, because they emit rays of light and love. Cino describes his yearning with such oxymorons as "sweet death" and "sweet delusion" (v. 10), thereby calling to mind the commonplace rhetoric of the love tradition that linked passion to death.[11] He closes by evoking the personifications of Pity and Mercy.

10A. C. d. Cinus de Pistorio ad ser Marinum narrans vagationes amoris et proprietates illorum qui filo amoris ligat sunt ponens hoc in se ipso[12]

  Io so' sì vago de la bella luce
degli occhie traditor' che m'ànno uciso
che là dov'io so' morto e so' deriso
la gran vaghezza pur mi ne conduce.
  E quel che pare e quel che me traluce
m'abbaglia tanto l'uno e l'altro viso
che, da ragione e da vertù deviso,
sieguo solo 'l desio che me conduce;
  el qual me mena pien tutor de fede
a dolce morte, sotto dolce enganno,
e non s'avvede, se no doppo danno.[13]
  Troppo me pesa del gabbato affanno,[14]
ma più m'encresce, lasso!, che se vede
meco Pietà tradita da Mercéde.

Ceccoli responds in kind, explaining the overwhelming power of love, from which no one can defend themselves. His mind dissolves like ice, a statement that echoes one found in poem 6. He consoles Cino by affirming that many other people suffer from amorous torments.

10A. Song [Sonnet] by Cino da Pistoia to Ser Marino that narrates the wanderings of Love and the properties of those whom Love binds by putting himself in them

> I'm desirous of the lovely light
> of those murderous eyes that have killed me,
> and yet that great desire leads me
> to where I am killed and derided.
> How it appears and how I perceive it
> both dazzle me so, with one and the other face,
> that I, separated from reason and virtue,
> only follow my desire as my guide.
> It leads me, still trusting so fully,
> to a sweet death, under sweet delusion,
> that is recognized only after it causes harm.
> The woe of betrayal weighs too greatly on me,
> but, alas, I regret it more to see
> Pity beside me betrayed by Mercy.

10B. Responsio ser Marini ad predicta ponens potentias Amoris et ludum ipsius

   Come pèr' giaccio, fòre andando, sdruce
nostro intelletto, contemplando fiso
quest'accidente, per cui pianto e riso
e altre passion' nove ·l'alma aduce,
   per che oltra natura te produce,
e il razional sentir devèn sommiso;
e quanto più se 'n vede, men proviso
è ciascun atto suo, ch'en noi induce;
   donqua foll'è chi nostra forza crede
scrimir dai colpe che sì dolce trànno
che spesso morte—parer vita fanno.
   De ciò molte consorte—a voi stanno,
e sì giocando, sè provar concede,
perché sua cognizion nel ciel risiede.

10B. Response by Ser Marino to the aforementioned expounding on the powers of Love and of Love's game

    Just as melting ice drips out,
our mind dissolves when it contemplates fixedly
that accidental property[15] for which the soul produces
tears and laughter and other strange passions
    for you, which occur beyond what is natural
and causes your reason to be submerged;
and the more one sees of it
the less foreseeable are one's responses.
    Thus, whoever believes he can defend himself
from Love's blows—which are sweet—is foolish
because they make death appear to be life.
    Many companions in this are dying with you:
Love, playing in this way, allows you to sense him,
because true knowledge of him resides only in heaven.

Poem 11: A sententious sonnet offering advice to someone identified only as Lord Guido after the death of his wife. Ceccoli encourages him to remain strong and trust in the healing powers of sleep. If necessary, Lord Guido should turn to God, who sends us tribulations in this life to inspire repentance. Ceccoli structures the poem around the metaphor of the reasoning of the mind as a scale; it needs to be corrected and prevented from wavering.

Ser Marinus ad d. Guidonem confortando eum de morte uxoris

   Quando sinistro alcun la mente affanna,
dèi lo 'ntelletto derizzar sua libra
a schiarir l'accidente, e poi delibra
a corruttibel dar notturna manna.
   Ben che l'effetto alcuna volta enganna
e 'l senso emmagenaio ma' non vibra,
né levar pò degl'autentiche libra
el savio provveder che non appanna.
   Però, signor, se vostra vertù engombra
l'esser rimaso solitario en ciambra,
prendet'el gran Saver, che sempre sgombra
   onne fumusità da la chiara ambra,
e non curate de morte né d'ombra,
ché chi più 'n cura, più confonde e adombra.

Ser Marino to Lord Guido comforting him about the death of his wife

    When something bad troubles your mind,
you should correct the scales of your intellect
to see clearly its properties, and then reflect on it
to bring the night's manna[16] to these worldly matters.
    Even though events sometimes trick us
and their apparent meaning never stops swaying,
nor can the heavy truth be raised up,
wise foresight never fails.
    However, my lord, if your solitary life
in your chambers encumbers your powers,
take the Great Sage to yourself, who always lightens
    all darkness from one's shining soul,
and have no care of death nor shadow,
for He sends more confusion and shadows to those He loves the most.

Poem 12: Ceccoli comforts his friend Monte, who failed to become a monk. To do so, Ceccoli cites Psalm 114:4 in Latin for the *incipit* verse, and he composes six other verses in Latin (vv. 4, 5, 8, 10, 12, 14). The world, which normally rejoices, is now grieving over this turn of events for Monte, and Ceccoli encourages him to remain steadfast in the face of adversity.

Ser Marinus ad Montem confortans eum quod se non monacheret

    Montes exultaverunt ut ariettes,
ei colli come agnel' se rallegraro;
or è disceso e·lloro un pianto amaro,
pro quo flere amarent pariettes.
    Albescit unus vestis[17] *variettes*
che sovra onn'altro fo sovrano e caro;
ora vien tempo che senza reparo,
a summo eius cadent[18] *abiettes.*
    El campo sirà ner s'el mont'embianca
et totus orbis fiet ita oscurus
che onne luce a lui deverrà manca.
    Ergo, pro Deo, sistat, sistat durus,
e vertù de fortezza stia sì franca,
quod viam vite non sit traslaturus.

Ser Marino to Monte comforting him because he did not become a monk

    The mountains were leaping like rams
and the hills like lambs were rejoicing,
but now a bitter weeping has come down to them,
for which even the stones would be crying.
    That mountain's variegated colors were fading,
it was higher and more beloved over all the others;
now the time comes from which there is no escape
when, from its summit, the vegetation will fall.
    The field will be black if the mountain turns white
and the whole world will become so dark
that all light will seem feeble to it.
    Therefore, for God, he should remain resolute
and he should remain strong in the virtue of fortitude,
for he shouldn't ignore the path of life.

Poem 13: An allegorical poem about the four cardinal virtues (prudence, justice, temperance, and fortitude), personified as four Ladies. They are normally able to combat the four vices that poison the human mind. Now, however, the four Ladies have been abandoned by humanity, and they lament that they have no escorts as they walk through dangerous areas. It is likely that this sonnet was influenced by Dante's *canzone* "Three women have come round my heart" ("Tre donne intorno al cor mi son venute"), which portrays

Ser Marinus de iiij.^{or} virtutibus et ij.° passionibus anime et imparis potentijs

     Le quattro donne, che 'l moral destingue,
ch'a le quattro passion' dàn téma e freno
(e ·l'animato[20] gettarian veneno,
se non che ciascheduna la sua stingue),
     envestigate fuor per molte lingue,
ché da natura aver non se podeno;
perché[21] schiuser da sé e 'l troppo e 'l meno
e, fuor del mezzo, onn'altro fièro elingue.
     Ora se ·vanno en oscura contrada
et àn lasciate loro spose morte
e non se trova chi a parlar lo' vada;
     l'una con l'altra se lamentan forte,
cridando a quei che passan per la strada;
e dicono: "Or pur non ci avesse scorte!"
     Sonetto mio, ben che te mostre oscuro,
agl' entendente pur se' chiaro e bello,
ma, per quest'altre, tu vori' un mantello.

the three Christian virtues, faith, hope, and love, as rejected by society.[19] Ceccoli composes this poem as a seventeen-verse *sonetto caudato*, a sonnet to which he adds a tercet.

Ser Marino, regarding the four virtues and two passions of the soul, and the odd-numbered powers

    The four Ladies, who are distinguished by ethics,
bring fear and restraint to the four passions
that would cast venom into the human mind
if they weren't extinguished by their counterparts—
    they were explained by many tongues,
and they couldn't be acquired by nature alone;
because they reject every excess or lack
and, except for the measured, they render all else silent.
    Now they walk in dark neighborhoods
and they've left their spouses for dead
and they can't find anyone who'll speak to them.
    Each one laments harshly to the other
crying to whomever they pass on the street,
and they say: "Oh, if only we had a companion!"
    My sonnet, even though you appear dark,
you are clear and beautiful to those who understand,
but to other people you wear a cloak.

Poem 14: A political poem about Perugia, personified as a Lady, as in Nuccoli's poem 17. Ceccoli describes her as a mistress with an unstained name, who governs provinces, seemingly echoing Dante's satiric characterization of Italy (*Purgatorio* 6:76–78). Perugia has been struck by adverse fortune, and it is therefore growing feebler. It is not clear what specific circumstance has beset Perugia, however. Nonetheless, Ceccoli calls on the city's residents to come to its defense before the situation becomes too dire. Ceccoli crafts this poem as a sixteen-verse *sonetto caudato*, appending a couplet to the sonnet.

Ser Marinus tractans de desolatione urbis perusine

   L'esento nome e 'l singolare arbitro,
che sempre ficer posa en quista donna,
sì che descritta fo regal madonna,
de terre e de province specchio e vitro,
   veggio percòter da mortal tonitro
e desquatrar per mezzo tal colonna;
e veggio metter sorte de sua gonna,
et a cui tocca chiudete el palpitro.
   E però prego che ciascun se sveghie,
prima che quista fiamma colga campo,
et a tener suo stato salvo veghie.
   Ché, po' lo stroppo, tardo vien lo scampo,
popol, se, 'nanze tratto, non reveghie
l'usate forze, ad arcovrar lo campo.
   Guárdate, donna, che non face el terzo,
a l'altre che fatt'ài rentrar per terzo.

Ser Marino writing about the desolation of the city of Perugia

     The unstained name and exceptional will
that always resided within this Lady,
such that she was always called a Royal Mistress,
mirror and looking glass of lands and provinces,
     I see her struck by a deadly thunderclap
and her supporting column weakened,
and I see her put on a dress of good fortune,
and whoever she touches closes his eyes.
     However, I beg everyone to wake up,
before this flame claims the fields,
and to be alert to keep their state safe.
     Because after the devastation, safety comes too late.
People, don't wait too long to reclaim
your old strength and recover the fields.
     See, Lady, that you don't become third
to the others whom you considered third to you.

Poem 15: Another poem about the political situation in Perugia. He opens by echoing Matthew 15:14: "If the blind lead the blind, both will fall into a pit." However, Ceccoli uses the biblical verse to criticize the lack of unity among the citizens of Perugia. He anticipates that their divisions will result in eventual defeat. He presents himself as a modern-day Erichtho, the witch from Lucan's *Pharsalia* (book 6), who prophesied the outcome of the Battle

Ser Marinus tractans de diversitate gentium civitatis Perusie

      Io trovo che l'un ceco l'altro guida;
e trovo gente de suo danno vaga,
la quale en asto nel profondo alaga,
et a se stessa su' bruciare aída;
      e trovo gente ch'in speranza fida,
ch'aspetta che da cel venga la paga;
e gente trovo che da fin già smaga,
credendo de dí en dí sentir glie strida.
      Et io, quase Eritòn, già m'alegro,
la qual predisse de Tissaglia el sangue,
che fe' 'l roman senato venir egro;
      poi che cossì la cosa fra sé langue,
e, lavorando de poco, en pelégro
crescendo va, sì come al suo loco angue,
      come la gente è infra sé partita,
cusì tien' tu la terra per perita.

of Pharsalus, near Thessaly. Ceccoli adds a couplet to this sonnet, rendering it a sixteen-verse *sonetto caudato*.

Ser Marino writing about the opposition of the peoples of the city of Perugia

  I find that one blind man guides the other,
and I find people desirous of their own harm,
because they sink into the deepest hatred
and they ruin any assistance to themselves,
  and I find people who put trust in hope,
and await heaven's just punishments;
and I find people that are lost in the end
believing that their cries will be heard from one day to the next.
  And I am already joyful,[22] almost like Erichtho,
who predicted the blood of Thessaly
that made the Roman Senate fall ill.
  The risk grows, like a snake in its hole,
since things are left to languish
and so little work is done in the face of danger.
  When the people are divided among themselves,
the land should thus be considered lost.

Poem 16: On 1 November 1333, heavy rains struck central Italy, causing the Arno to flood Florence on 4 November. The deluge swept away dams and houses, and killed 300 people. In this sonnet, Ceccoli describes the flood in mythological terms, mentioning Eurus, the god of the east wind, who was associated with bad weather; Eurus sent the lightning that sparked the downpour. Ceccoli then describes the flood surge as caused by the actions of Scylla and Charybdis, and he explains that Nature itself was in a rage. Giovanni Villani provides an ample description of the flood (*Nuova cronica*, bk. XII,

Ser Marinus exclamans ad Iovem causa diluvij florentinij

   Resciolsese dai ciel' novo dilluvio,
aceso già da l'eoropal favilla,
da cui la fiamba acuta se destilla,
ch'à 'n sé rechiuso l'universo engluvio.

   Oltra natura l'onde crude al fluvio
ve fuor proddutte da Caridde e Scilla,
en ira fo deglie elemente Quilla,
sé confondendo sotto el corso pluvio.

   Aspro destin, da le pianete messo
nei fredde segne, par ch'e·lleie s'anide,
sí dai sinistre è visitata spesso.

   Onde convene ormai ch'a Quel se gride,
ch'è Uno e Tre, e Tre sono Uno stesso,
ché la conduca sì ch'a sé la guide.

chaps. 1–4), and he mentions that in its aftermath a debate raged as to whether the flood was the result of divine punishment, or if instead it had been caused by astrological influences.[23] Ceccoli seems to bridge the two sides in the debate when he suggests that people should pray to God to control Nature via the movements of the planets. Other poets who discussed the flood of 1333 include Adriano de' Rossi (d. 1400) and Antonio Pucci (1310–88).[24]

Ser Marino calling out to Jove [God] because of the flood of Florence

> A new flood was released from the heavens,
> lit suddenly from the spark of Eurus,
> from which the sharp flame is distilled
> that contains the universe's destructive force.
>
> The river's rough waves were produced
> beyond Nature by Charybdis and Scylla—
> she was in a rage with the elements,
> confounding them under the hard rain.
>
> Harsh destiny, sent from the planets
> in the cold signs, seems to be hidden in her
> since she's often visited with disasters.
>
> Hence it's necessary to cry out to
> He who is One and Three, and Three are One,
> to guide her, so that He can control her Himself.

Poem 17: A complaint against the god of love, for whom Ceccoli has endured great tribulations, composed in the comic mode of vituperation. At first he expresses himself straightforwardly. He seemingly echoes the opening verses of *Inferno* 3 (vv. 1–3), which relate the warning at the gate of hell; here, Ceccoli repeats "Because of him" (*Per lui*, vv. 5–8), spelling out his suffering. By following Love, the poet writes, he has lost both Apollo (the god of poetry and knowledge) and Minerva (the goddess of wisdom). In the very last line, he returns to the infernal reminiscence by stating that love causes people to lose access to the stars (i.e., heaven).

At the start of the tercets, however, Ceccoli transforms the poem into an outright invective, saying that passion causes people to be damned to hell. At one point he rails against Love with a verse of great subtlety. He claims he

Ser Marinus Ceccholi conquerens de amore

    Si aíte dio Amor com'ei me serve
se non de cosa che non monta un aglio!
E dà biene[26] a veder ch'io poco i caglio,
quand'ei m'enfrasca con cotai mai serve.
    Per lui perdut'ò io le vene e i nerve,
per lui messo me so' ad onne retaglio,
per lui sofert'ò io briga e travaglio,
per lui perduto n'ò Apollo e Minerve.
    Ma io farò una fica e dirò: "Castra!
Fa' me 'l peggio che puoi, tènla tra gli occhie!
tu se' colui, c'ogne vizio amastra;
    tu se' colui, che, cèco, altrui adocchie;
tu se' colui, che tutta gente scastra;
tu se' colui, *pro quo perduntur astra.*"

will make the hand gesture called "a fig" (farò una fica, v. 9), famously depicted in Dante's *Inferno* 25:2 and mentioned by Meo dei Tolomei in his *caribetto* (poem 19, stanza X). The gesture consists of the thumb inserted between the index and middle finger, and its name literally indicates the female genitals; thus, by claiming he will make the gesture, Ceccoli literally states that he will make a vagina for himself, and the rhyme word of the very same verse is the exclamation "Castra!" (literally, "castrate"). The symptoms of love were believed to "unman" the lover, and part of the cultural anxiety of sodomy was that it overturned the proper relationship of men's dominance over women.[25] In other words, by complaining about his passion for another man, he imbues the verse with elements suggestive of gender inversion. Because of these characteristics, this sonnet seems to recall the poetry of Meo dei Tolomei.

Ser Marino Ceccoli complaining about love

>So may the god of love help me, even as he serves me,
>
>but with things that aren't worth even a garlic clove!
>
>And he shows that he doesn't care for me
>
>when he tricks me with his evil words.
>
>Because of him I've lost my veins and nerves,
>
>because of him I've put myself into such privation,
>
>because of him I've suffered troubles and strife,
>
>because of him I've lost both Apollo and Minerva.
>
>But I'll make a fig and say "Castra!"
>
>Do the worst you can to me; take it between the eyes!
>
>You're the one who instructs every vice,
>
>you're the one who, while blind, points out others;
>
>you're the one who tires out people,
>
>you're the one *for whom even the stars are lost.*"[27]

Poem 18: Ceccoli writes to someone identified only as "Tiberutium de Montemellino," about whom nothing is known. The poet implores him to leave Montemelino and to join Ceccoli down in the Tiber valley, where Tiberuccio's adored woman also can be found. As in sonnet 4, Ceccoli bases the sonnet on the contrast between life in the city (*urbanitas*) and life in the countryside (*rusticitas*); Nuccoli similarly wrote about that topic, underscoring the connections between the two poets. He tells Tiberutium that there

Ser Marinus Ceccholi ad d. Tibertutium de Montemellino dum ibi faceret residentiam scribendo quod revertatur

    O voi, che séte poste en alto colle,
il qual da lugne par ch'el mondo cove
e par c'ogne delletto ve se trove
(fuor d'uno, el qual la Teverina tolle),
    tornate qua, non siate tanto folle,
e no v'enganne l'abadare altrove,
ch'èccola che retorna en atte nove,
che scastra ogn'om che reguardar la volle.
    Or ve state là su, e noi qua entro;
e vederem costei, e voi le siepe
con cotai razze andar mo fuor mo entro!
    Ché certo chi cercasse de qui a Nepe,
ancor lo mondo tutto e 'l cielo e 'l centro,
contento non seria, se non véi l' "*e pe*."

are no greater delights to be found between Perugia and Nepi, a town just outside Viterbo in central Italy. In the manuscript, the last words of the sonnet, "*e pe*," are clarified as the woman's name; to the right of the poem appears the name "Pellola." There appears to be a connection between this sonnet and Nuccoli's poem 6, in which he discusses the origins of rivers.

Ser Marino Ceccoli to lord Tiberutium de Montemellino while he resides there [in Montemelino] writing for him to return

  Oh, you who have repaired to the high hill,
who, from afar, seem to have the world under your wings,
and it seems that every delight is found there
(except for one, which the Tiber valley takes from it):
  come back here—don't be so foolish!—
and don't be tricked when she looks about elsewhere,
for—here she is!—she returns with new behaviors
that make everyone crazy who wants to see her!
  Now, you're up there and we're here,
and we'll gaze upon her, but you'll see hedges
with such birds now going in, now going out!
  For whoever searched between here and Nepi—
indeed the whole world, the sky, and its center—
would not be content if they didn't see "e" and "p."

204 *Perugia*

Poem 19: Another sonnet addressed to "Tiberutium de Montemellino," apparently encouraging him again to leave his residence. As in the previous sonnet, Ceccoli contrasts life in the city to that of the countryside. In this poem, Ceccoli describes the swarms of mosquitoes that live outside Perugia, and he offers suggestions as to how to deal with them: importing their predators, ant lions, or burning *canuta* plants to drive them away.

Ser Marinus Ceccholi ad d. Tiberutium de Montemellino

    Se v'àn sí assidiato le cienciale,
che la partenza non sia sencia impaccio,
io verrò là con lo socurso vaccio
de grosse formicon', de quei con l'ale;
    e forse che mo fan defesa tale
che mo[28] campate de l'importun laccio
de quelle che tràn gli occhie, com'io saccio
(e già mur né fortezza non cie vale!)
    M'a ciò che la condutta sia con senno,
farite far de canútole un fumo
che più sentite sian, vedendo el cenno.
    E vederete com'io mo la schiumo,
se tosto non retornano a quel renno
onde lor nascemento en prima fenno.

Ser Marino Ceccoli to Lord Tiberutium de Montemellino

        If the mosquitoes have so attacked you
that you won't depart without some delay,
I'll come right away with the quick relief
of large ant lions, the ones with wings.
        And maybe then they'll provide you with such defense
that you'll make it out of that persistent trap
by tearing out their eyes, as I am sure
(neither city wall nor fortress is of any help).
        But if you act intelligently,
you'll produce the smoke of the *canuta* plant
and have its aroma spread across the marsh.
        You'll see, as I now conclude,
that they won't return to that realm
where they first were born.

Poem 20: A poem about the essence of love, which employs philosophical reasoning and language (*quia* and *quare*, vv. 2, 3). He uses the metaphor of a plant of love, claiming that he too is a devotee. As in his *tenzone* with Cino da Pistoia (sonnets 10A and 10B), Ceccoli raises the question as to whether love is a substance or an accident. Ceccoli notes that something without potentiality will lack the efficient causes to exist. Therefore, he asks about the origin of love, whether it is a by-product of matter or it has a transcendental

Ser Marinus Ceccholi

    Io so' de quei che van pur per le scorze
de l'amorosa pianta, senza *quia*,
ch'el *quare* san bien dire; ond'io vorria
en alcun verso sequitar lor forze.

    Cosa fuor da potenza par ch'esforze
natura, s'alcuno atto mena en via;
ché senza materia esser deveria
senza cagion de sé, valore e forze.

    Ora desio saper d'amor principio,
se da materia o forma fo produtto,
che fanno onne terrestro a sé mancipio;

    o s'ei fu fatto pur per sé condutto
e de ciascuno o nullo participio,
cercando vo per esser entrodutto.

nature that brought itself into being. This sonnet appears to be the start of a *tenzone*, but no response has survived.

Ser Marino Ceccoli

     I'm one of those who still cling to the bark
of the plant of love without a *because*,
since we know well how do say *why*; hence I'd want
to put their *maybe* into some verses.
     Something without potentiality seems to force
Nature if it should become a reality;
otherwise, without matter, valor, and force
it shouldn't truly exist, lacking the efficient causes.
     Now I want to know the origin of love:
whether it was produced by matter or form,
which render all earthly things as substance;
     or if it was brought forth by itself,
or if it is the product of everything, or of nothing?
I'm searching this out, just as a start.

Poems 21A, 21B, and 21C: A *tenzone* between Ceccoli, Nuccoli, and Gilio Lelli about the political strife between Perugia and the Tarlati of Pietramala, lords of Arezzo, which took place between 1335 and 1337. Nuccoli discusses the same situation in his sonnet 26.

Ceccoli begins this exchange by referring to the crest of the Tarlati, golden nuggets on a field of blue, describing it as crumbling and fading away. He sees the Tarlati as weakened and heading toward a sad end. They are impeded, he concludes, by Perugia, symbolized by its crest of a white griffon on a field of red.

Nuccoli replies to Ceccoli that the Tarlati, despite earlier appearances, seem to be returning to power. Fortune, Nuccoli writes, has a tendency to

21A. Ser Marinus Ceccholi tractans de statu illorum de Petramala

>Io veggio scolorir gli aurate sasse
e sgranellarse fuor del colle azuro
e l'uno e l'altro devenir sì oscuro
che quase paion d'ogne luce casse.
>>Le lor vertù sen van con lente passe,
forte piangendo per lo scoglio duro,
per trovar loco che lo' sia securo
dove riposen loro spirte lasse.
>>>Né mur né fosso, né poggio né ombra
non è che de costor si facia albergo,
ancie ciascun da sé glie schiude e sgombra.
>>>>Le lor vertute caminan ver' l'*ergo*;
la cruda petra un griffon bianco ingombra,
cinta dintorno d'un vermiglio asbergo.

turn, lifting up the people who are at their lowest points. Gilio Lelli answers Nuccoli, saying that if the Tarlati returned to power, it would be because of God's will. Lelli notes that any power, even that which destroyed the Catiline conspiracy in ancient Rome, is granted by God and not through the actions of human beings.

Through the reference to the crest of the Tarlati, this *tenzone* shows strong similarities to Nuccoli's sonnet 26. Ceccoli will again discuss this topic in the *tenzone* with Ceccolo in sonnets 24A and 24B.

21A. Ser Marino Ceccoli writing about the state of the people of Pietramala

      I see the golden stones fading
and crumbling away from the blue hill,
and one and the other becoming so dark
that they almost seem deprived of light.
      Their virtues move away with slow steps,
crying hard about the harsh cliff
to find a place that is secure for them
where they can rest their weary spirits.
      There is no wall nor ditch nor knoll nor shade
that provides them with refuge,
but instead each one shuts them out and drives them off.
      Their virtues walk toward a conclusion:
the crude rocks are encumbered by a white griffon
that is girded by vermillion armor.

21B. Responsio Ser Cecchi

    Non se credea che mai discolorasse
la orata petra fuor del franco muro
con l'agiur campo nel qual la figuro
ma che vigore e forza radoppiasse.
    E ben che mo ritrosa si voltasse
sua prospera fortuna, poco curo,
sperando sempre ch'el tempo futuro
subito fa salir quai son più basse.
    Tu vederai, se morte no l'adombra,
farne voltar, com'altra volta, el tergo
e tramar più che non fa la codombra,
    fuggendo come el pesce innanzi a mergo,
non ci varrà recar pietre né ombra.
Di cotal chiosa mia risposta vergo.

21B. Response by Ser Cecco

    No one believed that the golden rock
would fade apart from the secure wall
with the blue field, on which they're depicted,
but instead that their vigor and force would double.
    And although now its prosperous fortune
comes back unwillingly, I care little,
because I always anticipate that future times
make the things farthest down rise up again.[29]
    If Death doesn't darken things, you'll see
it turn its buttocks to you yet again
and tremble more than the wagtail does,
    fleeing like the fish before the duck;
it will not be worth it to cast rocks or a shadow.
I write my response with such a meaning.

21C. Responsio Gillij Lelli ad ser Marinum predictum

  Se l'antica potenza ritornasse,
che strusse Catellina dal congiuro,
s'io guardo ben con l'intelletto puro,
non credo che così vittoriasse;
  ma par che ·dDio tal opera destinasse
sì che non vale altrui l'esser maturo
né signoria, se bene il ver misuro,
che, com'è Suo voler, no 'l permutasse.
  Chi crede ch'altro sia, dico che ombra;
e può dir chi reggea: "S'io pur sommergo,
colpo de vostra spada no m'adombra!
  Ma se speranza, con la quale io pergo,
dall'aspera fortuna me disombra,
disfatto sia, s'ancor non vi dispergo!"

21C. Response by Gilio Lelli to the aforementioned Marino

    If the ancient power returned—
the one that destroyed Catiline the conspirator—
I don't believe that it would thus be victorious,
even if I look at it with a pure intellect.
    But it seems that God destined this work
such that it doesn't help if others are established,
nor will their lordship change,
if I consider the truth well, because it is His will.
    To whoever believes otherwise I say it's but a shadow,
and whoever reigned can say: "Even if I sink down,
the blows from your sword don't harm me!
    But if my hope, with which I walk,
distances me from the shade of harsh fortune,
may I still be undone if I don't scatter you all!"

Poems 22A, 22B, 22C, and 22D: A *tenzone* between Neri Moscoli, Simone da Pierile, and Marino Ceccoli about the nature of free will. Moscoli opens the exchange by asking if God's omniscience negates human freedom; specifically, he asks if God's foreknowledge predetermines our actions. Simone da Pierile answers that human beings have free will because, in its absence, punishments and rewards for actions would be unjust, and that is a position he considers unspeakable. Ceccoli concurs with Pierile, explaining that God's

22A. Idem Nerius domino Simoni de Perile

  El non par ch'abia libro arbitrio alcuno
poder montare a gloria ternale
e simelmente nel contrario male
non par che possa descender ciascuno;
  ché s'el Patre con quei che son Tre et Uno
sôn che dannar o salvar se dé tale,
mal operare o ben non noce o vale
ché 'l chiar saver non pòi deventar bruno.
  E perché questo mai non vide aperto
non perché 'l creder mio fedel non sia,
desío per voi, lettore, eserne certo.
  E ciò dimando non sol per la mia
volontà quïetar, ma per quî c'ànno
simel penser nei cori e quete stanno.

foreknowledge does not constrain human will, and therefore any merits or punishments for our actions are justified. Moscoli contributes a second poem that closes the *tenzone*, in which he asserts his adherence to the Christian teachings about human free will, but reiterating his confusion about the topic.

22A. By the same Neri [Moscoli] to Lord Simone de Perile

   It doesn't seem that anyone has free will
to be able to rise up to eternal glory,
and similarly, it doesn't seem that anyone
can descend to the opposite evil;
   because if the Father, with Those who are Three and One,
knows whom of us He will damn or save,
bad actions or good ones neither harm nor help us,
because His bright knowledge cannot then become dark.
   And because I've never seen this discussed openly,
and not because my belief is unfaithful,
I want to be assured by you, my reader.
   And I don't ask this only to quiet
my own will, but for those who have
similar thoughts in their hearts and are silent.

22B. C. d. Simon de Pierile responsio

       Io son sì al tutto de saver degiuno
ch' el mio conoscer troppo è desoguale
a l'alto vostro dimandar, del quale
passano molte co' scalzo per pruno.
       Ma per quel poco che tra me rauno
de sentimento, dico ch'animale
è om de pieno arbitrio; e scende o sale
per voglia non coatta ciascheduno.
       E se non fusse ciò, non avria metro
alcun de ben né pena de follia
e 'l giusto Scíentor serebe inesperto;
       quod est infandum; e perché la via
prevegia Dio o' gl'omeni vanno,
non prescir fa, ma prescir l'opre fanno.
       Ciò nel futuro fa divin savere
che nel presente umano chiaro vedere.

22B. Song [Poem] by lord Simone de Pierile, response

    I am so starved of wisdom
that my knowledge is far too unequal
to your high question, about which
many others pass barefoot among the thorns.³⁰
    But for that little sense that I can gather,
I can say that a man is an animal
of complete will; for he rises or falls
with a will completely unrestrained.
    And if this weren't so, no one would have
merit for goodness, nor punishment for folly,
and the Just Intelligence would be ignorant;
    *this would be unspeakable.*³¹ And simply because
God foresees the way where men will go,
their actions—not His foreknowledge—cause the outcomes.
    Divine knowledge sees the future
in the way human knowledge sees the present.

22C. Idem Ser Marinus Ceccholi Nerio predicto

   La prescienzia de Quel ch'è Terzo et Uno,
per che proveggia l'ordene fatale,
no n'impedisce arbitrio spander l'ale
sovra 'l propïo desio de ciascuno;
   come per volontà védesse[32] alcuno
andar, ch'egli ande non constringe tale
necessità al suo termen finale,
ch'andare e star fermo gli è comuno.
   Se bene entendo el vostro dir coperto,
el pressaper non giudica che sia
come destina, ma com'è suo metro
   receve chi via piglia bona o ria;
onde sian certe quei ch'errando vanno
che da cotal cagione albitrio trànno.

22C. The same Ser Marino Ceccoli to the aforementioned Nerio

      The foreknowledge of He who's Third and First
through which the order of fate can be seen
never prevented anyone's will from spreading
its wings over his own desire.
      It is seen how people move
according to their own will, for such necessity
does not constrain them to go to a Final End,
for the ability to go or stay is available to them.
      If I've understood well your veiled speech,
I don't judge foreknowledge to be
like a destiny; but they receive according to their merits
      whoever take the good or evil path.
So let whoever errs be certain
that they should understand free will from this case.

22D. Responsio Nerij predicti ad Ser Marinum[33]

   Non pense quel che scrisse esser pur uno
enfedel creder che cosa fatale
a qual vole andar su non rompa l'aile
né gionga 'n peso al scender de ciascuno.
   Ma come ciò sia non trovo alcuno
ch'el mostre per essemplo en modo tale
che chiar se végia ond'è l'atto finale;
e qui *de fede* ai cristian' comuno.
   Né se porria veder, sì è coperto,
per alcun, tanto che nel mondo sia,
per ciò che fede perderia suo merto.
   Io lasso la contesa ormai per ria;
ché quei che troppo altier volando vanno
espesse volte al più basso se trànno.

22D. Response by the aforementioned Nerio to Ser Marino

     Please don't think that he who wrote to be
of an infidel belief: that it is fate
for whoever wishes to rise to not break his wings,
nor whoever descends to find weights on his feet.
     But how is it so? I can't find anyone
who can show with an example, and in such a way
that it is clear how actions lead to the Final End;
though in this I adhere to the Christian faith.
     Nor could it be seen—for it is hidden—
for some, as many as there are in the world,
would lose their merits just because of their faith.
     I'm leaving this debate, which has now become coarse,
because those who go flying too high
too often are pulled to the lowest level.

Poems 23A, 23B, and 23C: A poetic exchange between Marino Ceccoli and Lord Ugolino of Fano. In his sonnet, Ceccoli asks Ugolino about the identity of the woman whom he had accompanied to the Festival of the Assumption of Mary (15 August). Ceccoli asks if the Lord of Love struck him with the golden arrow, a traditional image for falling in love. In his response, Ugolino explains through astrological reasoning that he fell in love with a woman who, he claims, bears a resemblance to the Virgin Mary. He mentions that a

23A. Ser Marinum Ceccholi d. Ugolino de Fano

    Diteme, ser Gulin, qual fu la donna,
che nella calda festa fu più vaga,
di cui più dolce el vostro cor s'appaga
vederla enella mente per colonna?
    E qual fu quella ch'en la strada, in gonna,
sola trovaste, di color di fraga,
ch'a rendervi salute non ismaga,
quando diceste: "Ben stiate, madonna"?
    Giònsivi Amor con sua saietta d'oro
alor sì che per Lui ve risovegna
d'i dolce colpe che ve dièr costoro?
    O cun qual d'esse l'anima s'ingregna
di rivedersi nel beato coro,
ove, col suo poter, te Amor sì regna?

bright star appears in the "Hebrew bull" (presumably the constellation of Taurus), which radiates the power that causes him to feel passionately toward her.

23A. Ser Marino Ceccoli to Lord Ugolino de Fano

    Tell me, Ser Ugolin, who was the lady
who, during the hot festival, was the loveliest,
and about whom your heart is most sweetly satisfied
to consider as the very basis[34] of your mind?
    Who was the one in a skirt on the street
whom you found in a strawberry color,
who didn't delay to respond to your greeting
when you said, "May you be well, milady?"
    Did Love arrive there with his golden arrow,
or when, through his strength, you call to mind
the sweet wounds that he then caused you?
    Or with which of them does your soul use its wits
to see itself in the blessed choir
where Love reigns with his power?

23B. Responsio d. Ugholinj de Fano Ser Marino[35]

    Nella festività di Nostra Donna,
sotto un bel manto vidi saggia e saga
tal, ch'a mirar, par che gli occhie si traga
per simiglianza di lontana monna,
    di cui la vita mia fu serva alonna;
poi, ritornando ove Amor più s'alaga,
da buona facia uscier parole in fraga,
ch'un ramo di dolcezza al cor m'antonna.
    Movesi ancor de l'ebraïco toro
una stella chiarita en cui s'aligna
Amore assai più forte ca in coloro.
    Cotal vaghezza la mia mente impregna,
ma, pur membrando el mio proprio tesoro,
ogn'altra gioia per me si desdegna.

23B. Response by Lord Ugolino de Fano to Ser Marino

    On the Feast Day of Our Lady
I gazed upon her—wise and prudent beneath a beautiful mantle—
who seems to take your eyes away when you look at her
because of her similarity to another, more distant Lady,
    of whom my life was a faithful disciple.
Then, to return to where love grows the most,
soft words came from her lovely face to me
to guide me with her sweet rudder on my heart.
    From the Hebrew bull[36] a bright star
still moves, in which love aligns
more strongly than in them.
    Such beauty permeates my mind
that, while still remembering my own treasure,
every other joy is scorned by me.

Poems 24A and 24B: A *tenzone* between Ceccoli and someone named Ceccolo about the political strife between Perugia and Arezzo. The same topic was debated by Ceccoli in the *tenzone* with Nuccoli and Gilio Lelli (sonnets 21A, 21B, and 21C) and was discussed by Nuccoli (sonnet 26 in his corpus).

In the opening sonnet of this exchange, Ceccoli addresses the city of Arezzo, citing the first verse of the biblical book of Lamentations (*Quomodo sola sedes*); Dante uses this very same passage to indicate the death of Beatrice in the *Vita Nuova* (ca. 1294). Nuccoli states that, in the hands of the Tarlati family, Arezzo's political fortunes are about to take a turn for the worse, and Neri Uguccione della Faggiuola will lead Perugia's army against it. In April 1335, Faggiuola did indeed take up arms against Pier Saccone Tarlati because

24A. Ser Marinus Ceccholi tractans de statu aritino

Quomodo sola sedes, città 'retina,
vedova donna dei tuoi bei tribute!
Pianger ti veggio e chiamare aiute,
ma 'l gran pastore ogni tuo varco spina.
    Conviente al certo la final ruina
portarla in pace col' tuo' signor' glute,
qual' per più tempo sforzar hon volute
città e castella et amistà vicina.
    Gierusalèm Gierusalèm, giudeo
Arezzo, dir ti puoi coi tuoi Tarlate;
convèrtete tosto al tuo Signore Deo
    e no aspettare el fin de' dir' trattate,
qual si fan contra te al tempo giusto,
per rifrenare el tuo pensiere ingiusto.
    E tosto vederai la chiara ensegna,
sovre dei sassa star l'uciel grifone,
e colla spada in man Ner d'Ugucione.

he had lost mountain castles to Pier Saccone over the years.³⁷ In writing about the conflict, Ceccoli characterizes Arezzo as traitorous, building upon the medieval Christian stereotype of the Jews.

Ceccolo responds with the same rhymes (*per le rime*), and like Ceccoli he composes a seventeen-verse *sonetto caudato*. He asserts that Perugia, the "Queen . . . over all cities," will be victorious, and will no longer pay tribute to Arezzo nor to the Tarlati; he refers to the latter through their crest of golden nuggets on a field of blue. Divine Justice will favor Perugia, and her standard will rule over everyone.

24A. Ser Marino Ceccoli writing about the state of Arezzo

How you sit alone,³⁸ Aretine city,
widow bereft of all your nice tributes!
I see you weep and call for help,
but the great shepherd pushes past all your limits.
    It's necessary for you to sue for peace
at this final ruin, because of your gluttonous lords
who for a long time wanted to force themselves
on cities and castles and nearby friends.
    Jerusalem, Jerusalem!—Arezzo the Jew³⁹
you can call yourself, with your Tarlati!
Turn at once to your Lord God!
    Don't wait till the end to make the treaties
that will be made against you at the right time
to restrain your unjust ideas.
    And soon you'll see the bright banner:
the griffon will be above the rocks,
and, sword in hand, Neri d'Uguccione.

24B. Sonectus Ceccholi

      Sovra di tutte ogni città regina,
ben per soverchio sovran'à salute;
divina Sapïenza à provedute
l'esciellente sue guardie a chi non fina;
      onde superbia alquanto s'inchina
per glie gravose colpe recevute,
i qual di giorno in giorn'òn procedute,
poi che licenza concessa fu piena.
      Non renderan più, trebutarie, feo
a l'artina città né ai sasse orate
i qual, disposta signoria, più reo
      dal possente Signor son condannate
Santa Giustizia fa sentir lor gusto
di novi tormenti et anco di combusto.
      O alta Maiestà tanto benigna,
reale dono dà a Prosa: il confalone,
che regga l'universo col leone.

24B. Sonnet by Ceccoli

      The queen over everyone, and over all cities,
has the robustness for her superior sovereignty.
Divine wisdom has provided for
her guards, whose excellence never ends;
      whence all pride must bow down
because of the heavy blows it received
that came to it day after day,
since full license to do so was conceded to her.
      She will not pay tribute any longer
to the Aretine city, nor to its golden stones
that with the lordship, now most cruelly deposed,
      are condemned by the powerful Lord;
Holy Justice, have them rightly feel
new punishments, even of burning.
      Oh, the highest Majesty, most benign,
gives to Perugia a royal gift: the standard
with a lion, which will rule the universe.

Poem 25: A *canzone*, a long, multistanza composition, about Love and the spiritual basis for loving.[40] Ceccoli depicts people who do not feel Love's power as lacking in virtue; their souls will never mature and, hence, they risk eternal damnation. He explains that Love endows people with valor and, thus, it drives away all vice. He connects Love to the zodiacal cosmos, associating it to the planet Venus, and repeatedly mentioning the celestial orbits; in this manner, Ceccoli evokes Dante's poem "All you who, knowing, make

C. dulcis invitatio ad Amorem vulgari sermone facta per ser Marinum Ceccholi de Perusio

Vita, che senza Amor nel tempo corre,
senza nulla vertù suo cerchio volta,
et è privata e tolta
dal primo fine a ch'ella fo ordenata.
Perdendo el corso, suo viver trascorre,
però ch'ell'è da quel pianeto sciolta,
sotto 'l quale è ricolta
onne vertù ch'è nel sentir creata.
L'anima da se stessa è ignorata,
et, ignorando sé, deventa nulla.
Poscia, così fanciulla,
se n'anda al loco ove non luce sole
e 'l Ben perduto, più che 'l martir, dole.

Cosa, che senza Amor l'anima adopre,
mai non aspette premio de fatiga;
ma quanto più ciò briga
tanto più perde ciascun ben che face.
Amor sol de valor glie spirite copre,
onne vizio dal cor caccia e metiga;
Amore sesta e riga
la terra e 'l ciel secondo ch'a Lui piace.
Donqua, van'è ciò che fuor d'Amor giace,

the Third Sphere move" ("Voi ch'intendendo il terzo ciel movete").⁴¹ Further underscoring the relationship to Dante, Ceccoli then writes that Love is related to the Christian virtue of charity, which he personifies as a Lady.⁴² Charity drives to hell everyone who had no interest in her. He then draws the connection between Love and the divine, claiming that Love is as eternal as the First Cause, that is, God.

A sweet poetic invitation to love, a sermon in the vernacular made by Ser Marino Ceccoli of Perugia

Life, which without Love runs across time,
will close its circle without any virtue
and is bereft and lost
from its first aim toward which it was ordered.
Losing its course, it forgets to live
because it is unbound from the planet
under which is collected
every virtue that is created in feeling.
The soul is ignored by itself,
and, ignoring itself, becomes nothing.
Then, so immature,
it goes to the place where the sun never shines
and it suffers more from loving the Good than any punishment.

Something without Love that possesses a soul
should never expect a reward for its trouble,
but for as much as it struggles at it,
the more it will lose any of the good it earns.
Only Love covers spirits with valor,
it chases off or mitigates all vice;
Love measures and encompasses
the Earth and Heaven according to its will.
Therefore, anything that resides outside of love is empty,

e quanto à l'om d'Amor tant'à de bene;
e però se convene
aver prima Signor la mente nostra
Quel, senza 'l qual se perderia ogne giostra.

Nel sen de Caritade Amore alberga,
e chi non sente Lei né Lui non sente.
Carità realmente
onne vertude en sé ferma rechiude,
Ella retiene en sé la real verga
del sommo Giove et è sì possente
ch'amica fa la mente
a Quel che l'universo en sé conchiude.
Ella fa andar nell'altro mondo nude
gli spirte, che de Lei no n'eber cura.
Ell'è libera e pura,
et altrui, come sé, sempre conduce
e tanto en altre quant'en sé produce.

Ogne vertute en Amor se specchia
e quanto luce en Lei tant'à de luce;
ov'Esso non traluce,
cosa nïuna mai nasce perfetta.
Colla Prima Cagion s'antiqua e invecchia;
et Ella creò Lui ministro e duce,
sotto 'l qual se reduce
ogne animato che veder l'aspetta.
Errar non può chi ben fier soa saietta,
ma alegro, dolce e senza cura vive;
poi che glie spirte prive
dal corpo son, se 'n va l'anima santa
nel loco ove de Lui sempre se canta.

O canzon mia, che tanto lode Amore,
chi te dimanda chi te fice, diglie
che non t'engenerò altre che Eglie.

and a man has as much goodness as he has love,
and for that reason it's necessary
to have it as our mind's first lord,
without whom every joust will be lost.

Love resides in the breast of Charity,
and whoever doesn't feel her won't feel him either.
Charity truly
solidly encircles every virtue within it;
she holds within herself the royal staff
of Jove, and she's so powerful
that she is the friend of the mind
of Him who encloses the whole universe.
She drives to the other world the nude spirits
who had no concern about her;
she is free and pure
and she always induces others as if herself,
and produces in them as much as she produces.

Every virtue is mirrored in Love,
and they shine with him as much as he shines.
Where he doesn't shine
nothing is born perfect.
Love is as ancient and aged as the First Cause,
and it created Love as minister and leader
beneath which every being with a soul
is driven to see his face.
Whoever is wounded with his dart can't err,
but lives happily and sweetly, without cares,
and when their spirits are gone
from his body, their souls will go
to the place where they will sing of him forever.

Oh, my song, who praise Love so much,
whoever asks who made you, tell him
that only Love generated you.

Epistle 26: This epistle (*litera*) comes after an anonymous sonnet in manuscript Vatican Barberiniano Latin 4036 (f. 29r), which describes Fortuna as an obstacle to reason. Ceccoli responds by asserting the power of intellect and virtue, attributes that make a person resemble the gods. Those attributes induce people to grow and acquire knowledge, eventually turning away from secular concerns toward the spiritual. He compares such individuals to Atalanta, the mythological figure who was nursed by a she-bear and grew up to

Intellectus et ratio, que nos fatiunt superis fore congnatos, virtutum sublimes vias aperiunt earumque ardua scandere cor nostrum ardenti pede ac viribus indefessis alliciunt, ut, superatis inanis terre ponderibus, more Athalantis maximi, supremum celum invictis humeris nostra indomita volvat humanitas. Non igitur blande dee instab[i]li numina anime congnoscentis discreptio colla submictat, non eam noxius appetitus invadat, non astris tellurem preferat, non famam djis ascriptam, quam quisque sacer spiritus apetit, negligat. Ispius enim solius, ceteris cessantibus infimis, ymago perhennis mundi sigillatur in fronte, quivis igitur comodis, quaque pigra quiete, tenera patria, se sospitet, incoli quantumlibet cura solicited, nominee pretacto, eidem negatur adsensus. Nonne felicior est qui cum divinorum proceribus beata conversatione perficitur ac domesticus deorum scrinearus eligitur, ultra magis ampli Apolinis rengni universus heres instituitur, quam qui rudibus ineptisque vulgis miscendo se, ipsorum lapideo numero marmor ascribitur? Hijs ergo hec claudatur litera ut illos reliquisse sufficiat, et hominum filios belluarum gregibus anteferri.

Marinus
conpassor

be a virginal hunter and devoted herself to the goddess Artemis. The man who pursues divine knowledge is far better off than those who acquire worldly acclaim, even if he is not recognized by the society of his fatherland.

Intellect and reason, which make us be godlike, open the sublime ways of the virtues, and urge our hearts to climb the arduous ascents to them with an ardent foot and with unwavering strength; so that, having overcome the burdens of an empty land, in the manner of greatest Atalanta, our undefeated humanity may confront supreme heaven with our shoulders unconquered. Therefore, may the judgment of a flattering, unstable soul not fall on the neck of someone knowledgeable of the gods; may a harmful appetite not invade him; may he not prefer the earth to the stars, may he not neglect the fame that every sacred soul seeks, ascribing it to the gods. For, as other lowly things fade away, the image of the secular world is on the brow of this solitary man.

  I withhold my approval from the man who concerns himself with earnings rather than from some other quiet life. In his beloved fatherland—however much care of it causes him to live there—his name is kept silent; but isn't that man better off who is perfected by the blessed society with the greatest men of the Divine? He is chosen to be the secretary to the gods, and, even more, he is established as the universal heir of the wide kingdom of Apollo, rather than the man who, by mixing with the coarse and stupid masses, is added to their stony inscriptions on marble. Therefore, with these words let this letter be closed: it suffices to remember them, and to prefer the sons of men to the herds of wild beasts.

Marino
Fellow sufferer

Works Written to Marino Ceccoli

Poem 27: It is not known who wrote this poem to Ceccoli.[43] In it, the poet complains that Ceccoli delays returning to Perugia, again evoking the contrast of *urbanitas* and *rusticitas*. The poet wishes to engage in a *tenzone* with Ceccoli about the nature of love, but he does not explain his question in this sonnet. The poet employs identical rhymes throughout (A-rhyme: *sale*; B-rhyme: *pugni*; C-rhyme: *servo*; D-rhyme: *sole*).

    De, lascia ormai le contadine sale,
ser Marin mio, però che quanto pugni
a retornar, tanto mia mente pugni
e 'l gran dolor de ciò sovr'essa sale.
    È perché con lo tuo sapido sale
nïun non trovo contra cui non pugni
(io dico con la lingua, non con pugni);
e se son ver' le miei parole, sa' le!
    E le dottrine tuoi, le quale io servo,
ne la mia mente no ne stian sì sole
da te, fattor de lor, cui sempre servo.
    Questo te chièro, se quel chiaro sole
del gran signore Amor, de cui se' servo,
eterno luca en te come far sole.

	Ah, now leave your rustic halls.
My Ser Marino, since you delay
your return, you wound my mind terribly
and its great pain stands over it.
	And this happens because I find no one
whom you won't fight with your salacious statements
(and I mean with tongues, and not with fists);
and if my words are true, you know it!
	And may your doctrines, of which I am a servant,
not be kept apart in my mind
from you, their maker, whom I'll always serve.
	I ask this of you: may that bright sun,
the great lord, Love, of whom you are a devotee,
shine on you as he typically does.

28. Coluccio Salutati's letter to Marino Ceccoli: Roughly three decades after the compilation of the Vatican Barberiniano Latin 4036 manuscript, the proto-humanist Coluccio Salutati (1331–1406) addressed an epistle[44] to Ceccoli on 2 January 1369. A contemporary of Giovanni Boccaccio, Francesco Nelli, and Francesco Petrarca, Salutati was active in the cultural developments in Florence. Salutati also participated in Florentine politics, becoming the chancellor of Florence in 1374; he had also held the offices as chancellor of Todi in 1367, and of Lucca in 1370.

Preclarissimi eloquii viro domino Marino Cecholi de Perusio iurisperito musarumque familiari egregio, amico karissimo.

Iandiu, postquam tue virtutis lumen illuxerat, et, volitante fama, segnius quam res tanta merebatur, tui noticiam, imo tuorum meritorum habui, te avidis complexum lacertis imis in sensibus collocaram. Fui quidem semper admirator dilectorque virtutis et eius, que virtutis ornamentum est, eloquentie. Nam licet illa michi nulla vel ex parte contigerit, semper tamen magnifici quos vidi tam celesti munere decorari. Illa quidem iudicio meo hominum genus a ceteris animantibus maxime separat et multo magis virum secernit a viro, eoque plus quia, seu imbecilitate nature, seu difficultate scientie, seu infructuositate laboris, seu, quod mage reor, alio animos cupiditate flectente, nimis etate nostra eloquentie studia negliguntur et iam reges et principes non latine, sed gallice vel suis volgaribus scribunt. Nec contendo quod illud genus loquendi non possit etiam eleganter artificio quodam regi; sed indignor potius quod minor labor esse videatur maternam sequi dicendo rudem inscitiam verborum ornare corticem, quod est profecto puerorum, sententiarum ponderibus et argumentorum copia orationis facient admirabilem dignitatem? Quapropter cum aliquem audio ad huiusmodi studia animum applicuisse, fama delector et illum virum, etiam alias incognitum, admiror et diligo. Tu autem quantum in illa profeceris tibimet es conscius et ceteris iudicandi copiam multis rerum natumque, et permitte obsecro hoc, quanvis blandum videatur, ingenue, prout sentio, tecum loqui; vidi, inquam, dictamen stilumque tuum, in quo non modernorum lubricatione iocaris, non religiosorum rythmica sonoritate orationem instruis, sed solido illo prisco more dicendi

In this epistle, Salutati praises Ceccoli for his eloquence, calling it the ornamentation of a person's virtue. In particular, he values Ceccoli's skills with Latin rather than with the vernacular. Thus, the epistle provides evidence that Ceccoli's fame as a writer expanded beyond the sole extant manuscript from the 1330s, and his fame was still present at the end of the 1360s. The purpose of Salutati's letter, however, is entirely political: he seeks Ceccoli's assistance in acquiring the chancellorship of Perugia, an initiative that does not appear to have had success.

To Lord Marino Ceccoli of Perugia, man of brightest eloquence, legal expert and distinguished familiar of the muses, dearest friend

For the long time since the light of your virtue shone, and with fame fluttering away more slowly than such a great thing merited, I became acquainted with you and indeed with your merits: I will greet you, embraced with eager arms, in the deepest of my sentiments. Indeed, I have always been an admirer of and delighter in your virtue, and of this thing, eloquence, which is the ornamentation of that virtue. Although I'm not at all eloquent, you are to be praised, for it is fitting that great people be decorated with a celestial gift, however marvelous it may be. Indeed, in my opinion eloquence in particular separates the species of men from the other animals, and much more, it discerns one man from another man; much more so because either by having the natures of idiots, or by the difficulty of knowledge, or by the fruitlessness of the labor, or—what is the greater evil—because another person bends their minds with desire. In our age studies of eloquence are neglected too much and now they write about Kings or Princes not in Latin, but in Gallic or in their own common tongues. Nor do I assert that that vernacular speech can't still be elegantly regulated with a certain craft; but is it not rather unworthy? For it seems to be a lesser labor to follow the maternal tongue in speaking. To decorate the rude exterior of a language replete with uncultured words, they will create an admirable dignity with ponderous sentences and arguments and an excess of speech, such as children do. Thus when I hear someone has applied their mind to studies of Latin eloquence, I am pleased by his fame, and I admire and take delight in that man, even one who is otherwise unknown.

contentus, nil fucatum et maiore quam deceat apparatu comptum profers; de quo conceperam tecum ampliori epistola gratulari.

 Nunc autem cum aliud impulerit ut scriberem, a laudibus tuis abstinendum duxi, ne Gnatanici hominis videar te falgitiis adoriri. Contigit enim cum dominus meus, dominus Franciscus Bruni, te rogandum duceret ut pro me, licet immerito, pro posse Perusini cancellariatus officium procurares, ut et ego quadam confidential ipse idem preter meum morem pro me rogarem. Iam satis dictum puto, sed concludam expressius. Ego enim, etsi me indignum iudicem tanto honore, magnopere cupio ad illud officium evocari, ut aliquando emergam, et si quid studio vel natura bene partum habeo, possim in lucem educere. Tu obsecro his nostris conatibus fave, et quantum decens videris, laborato, ut, si in fatis fuerit, ego tecum tam corpore quam animo aliquando coniugar. Vale felix. Rome, die secunda ianuarii [1369].

By now you are aware of how much you have been instructive to me. An opportunity to rule over many other cases has arisen, however, so allow me to praise you; although it might seem like flattery, I speak naturally to you in exactly the manner that I feel. I saw, I say, your style in writing letters, in which you do not play around with the slipperiness of the moderns, you do not construct your speech with the rhythmic music of the religious, but you are content with that solid, old-fashioned manner of speaking, not at all dressed up but with no more elegance than what is fitting. I had intended to congratulate you about this in a longer letter.

Now, however, since one thing impels me to write to you, I thought that I must abstain from praising you, lest I seem to address you with the shameful statements of a sycophant. For it happens that my lord, Franciscus Bruni, thinks that you should be asked on my behalf that you might procure for me the office of chancellor of Perugia (although I'm not worthy of it), something I am doing with a certain boldness beyond my usual habit. Now I believe enough has been said, but I will close this letter with greater clarity. For although I judge myself unworthy of such honor, I very much wish to be summoned to that office, so that I will rise up some day, and if I have something by effort or by nature of good birth, I might be able to bring it to light. I kindly implore you, favor this attempt of mine, and as much as you seem worthy, work so that, if it is destiny, I will be joined with you as much in body—there in Perugia—as in mind. Farewell, fortunate one. In Rome, 2 January [1369].

NOTES

Introduction

1. For a complete description of the manuscript, see Berisso, *La raccolta dei poeti perugini del Va. Barberiniano Lat. 4036*; for a succinct description of the manuscript, see De Robertis, "Censimento dei manoscritti di rime di Dante (VI)," 435–36. The physical description of the manuscript is derived from Berisso (1); the reference to Gino Guidinelli da Castro San Piero is from De Robertis (433).

2. Berisso, *La raccolta dei poeti perugini del Va. Barberiniano Lat. 4036*, 148. By the late thirteenth century, notaries and judges were in an ambivalent category; they were classified as magnates, but they were treated as distinct from the magnates in the penal code. For information about the notaries, see Blanshei, "Perugia, 1260–1340," 17.

3. Berisso, *La raccolta dei poeti perugini del Va. Barberiniano Lat. 4036*, x.

4. Schiaffini, "Influssi dei dialetti centro-meridionali," 77–129.

5. Baldelli, "Lingua e letteratura di un centro trecentesco," 16.

6. Mengaldo, "Perugia," 443.

7. Elsheik, "Scavi Perugini," 287, 298.

8. See the footnotes throughout Marti, *Poeti giocosi del tempo di Dante*. He repeatedly shows how subsequent writers learned from Cecco Angiolieri in particular.

9. The major critical studies of Cecco Nuccoli and Marino Ceccoli are as follows: Corbucci, "L'antico poeta Perugino Marino Ceccoli"; Massèra, *Sonetti burleschi e realistici dei primi due secoli*; Marti, *Poeti giocosi del tempo di Dante*; Botterill, "Cecco Nuccoli: An Introduction"; Botterill, "Autobiography and Artifice in the Medieval Lyric"; Botterill, "Marino Ceccoli," 684–85; Botterill, "Cecco Nuccoli." See also Elsheik, "Scavi Perugini"; Berisso, *La raccolta dei poeti perugini del Vat. Barberiniano Lat. 4036*; and Baldelli, "Lingua e letteratura di un centro trecentesco."

10. Blanshei, "Perugia, 1260–1340," 13.

11. Blanshei, "Perugia, 1260–1340," 15–16. Note: a *quintale* is a unit of measurement roughly equivalent to 100 kilograms.

12. Blanshei, "Perugia, 1260–1340," 13.

13. Blanshei, "Population, Wealth, and Patronage in Medieval and Renaissance Perugia," 599.

14. Barker and Kleinhenz, "Perugia," 877.

15. Lewis, *The Allegory of Love*, 1. See also Burnley, *Courtliness and Literature in Medieval England*, 148; see also Lochrie, McCracken, and Schultz, "Introduction," xi.

16. Andreas Capellanus describes love as pertaining exclusively to the nobility; see Capellanus, *The Art of Courtly Love*, 149–50; Scaglione, *Knights at Court*, 34.

17. Jaeger, *Ennobling Love*, 171–78.

18. Regarding the subordination of the male lover to the woman, see Wack, *Lovesickness in the Middle Ages*, 125. Regarding the self-descriptions of the lovers as abject, see O'Donoghue, *The Courtly Love Tradition*, 5.

19. Evans, "Introduction: What Was Sexuality in the Middle Ages?," 10.

20. Marti, *Poeti del Dolce Stil Nuovo*, 17.

21. Rigo, *Lo stilnovo*, 12.

22. For an overview of the debate, see Pirovano, *Il Dolce Stil Novo*, 16–25.

23. Berisso, *Poesie dello stilnovo*, 8–100.

24. Petrocchi, "Il dolce stil novo," 736.

25. Berisso, *La raccolta dei poeti perugini del Vat. Barberiniano Lat. 4036*, 120.

26. O'Donoghue, *The Courtly Love Tradition*, 5.

27. Betella, *The Ugly Woman*, 10.

28. Cowell, *At Play in the Tavern*, 8–9; Bayless, *Parody in the Middle Ages*, 94.

29. DePierre, *A Brief History of Oral Sex*, 62–65.

30. Botterill, "Cecco Nuccoli: An Introduction," 22–23.

31. Botterill, "Marino Ceccoli," 684–85.

32. It is important to be circumspect about the statements found in the manuscript rubrics. Elizabeth Wilson Poe's study on the troubadouric *vidas* and *razos* acts as a cautionary tale. Instead of providing corroboration of a poem's biographical veracity, the prose blurbs (e.g., *vidas* and *razos*) were often derived from the poem itself; see Poe, *From Poetry to Prose in Old Provençal*, 61.

33. Corbucci, "L'antico poeta Perugino," 4.

34. All references to the *Decameron* are from Boccaccio, *Decameron*, ed. Branca.

35. In *Decameron* 8.8 you will find a modest bibliography. In recent decades, studies have focused primarily on its relationship to ethics. Olivia Holmes has studied it in terms of retributive justice, Ulrich Langer has applied the discourse of Aristotelian-Ciceronian morals to it, and Dino S. Cervigni examines it through the lens of Christian morality. See the following: Holmes, "Doing Unto Others, or Sienese Polyamory (VIII.8)"; Langer, "The Renaissance Novella as Justice"; and Cervigni, "Fiammetta's Song of Jealousy," 473. Louis Haas explores the story in relationship to the medieval concept of baptismal kinship, and Shirley W. Vinall and Peter S. Noble look at it through the lens of a female perspective; see Haas, "Boccaccio, Baptismal Kinship, and Spiritual Incest," 345; and Vinall and Noble, "Shrewd and Wanton Women," 146–47.

36. Information about Meo's biography is culled from Marti, "Tolomei, Meo dei." See also Berisso, *Poesia comica del medioevo italiano*, 225–27.

37. Marti, *Cultura e stile dei poeti giocosi del tempo di Dante*, 81.

38. Anna Bruni Bettarini treats it as a name; Franco Mancini treats it as a noun. See Bettarini, "Le rime di Meo dei Tolomei e di Muscia di Siena," and Mancini, ed., *Poeti perugini del Trecento*, 1:151.

39. "Ciampolino," in *Grande Dizionario della Lingua Italiana*, 3:107.

40. It also should be noted that in a sonnet of debated attribution, Meo dei Tolomei also refers to one Ciampolo (sonnet 23B).

41. See *Tesoro della Lingua Italiana delle Origini*, http://tlio.ovi.cnr.it/TLIO.

42. See Boggione and Casalegno, *Dizionario storico del lessico erotico Italiano*; and "Ciampolino," in *Grande Dizionario della Lingua Italiana*, 3:107.

43. For an analogous study of the slang usages of names, this time in the poetry of Rustico Filippi, see Gallarati, "Onomastica equivoca nei sonetti satirici di Rustico Filippi."

44. "Mascolino," in *Grande Dizionario della Lingua Italiana*, 9:880–81.

45. Minnis, "Authors in Love," 181 (emphases original).

46. Andrew Cowell, *At Play in the Tavern*, 6–8.

47. See Martin, *Alcohol, Sex, and Gender in Late Medieval and Early Modern Europe*, 62, and Valentini, *Mangiare nelle taverne medievali tra cibo, vino e giochi*, 10.

48. Bayless, *Parody in the Middle Ages*, 94.

49. Trexler, "Correre la Terra," 120–21.

50. See Todorović, "Who Read the *Vita Nova* in the First Half of the Fourteenth Century?"; and Indizio, "Dante as a Florentine Lyrical Author," 284.

51. Meo dei Tolomei's sonnet 22 appears in Vaticano Barberiniano Latin 3953. That sonnet, however, is atypical of Meo's lyric production, as it deals

sententiously with nobility, and not about his three enemies. Therefore, it offered no guidance to literary scholars about the nature of Meo's poetics. For a complete description of the manuscript, along with diplomatic transcriptions of all the poems therein, see Lega, *Il canzoniere Vaticano Barberiniano Latino 3953 (già Bar. XLV. 47)*.

52. The sonnets in Meo dei Tolomei's corpus from Chigiano L.VIII.305 are 2, 3, 4, 5, 6, 7, 8, 9, 10, 11, 12, 13, 14, 15, 17, 18, 21, 22, and 23B. For a complete description of the manuscript, along with diplomatic transcriptions of the poems, see Monaci, "Chigiano L. VIII. 305." For more recent analyses of the Chigiano L.VIII.305 manuscript, see Borriero, "Quantum illos proximius imitemur, tantum rectius poemetur"; see also Rea, "Lo Stilnovo secondo Dante."

53. Borriero, "Considerazioni sulla tradizione manoscritta," 389.

54. See, for instance, Massèra, *I sonetti di Cecco Angiolieri*, lvii; and Angiolieri, *Il canzoniere*, ed. Steiner.

55. Sonnets 1, 3, 12, 13, 15 in this book are from Escorialense e.III.23 and are attributed to Meuçço, and poem 19 is attributed to Meo. For a complete description of the manuscript, see Barbi, "Un nuovo codice di rime antiche molto importante"; see also De Robertis, *Il canzoniere escorialense*.

56. Throughout this book, Meo dei Tolomei is cited from Bettarini, "Le rime di Meo dei Tolomei e di Muscia di Siena." For a fuller study of Meo's rewriting of Angiolieri's sonnet, see Alfie, "I' son sì magro che quasi traluco."

57. Marti, *Poeti giocosi del tempo di Dante*, 16–17.

58. For a fuller study of Angiolieri's antipaternal sonnets, see Alfie, *Comedy and Culture*, 115–44. For a fuller study of Meo's antimaternal sonnets, see Alfie, "The Violent Poetics of Inversion, or the Inversion of Violent Poetics."

59. Marti, "La tecnica del 'vituperium' in Meo dei Tolomei di Siena," 78.

60. For a recent study of Angiolieri's dialogues, see Schwarts, *Rogue Poetry*, 2–8.

61. Baldelli, "Lingua e letteratura di un centro trecentesco: Perugia," 8.

62. The original verse reads, "la donna, la taverna, e 'l dado." Except for the four pseudo-Angiolieri sonnets and those in chapter 1, on Meo dei Tolomei, the translations of Cecco Angiolieri are from Angiolieri, *Sonnets*, trans. Scott and Mortimer.

63. The verse reads, "io la farei grattar con diece dita" (v. 14), from "Today no joy unto my heart accrues" ("Lo mi' cor non s'allegra di covelle").

64. The verse reads, "Cecco, va', che sie fenduto!" (v. 14), from "Dad, my Becchina, Love and then my mother" ("Babb'e Becchin, l'Amor e mie madre").

65. For a study of Cecco Angiolieri's persona, see Barrett, "'Rogue,' 'Scamp': The Elusive Persona of Cecco Angiolieri," 121.

66. See note 46, above.

67. Schultz, "Heterosexuality as a Threat to Medieval Studies."

68. For an overview of the debate of essentialists versus constructivists, as it stood at the time, see Sedgwick, *The Epistemology of the Closet*, 40. For other examples, see Halperin, *How to Do the History of Homosexuality*, 28; Clark, *Desire*, 5–6; and Stevens, "Homosexuality and Literature: An Introduction," 2–3.

69. Hollywood, "The Normal, the Queer, and the Middle Ages," 173.

70. Mills, "Homosexuality: Specters of Sodom," 57–58. See also Lochrie, *Heterosyncrasies*, xv, and Davidson, "Sodomy in Early Modern Venice," 66.

71. Dante's *Divine Comedy* has two episodes that deal with sodomy (*Inferno* 15 and 16, and *Purgatorio* 26), which offer divergent ideas about the damnation—or salvation—of sodomites. For a study of Dante's nuanced views on sodomy, see Alfie, "Sinful Wives and Queens." Additionally, Boccaccio's *Decameron* contains a tale about Pietro di Vinciolo, a man sexually oriented to other men and unhappily married (5.10).

72. There is currently little evidence about same-sex desire or activities between women. A notable exception occurred in Bologna in 1295 when a woman named Guercia was accused of "sodomitic activities" with twelve women using *virilia* (presumably, implements shaped like a penis). For information about Guercia, see Evans, "Introduction: What Was Sexuality in the Middle Ages?," 13. Also, toward the end of the fourteenth century, the Lucchese author Giovanni Sercambi composed a comic tale in which nuns employ a similar apparatus to have sex with one another; for a study and translation of Sercambi's narrative, see Alfie, "Giovanni Sercambi: Story 31."

73. Stehling, *Medieval Latin Poems of Male Love and Friendship*. See also Boswell, *Christianity, Social Tolerance, and Homosexuality*, 234.

74. Méndez, "Humor and Sexuality."

75. Woods, *A History of Gay Literature*, 43. See also Boswell, *Christianity, Social Tolerance, and Homosexuality*, 210.

76. Jordan, *The Invention of Sodomy in Christian Theology*, 29.

77. Patrone, *Il messaggio dell'Ingiuria nel Piemonte del tardo medioevo*, 17–18.

78. The translations of Guido Cavalcanti and Lupo degli Uberti are from Cavalcanti, *Complete Poems*, trans. Mortimer. Note that Mortimer lists Lupo Farinata as Lapo Farinata.

79. Rea, *Stilnovismo cavalcantiano e tradizione cortese*, 20.

80. Lupo degli Uberti is cited from *Poesie dello stilnovo*, ed. Berisso, 467–68.

81. Jordan, *The Invention of Sodomy in Christian Theology*, 52.

82. Interestingly, Muscia's third sonnet is an insult of Guido Cavalcanti, who had failed to complete a pilgrimage to Compostela. However, there are no textual indications of any sort insinuating Cavalcanti's sexuality.

83. DePierre, *A Brief History of Oral Sex*, 62.

84. Violante, "Le *noie* cremonesi nel loro ambiente culturale e sociale," 102. The translations of Niccola Muscia of Siena, Iacomo de' Tolomei, and Rustico Filippi are from Alfie, *Rustico Filippi: The Art of Insult*.

85. Alfie, "Black Comedy," 198–99.

86. Mills, *Seeing Sodomy in the Middle Ages*, 3–4.

87. Bullough, "The Sin against Nature and Homosexuality," 55.

88. Peter Damian, "Letter 31," 5.

89. Peter Damian, "Letter 31," 6–7.

90. Salih, "Sexual Identities: A Medieval Perspective," 113.

91. Historians of sexuality have repeatedly emphasized the definition of medieval sodomy as any sex act with no potential for procreation. See Davidson, "Sodomy in Early Modern Venice," 66; Mills, *Seeing Sodomy in the Middle Ages*, 296; Frantzen, "The Shadow of Sodom: Same-Sex Relations in Pastoral Prose and Poetry," 209; Hergemoller, *Sodom and Gomorrah*, 62.

92. Laqueur, *Solitary Sex*, 148.

93. Karras, *Sexuality in Medieval Europe*, 120.

94. Dinshaw, *Getting Medieval*, 6.

95. Brundage, *Law, Sex and Christian Society in Medieval Europe*, 472.

96. Boswell, *Christianity, Social Tolerance, and Homosexuality*, 293. See also Bullough, "The Sin against Nature and Homosexuality," 55.

97. Goodich, *The Unmentionable Vice*, 83–84.

98. Rocke, *Forbidden Friendships*, 21.

99. Degli Azzi, ed., *Statuti di Perugia dell'anno MCCCXLII*, 79.

100. See, for instance, Michel Foucault, who talked about the cultural change that occurred in Europe after the coining of the word "homosexual"; the focus shifted from acts to identities. "The sodomite had been a temporary aberration; the homosexual was now a species" (Foucault, *The History of Sexuality*, 1:43).

101. Mills, "Homosexuality: Specters of Sodom," 57.

102. Moore, *The Formation of a Persecuting Society*, 160.

103. Moore, *The Formation of a Persecuting Society*, 88; see also Karras, "The Regulation of 'Sodomy' in the Latin East and West," 982.

104. Bonazzi, *Storia di Perugia dalle origini al 1860*, 318.

105. See Goodich, *The Unmentionable Vice*, 84–85. See also Rocke, *Forbidden Friendships*, 7, and Crawford, "The Good, the Bad, and the Textual," 29.

106. Rocke, *Forbidden Friendships*, 3–6.

107. Trumbach, *Sex and the Gender Revolution*, 4. Recently, Dyan Elliott has noted how expressions of same-sex attraction at the time could also be a cover for sexual abuse of boys; see Elliot, *The Corrupter of Boys*, 93–94.

108. Trumbach, "The Transformation of Sodomy," 832.

109. The parallels with the sumptuary laws are striking. Throughout the Middle Ages, about 40 cities passed more than 300 laws to regulate the consumption of luxury goods. The concern was that public displays of luxury could erode class distinctions, particularly the exclusive status of the nobility. See Killerby, *Sumptuary Laws in Italy*, 2–7. See also Killerby, "Practical Problems in the Enforcement of Italian Sumptuary Law."

110. Clark, *Desire*, 2.

111. Baldassano, "Talking Back," 58.

112. Rocke, *Forbidden Friendships*, 12–13.

113. Callahan, *Writing the Voice of Pleasure*, 4; and Wack, *Lovesickness in the Middle Ages*, 65. See also Alfie, "Men on Bottom."

114. DePierre, *A Brief History of Oral Sex*, 66.

115. Morrison, "The Body: Unstable, Ungendered, Theorized," 111.

116. Marti, *Poeti giocosi del tempo di Dante*, 658.

117. The passage from Marti warrants examination in full: "We find repulsive the thought that truly perverted men would make a banner of their perversion and would exalt their shame" (A noi repugna il pensiero che uomini veramenti pervertiti si facciano della loro perversione una luminosa bandiera e si esaltino della loro vergogna) (Marti, *Poeti giocosi del tempo di Dante*, 658; my translation).

118. Berisso, *La raccolta dei poeti perugini del Va. Barberiniano Lat. 4036*, 153.

119. Dillon, "Representing Obscene Sound," 62. Regarding the history of the word "cazzo," see the entry in *Grande Dizionario della Lingua Italiana*, 2:935. For other examples of this sonnet as an early example of the word, see the entry for "cazzo" in *Dizionario etimologico italiano*, 1:833; and *Dizionario etimologico della lingua italiana*, 1:220.

120. Mohr, *Holy Shit*, 41.

121. Irvine, "Leaky Registers and Eight-Hundred-Pound Gorillas," 18–20; Boggione and Casalegno, *Dizionario storico del lessico erotico Italiano*, viii.

122. Mattews-Grieco, "Satyrs and Sausages," 36.

123. Leap, "Language, Sexuality, and the Suspension of Taboo," 246–47.

124. Leap, "Studying a Not-So-Secret 'Secret Code,'" 51.

125. Minnis and Scott, *Medieval Literary Theory and Criticism*, 282–84. See also Allen, *The Ethical Poetic of the Later Middle Ages*, 19–20.

126. Miller, "John Gower, Satiric Poet," 80–81.

127. Matthew of Vendôme, *The Art of Versification*, 1.58.

128. Mieszkowski, "Old Age and Medieval Misogyny," 299. For representative readings of the topoi of misogyny and *vituperium in vetulam* in the fourteenth and fifteenth centuries, see the following studies: Bentivogli, "Sonetti misogini da codici quattrocenteschi"; Zancani, "Misoginia padana del Quattrocento e testi scurrili del Cinquecento"; Percan, *"Femina dulce malum"*; Rossi, "Aspetti dell'invettiva nell'Occitania del XIII secolo"; and Alfie, "Like She-Cats in January."

129. Alfie, "Old Lady Avignon," 104.

130. For an overview of the influence between Cavalcanti and Meo dei Tolomei, along with the poetry of Guido Guinizelli, see Orvieto and Brestolini, *La poesia comico-realistica*, 16–22. See also Gorni, "Manetto tra Guido e Dante."

131. Wack, *Lovesickness in the Middle Ages*, 107.

132. Alfie, "The Violent Poetics of Inversion, or the Inversion of Violent Poetics," 216.

133. Jones, *The Italian City-State*, 313.

134. Larner, "La nobiltà," 171. See also Waley, "A Blood-Feud with a Happy Ending," 47–48.

135. Lansing, *The Florentine Magnates*, 221–22.

136. Lansing, *The Florentine Magnates*, 212. See also Jones, *The Italian City-State*, 317.

137. Hatty and Hatty, *The Disordered Body*, 171.

138. Park, *Doctors and Medicine in Early Renaissance Florence*, 51.

139. Grigsby, "Medical Misconceptions," 142.

140. Cardini, "Tradizioni magiche e 'medicina popolare,'" 36.

141. Ciasca, *L'arte dei medici e speziali*, 329.

142. Siraisi, *Medieval & Early Renaissance Medicine*, 118.

143. Metzler, *Disability in Medieval Europe*, 19. See also Singer, "Disability and the Social Body."

144. Wheatly, *Stumbling Blocks before the Blind*, 11–13.

145. Bragg, "Visual-Kinetic Communication in Europe before 1600," 20.

146. Cockcayne, "Experiences of the Deaf in Early Modern England," 504. See also Singer, "Deafness: Reading Invisible Signs."

147. Angiolieri, *I sonetti di Cecco Angiolieri*, ed. Massèra, 160–61.

148. Wis, "Mito e leggenda in un sonetto di Meo dei Tolomei," 333.

149. Jacobus de Voragine, *The Golden Legend*, 61–62.

150. A version of Nicholas the Fish from more recent centuries appears in Italo Calvino's collection, *Italian Folktales*, translated under the title of "Nick Fish."

151. Jones, "Wicked Willies with Wings," 259; see also "naso" in Boggione and Casalegno, *Dizionario storico del lessico erotico italiano*, 310.

152. Sposato, *Forged in the Shadow of Mars*, 3.

153. Lansing, *The Florentine Magnates*, 156.

154. Jones, *The Italian City-State*, 158.

155. For an overview about the flood, see the following studies: Moulinier and Redon, "L'Inondation de 1333 à Florence"; Salvestrini, "L'Arno e l'alluvione Fiorentina del 1333"; Schenk, "More Resilient with Mars or Mary?"; Schenk, "Prima ci fu la cagione de la mala provedenza de' Fiorentini."

156. For an overview of the literary and cultural discussion of the flood, see Alfie, "A New Flood Was Released from the Heavens."

157. Giovanni Villani, *Nuova cronica*, bk. XII, chap. 2.

158. Information about the struggles between Pier Saccone Tarlati di Pietramala and Perugia is culled from Heywood, *A History of Perugia*, 162–68; see also Bonazzi, *Storia di Perugia dalle origini al 1860*, 324–30.

159. Leap, "Language, Sexuality, and the Suspension of Taboo," 247.

160. Ferm, "Form: Its Expressions and Manifestations," 22.

161. Lanza, *Polemiche e berte letterarie*, 170.

162. The passage reads as follows: "Vidivi il soddomito Corso Cei, / quel che ha speso presso che contanti, / e 'l Minchia Amier, che sempre grida: 'Omei!'" (cited from Finiguerri, *I Poemetti*, ed. Lanza; my translation).

163. The passage reads as follows: "Vedi uno ch'è bussato, ch'io ne godo, / dal Ciampellin perché non sa vogare: / Bussotto ha nome, che mi diè il mal lodo."

164. Gallarati, *Rustico Filippi: Sonetti Satirici e giocosi*, 38–41.

165. Pasquini, "Il 'secolo senza poesia' e il crocevia di Burchiello," 35.

166. See Crimi, "Burchiello e le sue metamorfosi," 91, and Watkins, "Il Burchiello (1404–1448)," 22. See also Marrani, "La poesia comica fra '200 e '300," 109.

167. Piromalli, "Aspetti della cultura e della poesia giocosa in Toscana nel Quattrocento," 4; see also Tartaro, "Burchiello, dell'immaginazione grottesca," 141.

168. Piromalli, "Aspetti della Cultura," 4. See also Messina, ed., *Burchiello: Sonetti inediti*, 14–15; and Berisso, "Preistoria (mancata) del *nonsense* nella poesia medievale italiana," 36–37.

169. Fubini, "Sulla poesia del Burchiello," 29.

170. Zaccarello, "Off the Paths of Common Sense," 91.

171. See Zaccarello, "Una forma istituzionale della poesia burchiellesca," 47, and Smith, "Fraudomy," 84–103.

172. The translation of Burchiello is cited from Di Giovanni, *The Poetry of Burchiello*, trans. Alfie and Feng.

173. Angiolieri, *The Sonnets of Cecco Angiolieri of Siena Done into English Doggerel*, trans. Scott. Scott's translations have recently been reissued, but edited and with the appropriate attributions; see Angiolieri, *Sonnets: Cecco Angiolieri*, ed. Scott and Mortimer.

174. Chubb, *The Sonnets of a Handsome and Well-Mannered Rogue*.

175. Vitale, ed., *Rimatori comico-realistici del Due e Trecento*.

176. Regarding Meo dei Tolomei's corpus, see Bettarini, "Le rime di Meo dei Tolomei e di Muscia da Siena." In the recent anthology of comic poetry by Marco Berisso, the section on Meo dei Tolomei is based upon Bettarini's work; see Berisso, *Poesia comica del medioevo italiano*, 225–40. Regarding the poetic productions of Nuccoli and Ceccoli, see Mancini, ed., *Poeti perugini del Trecento*, Vol. 1, *Marino Ceccoli, Cecco Nuccoli e altri rimatori in tenzone*.

177. Angiolieri, *Le rime*, ed. Lanza.

Chapter 1. *Meo dei Tolomei*

1. Pasquini, "Il 'secolo senza poesia,'" 55.

2. The translations of the sonnets 1A, 1B, and 1C are cited from Di Giovanni, *The Poetry of Burchiello*, 244–47. For a fuller analysis of Meo's rewriting of Angiolieri's sonnet, and the version by the fifteenth-century poet Burchiello, see Alfie, "'I' son sì magro che quasi traluco," 5–28.

3. Massèra (who attributes this sonnet to Cecco Angiolieri), Marti, and Vitale all have "vesto il luco."

4. Marti and Vitale both have "di."

5. This sonnet was translated by Thomas Caldecott Chubb as "I am so lean that light well-nigh shines through me" (attributed to Cecco Angiolieri); see Angiolieri, *The Sonnets of a Handsome and Well-Mannered Rogue*, 56.

6. This version of Angioleri's sonnet is found in the Chigiano L.VIII.305 manuscript (f. 105v); forms of version 2, which more closely resembles Meo dei Tolomei's version (see v. 2), appear in Escorialense e.III.23 (f. 86v), Capitolare Veronese 445 (f. 61), Ambrosiano O 63 supra (f. 16r), Ambrosiano C 35 (f. 16r), and Laurenziano Acquisti e Doni 759 (f. 243v).

7. This version by Angiolieri is cited from Contini, "Postilla angiolieresca," 584.

8. For a more detailed analysis of Meo dei Tolomei's sonnets about his mother, see Alfie, "The Violent Poetics of Inversion," 207–23.

9. Vitale has "tolto."

10. Massèra, Marti, and Vitale all have "potreste."

11. Massèra, Marti, and Vitale all have "che mi."

12. This sonnet was translated by Chubb, and by C. H. Scott and Anthony Mortimer, as "My mother said to me the other day" (attributed in both editions to Angiolieri). See Angiolieri, *The Sonnets of a Handsome and Well-Mannered Rogue*, 57; and Angiolieri, *Sonnets: Cecco Angiolieri*, 112.

13. Vitale, *Poeti comico-realistici del Due e Trecento*, 28–29.

14. This sonnet was translated by Chubb as "I was so desperate sick the other day," and by Scott and Mortimer as "So ill in fact was I two days ago" (attributed in both editions to Angiolieri). See Angiolieri, *The Sonnets of a Handsome and Well-Mannered Rogue*, 58; and Angiolieri, *Sonnets: Cecco Angiolieri*, 115.

15. According to the *Regimen Sanitatis Salerni*, peaches were to be avoided by people prone to melancholy, as were beef and cheese: "Persica, poma, pyra, lac, caseus, et caro salsa, et caro cervina, leporine, caprina, bovina: haec melancholica sunt infermis inimica" (chap. 7, "De cibis melcancholicis vitandis"). Moreover, according to the *Regimen Sanitatis Salerni*, eels are bad for the voice, and should not be eaten in great quantities with cheese (chap. 31, "De anguilla"). See *The School of Salernum*.

16. This sonnet was translated by Chubb as "My mother taught me to use medicine," and by Scott and Mortimer as "Now medicine unto me my mother teaches" (attributed in both editions to Angiolieri). See Angiolieri, *The Sonnets of a Handsome and Well-Mannered Rogue*, 58; and Angiolieri, *Sonnets: Cecco Angiolieri*, 114.

17. Quartan fever is a malarial fever with recurrences every seventy-two hours; similarly, tertian fever is a malarial fever with recurrences every forty-eight hours.

18. *La colla* was a form of torture in Italian communes, in which the person was suspended from his hands that were tied behind his back.

19. This sonnet was translated by Chubb as "The other day I lay upon my bed," and by Scott and Mortimer as "One night when I was dozing off to sleep" (attributed in both editions to Angiolieri). See Angiolieri, *The Sonnets of a Handsome and Well-Mannered Rogue*, 57; and Angiolieri, *Sonnets: Cecco Angiolieri*, 113.

20. Marti and Vitale both have "alcuna fiata, ma non ne fie nulla."

21. Marti and Vitale both have "ch'i' mi vad'affogar."

22. This sonnet was translated by Chubb as "When Mino Zeppa sees an enemy," and by Scott and Mortimer as "The flight of Mino Zeppa when he knew" (attributed in both editions to Angiolieri). See Angiolieri, *The Sonnets of a Handsome and Well-Mannered Rogue*, 66; and Angiolieri, *Sonnets: Cecco Angiolieri*, 131.

23. See, for example, Angiolieri's poems, "'Stop thief! Stop thief! Stop thief! Help! Succor! Aid!'"; "'You've said enough! I beg you no more speak!'"; "'Becchina love, one time I did hate you'"; "'Becchina mine!' 'Cecco, I am not thine'"; and "'Becchin', my love!' 'What want you, false traitor?'" For a recent study on Angiolieri's dialogue sonnets, see Schwarts, *Rogue Poetry*, 2–8.

24. Massèra (who attributes this sonnet to Cecco Angiolieri), Marti, and Vitale all have "—Oimè lasso, ben posso dir ch'imi- / ti un."

25. Massèra, Marti, and Vitale all have "Omè amor."

26. Massèra, Marti, and Vitale all have "Ché non fia nessun, che possa dirmi mi."

27. This sonnet was translated by Chubb as "Zeppa, you are so vile one puny blade," and by Scott and Mortimer as "Now by the Holy Rood, Min Zeppa, say" (attributed in both editions to Angiolieri). See Angiolieri, *The Sonnets of a Handsome and Well-Mannered Rogue*, 66; and Angiolieri, *Sonnets: Cecco Angiolieri*, 130.

28. Boggione and Casalegno, *Dizionario storico del lessico erotico italiano*, vii. See also "pène" in *Dizionario etimologico della lingua italiana*, 4:901. For the history of the word "cazzo," see "Cazzo" in *Grande Dizionario della Lingua Italiana*, 2:935. For other examples of this sonnet as an early example of the word, see the entry for "cazzo" in *Dizionario etimologico italiano*, 2:833; and *Dizionario etimologico della lingua italiana*, 1:220.

29. Dean, "Gender and Insult in an Italian City," 219.

30. See, for instance, Manca, "Dante e la poesia realistico-borghese," 34–35; Suitner, "Dante e la poesia satirica del suo tempo," 75–76; and Chiarini, "Ben so che fosti figliuol d'Alighieri," 590.

31. Massèra and Vitale both have "sciaurati."

32. This sonnet was translated by Chubb as "By God, Min Zeppa, now the truth is out," and by Scott and Mortimer as "Min Zeppa, rouse! Your foes are at the door" (attributed in both editions to Angiolieri). See Angiolieri, *The Sonnets of a Handsome and Well-Mannered Rogue*, 67; and Angiolieri, *Sonnets: Cecco Angiolieri*, 13.

33. This sonnet was translated by Chubb as "Long after curfew, with his arms outspread," and by Scott and Mortimer as "Prone on his belly outside Pina's door" (attributed in both editions to Angiolieri). See Angiolieri, *The Sonnets of a Handsome and Well-Mannered Rogue*, 65; and Angiolieri, *Sonnets: Cecco Angiolieri*, 129.

34. The sense of this verse is that the money was counterfeited by Capocchio.

35. Cohen, "Jews as the Killers of Christ," 5–10.

36. According to the *Regimen Sanitatis Salerni*, fennel was effective in treating eye ailments (chap. 79, "De confortantibus visum"). Although *finocchio* ("fennel") is a slur against homosexuals nowadays, the term appears to have acquired its offensive connotation only centuries after Meo dei Tolomei. Alberto Menarini argues that the slander originally referred not to the plant but to a similarly named character of the *Commedia dell'arte* who behaved in effeminate and affected ways; the earliest reference to the character Finocchio is from 1560. See Menarini, "Finocchio in senso osceno," 57–58.

37. Massèra (who attributes this sonnet to Cecco Angiolieri), Marti, and Vitale all have "per ciò."

38. This sonnet was translated by Chubb as "When Zeppa went to church, he used to say," and by Scott and Mortimer as "When Zeppa enters Church, he bids goodday" (attributed in both editions to Angiolieri). See Angiolieri, *The Sonnets of a Handsome and Well-Mannered Rogue*, 65; and Angiolieri, *Sonnets: Cecco Angiolieri*, 128.

39. Roberto Wis suggests that "Uvil" is the linguistic variation on the name Uliva, and that Meo is referring to a legend of Saint Uliva. See Wis, "Mito e leggenda in un sonetto di Meo dei Tolomei," 333.

40. Meo appears to be conflating John the Baptist with John the Evangelist in this verse. According to Jacobus de Voragine, the high priest at the temple of Diana at Ephesus challenged John the Evangelist to drink poison. John was able to do so without harm, thereby demonstrating the power of the Christian God. See Jacobus de Voragine, *The Golden Legend*, 61–62.

41. A man from Messina, Nicola Pesce or Colapesce, was swimming when his mother cursed him, causing him to be transformed into a fish. The legend is reported in numerous medieval sources, including the *Cronica* by Salimbene de Adam and the *Dittamondo* by Fazio degli Uberti. A version from more recent centuries appears in Italo Calvino's collection, *Italian Folktales*, translated with the title "Nick Fish."

42. For an in-depth study of Angiolieri's antipaternal sonnets, see Alfie, *Comedy and Culture*, chap. 6, 115–43.

43. This sonnet was translated by Chubb as "If you should hack off Mino Zeppa's head," and by Scott and Mortimer as "If Mino Zeppa were decapitated (attributed in both editions to Cecco Angiolieri). See Angiolieri, *The Sonnets of a Handsome and Well-Mannered Rogue*, 68; and Angiolieri, *Sonnets: Cecco Angiolieri*, 134.

44. This sonnet was translated by Chubb as "If all the inflaming drugs from oversea," and by Scott and Mortimer as "If all the theriac from beyond the seas" (attributed in both editions to Angiolieri). See Angiolieri, *The Sonnets of a*

Handsome and Well-Mannered Rogue, 67; and Angiolieri, *Sonnets: Cecco Angiolieri*, 132.

45. "Radda": Scholarship isn't clear on this expression. Marti and Vitale both believe "radda" to be a form of "radere" (to shave), thus punning on the idea that he is a thief who shears others. Massèra and Bettarini, conversely, both interpret Radda as the castle Radda, besieged by Siena in 1230. In this interpretation, the verse represents Mino as a defeated soldier.

46. Cowell, *At Play in the Tavern: Signs*, 8–9; Bayless, *Parody in the Middle Ages*, 94.

47. See Angiolieri's sonnet "There are three things that give me great delight."

48. Collegari, "Grey Partridges and Middle-Aged Mutton," 182–84. In addition, one citation in particular from the *TLIO* contributes further to Collegari's finding. In the *Tesoro volgarizzato*, Brunetto Latini states: "The partridge is a bird that, because of the goodness of its meat, is always hunted by hunters; but they are sinful with the heat of lustfulness. They [partridges] fight over the females in such a way that they lose awareness of their natures, and they have sex with other males as if they were females" (Pernice è uno uccello che per bontà di sua carne sempre è cacciata per gli uccellatori. Ma molto sono peccatrici per lo calore della lussuria. Elle si combattono per le femine in tal maniera ch'elle perdono la conoscenza della loro natura, ed usano li maschi insieme sì con le femine). Given both the reference to male–male sexuality (among birds) and the source of the quote—Brunetto Latini, whom Dante meets in hell's circle of sodomites—this highlights the potentially sodomitic connotations to Meo's choice of delicacy.

49. *Tesoro della lingua Italiana delle Origini* (*TLIO*) cites Agostino da Scarperia (ca. 1390), who uses the term to denote the penis; it also cites this poem as a source for interpreting "mascolino" as a male lover; http://tlio.ovi.cnr.it/TLIO/. Conversely, the *Grande Dizionario della Lingua Italiana* makes no reference to Agostino da Scarperia or the interpretation of "mascolino" as the penis; however, it too cites this poem to derive the definition of homosexuality. See "Mascolino," in *Grande Dizionario della Lingua Italiana*, 9:880–81.

50. See "Diritto" in *Grande Dizionario della Lingua Italiana*, 4:541–47; the definition as "loyal" is found on page 545; the definition as "vertical, erect" or "rigid" appears on page 542.

51. This sonnet was translated by Chubb as "My heart I've torn from you, O Ciampolino," and by Scott and Mortimer as "My heart I sunder from you, Ciampolino" (attributed in both editions to Angiolieri). See Angiolieri, *The Sonnets of a Handsome and Well-Mannered Rogue*, 63; and Angiolieri, *Sonnets: Cecco Angiolieri*, 124.

52. This sonnet was translated by Chubb as "My Ciampolino, you are now so broke," and by Scott and Mortimer as "Your candle, Ciampolino, is burnt so low" (attributed in both editions to Angiolieri). See Angiolieri, *The Sonnets of a Handsome and Well-Mannered Rogue*, 64; and Angiolieri, *Sonnets: Cecco Angiolieri*, 127.

53. "Tossed in the ditches . . . dying in prison": that is, if Ciampolino isn't already dead and buried as a pauper, he'll be alive but dying in debtors' prison.

54. This sonnet was translated by Chubb as "If you are strong and valiant, Ciampolino," and by Scott and Mortimer as "With valour, Ciampolino, do you burn?" (attributed in both editions to Angiolieri). See Angiolieri, *The Sonnets of a Handsome and Well-Mannered Rogue*, 64; and Angiolieri, *Sonnets: Cecco Angiolieri*, 126.

55. "Coward": literally, "Burgundian." The soldiers from Burgundy were apparently renowned for their cowardice.

56. This sonnet was translated by Chubb as "My mother's cheated me, nor's Ciampolin'" (attributed to Angiolieri). See Angiolieri, *The Sonnets of a Handsome and Well-Mannered Rogue*, 56.

57. "Pound water in a mortar": this expression seems to mean that Meo should engage in another useless activity.

58. This sonnet was translated by Chubb as "I made myself another Ciampolino," and by Scott and Mortimer as "Like Ciampolino I myself became" (attributed in both editions to Cecco Angiolieri). See Angiolieri, *The Sonnets of a Handsome and Well-Mannered Rogue*, 63; and Angiolieri, *Sonnets: Cecco Angiolieri*, 125.

59. "Didn't make the mill any whiter for me": the wheat didn't result in any new flour for me; that is to say, my trust in him didn't profit me in any way.

60. This sonnet was translated by Chubb as "The jewels I've brought from Venice, take you," and by Scott and Mortimer as "Take these Venetian gems I've brought for you" (attributed in both editions to Angiolieri). See Angiolieri, *The Sonnets of a Handsome and Well-Mannered Rogue*, 72; and Angiolieri, *Sonnets: Cecco Angiolieri*, 142.

61. Spitzer, "Parole di Dante," 65–66.

62. Marti and Vitale both have "già di."

63. Marti skips this line.

64. Marti and Vitale both have "voglia."

65. Marti has "'mpazzo." Vitale has "'mpaccio."

66. Marti and Vitale both omit the reference to a missing verse.

67. Marti and Vitale both have "che."

68. "Later": the statement is unclear (*'nn-otto*), but the poet appears to create a linguistic parallel with the earlier phrase "in an instant" (*enn-una*, v. 6).

69. It is possible that the nose is a euphemism for the penis because that was a common metaphor. See Jones, "Wicked Willies with Wings," 259; see also "naso" in Valter Boggione and Giovanni Casalegno, *Dizionario storico del lessico erotico italiano*, 310.

70. "Give him the figs": the figs were an obscene gesture, in which the thumb was inserted between the first and second fingers, and the hand was closed like a fist. The gesture of the figs appears in Dante's *Inferno* (25.1–3), where the thief Vanni Fucci directs them at God, and in Ceccoli's poem 17.

71. See, for instance, Angiolieri's poems "Such is my melancholy and so great," "Dame Poverty proclaims I am her son," and "I am so wrapped and robed in melancholy."

72. Mario Marti attributes this sonnet directly to Meo. Maurizio Vitale considers this sonnet to be among those of dubious attribution to Meo. Anna Bruni Bettarini does not reproduce this sonnet at all; rather, she argues that any biographical references to Meo's biography therein are unfounded. See Bettarini, "Le rime di Meo dei Tolomei e di Muscia da Siena," 39–40. The sonnet is cited from Marti, *Poeti giocosi del tempo di Dante*.

73. This sonnet was translated by Chubb as "Dearly has cost me my deep melancholy" (attributed to Angiolieri). See Angiolieri, *The Sonnets of a Handsome and Well-Mannered Rogue*, 35.

74. This sonnet was translated by Chubb as "I had a sudden whim not long ago" (attributed to Angiolieri). See Angiolieri, *The Sonnets of a Handsome and Well-Mannered Rogue*, 31.

75. Jones, *The Italian City-State*, 224.

76. Marti considers this to be of dubious attribution to Meo. Neither Bettarini nor Vitale includes this sonnet among Meo's works. Furthermore, Stefano Carrai definitively attributes it to Maestro Rinuccino of Florence; see Carrai, *I sonetti di Maestro Runuccino di Firenze*, 40–44. The sonnet is cited from Marti, *Poeti giocosi del tempo di Dante*.

77. In other words, a delayed gift becomes a transaction, and no longer constitutes recognition of valor.

78. For general studies about *vituperium in vetulam*, see Pratt, "*De vetula*," 321–42. See also Mieszkowski, "Old Age and Medieval Misogyny," and Alfie, "Old Lady Avignon."

79. Opinions differ about the identity of the recipient of the sonnet, Manetto. Conjectures include Manetto Portinari, Manetto Scali, and Manetto Cavalcanti. For an overview of the debate, see Cavalcanti, *Rime*, ed. Cassata, 150.

80. For an interpretation of Cavalcanti's sonnet, see Howard, "An Interpretation of Cavalcanti's 'Guata, Manetto,'" 183–87.

81. For an overview of the influence between Guinizelli, Cavalcanti, and Tolomei, see Orvieto and Brestolini, *La poesia comico-realistica*, 16–22. See also Gorni, "Manetto tra Guido e Dante," 25–39.

82. Guido Cavalcanti's poem is cited from Pirovano, ed., *Poeti del dolce stil novo*.

83. No scholarly consensus exists about the attribution of this sonnet. The manuscript Chigiano L.VIII.305 (*unicus*) presents it as anonymous, and therefore it is of no assistance, but the presence of "Ciampol" (Ciampolino) suggests Meo dei Tolomei. Todaro ascribes it to Meo; Bettarini attributes it to Muscia da Siena. Marti and Vitale both consider it to be of dubious attribution to Cecco Angiolieri.

84. This sonnet was translated by Chubb as "Ugh, do observe that ancient hag," and by Scott and Mortimer as "Look, Ciampolo, 'twill fill you with amaze" (attributed in both editions to Angiolieri). See Angiolieri, *The Sonnets of a Handsome and Well-Mannered Rogue*, 71; and Angiolieri, *Sonnets: Cecco Angiolieri*, 140.

85. In his edition of Dante's lyrics, Domenico De Robertis claims that Dante addresses this sonnet to Meo dei Tolomei, as do Cudini, ed., in Alighieri, *Le Rime*, and Del Monte, ed., in Alighieri, *Opere minori*. See also Scotti-Porcelli, "Dante e Cecco cantori della Maremma," 178, and Marti, "Sulla genesi del realismo dantesco," 11.

86. Cited from Alighieri, *Rime*, ed. De Robertis.

87. Regarding the interpretation of the addressee to be Meo dei Tolomei, see Pirovano, ed., *Poeti del dolce stil novo*.

88. The poem is cited from Pirovano, ed., *Poeti del dolce stil novo*.

89. Two versions of this sonnet are extant, both of them appearing in Chigiano L.VIII.305 (f. 103r, and again on f. 112v).

90. Moco di Pietro Tolmei (ca. 1285–1306), whose house was nearby Angiolieri's. Little is known about this individual except that Angiolieri suggests his sexual proclivities in this sonnet.

91. "Min(o) di Pep(p)o Accorridore (Petroni)": nothing is known about this individual except that Angiolieri indicates his cowardice in this sonnet.

92. "Tano": Nothing is known about this individual.

93. "Migo": Nothing is known about this individual, except that Angiolieri suggests his heretical beliefs in this sonnet.

Chapter 2. *Pseudo-Cecco Angiolieri*

1. For an in-depth reading of this sonnet, along with the three that follow, see Alfie, "Men on Bottom."
2. "Pink, and white, and red": the colors that love spreads across the face of someone in love.
3. The sense of this verse is, "we don't believe that he'll show those colors to you," meaning that he will not be in love with you.
4. Chubb translates this sonnet as "One Corso from Corzan's so wounded me"; see Angiolieri, *The Sonnets of a Handsome and Well-Mannered Rogue*, 62.
5. "Centaurea": in folk medicine, centaurea was a purgative. See *Ricettario fiorentino*, 29–30.
6. "Enema": according to the *Grande Dizionario della Lingua Italiana*, "argomento" can mean both "argument" and "enema." Given the medicinal references in the sonnet, the latter seemed more appropriate for the translation.
7. See, for instance, Angiolieri's sonnet "Love, when you brought me down to such a state," where he compares himself to a horse: "you've put a bit between my teeth, and I / Champ on it, knowing that it's there forever" (vv. 13–14). See also "By how much is a millet seed less," where he concludes that he has less ability to free himself from love than a chick to hatch before its time (vv. 12–14).
8. Chubb translates this sonnet as "Whenever that love lodges in your heart"; see Angiolieri, *The Sonnets of a Handsome and Well-Mannered Rogue*, 62.

Chapter 3. *Cecco Nuccoli*

1. O'Donoghue, *The Courtly Love Tradition*, 5.
2. This sonnet was translated by Jill Claretta Robbins as "Since I abandoned and tied my soul"; see "Cecco Nuccoli," in *The Columbia Anthology of Gay Literature*, 139.
3. See, for instance, Mott, *The System of Courtly Love*, 8.
4. Massèra and Marti both have "per che."
5. Massèra and Marti both have "tempio."
6. This sonnet was translated by Dante Gabriel Rossetti (attributed to Cecco Angiolieri) as "Never so bare and naked was church-stone"; see Rossetti, *Dante and His Circle*, 199.
7. Lelli refers to the parable of the Prodigal Son in Luke 15:11–32.
8. "Pair of leggings . . . similar zither": that is, no matter what Nuccoli requested, his father would always make a similar complaint.

9. "Provost" (*proposto*): presumably this is a reference to Nuccoli's father.

10. This sonnet was translated by Robbins as "You have the light of my life"; see "Cecco Nuccoli," in *The Columbia Anthology of Gay Literature*, 139.

11. Dante mentions that geminate consonants are typical of the comic style in his treatise on literature and language, *De vulgari eloquentia* (2.7.5).

12. "Black lines and the nice vermillion": the meaning of this line is unclear. Marti interprets it as a reference to writing, with black lines and red rubrics on a page. Mancini, conversely, interprets it as depicting the colors on Nicolò's crest.

13. Literally, "warts." However, *TLIO* notes that "lebbre" could mean either warts or, more generally, flaws. The latter definition makes more sense in the context of this sonnet.

14. "Chiana valley . . . Tiber valley": these were two areas dominated by the Perugian commune, the Chiana valley to the west and the Tiber valley to the south; see Blanshei, "Perugia, 1260–1340," 13.

15. There has been some debate as to what—or who—Monna Raggia was. Massèra proposed that Monna Raggia was a donkey, while Marti offered that it was a bird, perhaps a falcon, an interpretation that seems most likely given the reference to a wing (v. 17). Additionally, Mancini notes that, whatever Monna Raggia was, the sonnet may employ subtle language, at the same time making a veiled reference to the mistreatment of a woman.

16. See the sonnet "Today no joy unto my heart accrues," in which Cecco Angiolieri concludes that he would scratch her with all ten fingers: "I'd scratch her up and down with my ten fingers" ("io la farei grattar con diece dita," v. 14). Angiolieri's sonnet appears only in the Chigiano L.VIII.305 manuscript (f. 103v).

17. "Him who fell at the sovereign's hand": Tristan, whom King Mark had killed.

18. This verse appears to contradict the overall message of the sonnet, as does the penultimate.

19. See Angiolieri's sonnet "At night, when all the day I failed to see" ("Qualunque giorno non veggio 'l mi' amore"). Angiolieri's poem only appears in Chigiano L.VIII.305 (f. 109v).

20. See, for instance, "Dear companion of my companion" ("Cara compagna del compagno mio") by Adriano de' Rossi.

21. "Giovannel's . . . test": the meaning of this verse is unclear. It is possible that Giovannel is another man similarly enduring sexual dysfunction.

22. See "becco" in Boggione and Casalegno, *Dizionario storico del lessico erotico italiano*, 283.

23. DePierre, *A Brief History of Oral Sex*, 62–65.

24. The final word of the sonnet (*becco*) can denote either a beak or a ram. Given the other avian references in Nuccoli's corpus, the translation as beak seems preferable. In either instance, the sexual innuendo in Cecco's statement is clear.

25. "Shoot a crossbow bolt at him": the probable meaning of this phrase is that Cucco should use more than words to win over his beloved.

26. Gratian (d. ca. 1159), who composed the Decretals on canon law.

27. "I'll ride in the saddle while you run alongside the mane": the verse probably means that Nuccoli will ride victorious, while Cucco, the loser, must run on foot.

28. Lake Trasimeno provided nearly 5,000 *quintali* of fish to the Perugian commune annually, including eels, tenches, and freshwater mullets; see Blanshei, "Perugia, 1260–1340," 15–16.

29. Massèra and Marti both have "per."

30. Massèra and Marti both have "lascio mo'."

31. Massèra and Marti both have "Est ist gut got mich hungerte."

32. "*By God, I'm hungry*": this line is in a garbled German (*Les is gut nich nengert*), which Massèra interpreted as *Es is gut got miche hungerte*; Massèra's reading for the line has been accepted by most editors and is therefore the basis for this translation.

33. "Opens": presumably, he opens his hands to spend.

34. "But I believe . . . somersaults behind him": these verses appear based upon a sexual double entendre.

35. "Fuia," denoting "furious," was also a way to refer to sexual excitement.

36. The reference to Jason is not clear. A possible interpretation is that another man will win over a member of the Montemelino family (*monte*, "hill") by chasing away the women.

37. See Angiolieri's sonnet "Dad, my Becchina, Love and then my mother," which closes with his mother cursing him: "Go and get yourself impaled" ("Cecco, va', che sie fenduto!," v. 14). This sonnet appears in two manuscripts, Chigiano L.VIII. 305 (f. 106v) and Vaticano Latino Barberiniano 3953 (f. 156).

38. For a fuller discussion of "Ciampolino" and "Ciamprolino," see my introduction to this book.

39. See Cecco Angiolieri's poem "There are three things that give me delight" where he enumerates the items: "woman, the tavern and a game of dice" ("la donna, la taverna e 'l dado," v. 3). This sonnet appears in two manuscripts, Chigiano L.VIII.305 (f. 105v) and Escorialense e.III.23 (f. 86v).

40. Jones, *The Italian City-State*, 158. For another example of the literary denigration of *rusticitas*, see Alfie, "S'e' non ti cagia la tua santalena," 309–21.

41. "Patarines": a reform movement, eventually considered heretical, of the mid-eleventh century, which opposed ecclesiastical corruption and the papacy's temporal powers.

42. Zaccarello, "Off the Paths of Common Sense," 90–91.

43. Bonazzi, *Storia di Perugia dalle origini al 1860*, 318.

44. Massèra and Marti both have "posso."

45. Massèra and Marti both have "senza."

46. This sonnet was translated by Robbins as "Since I abandoned and tied my soul"; see "Cecco Nuccoli," in *The Columbia Anthology of Gay Literature*, 139–40.

47. See, for instance, Falini, "Gli 'oggetti' della poesia comico-oscena," 39–40.

48. "William of Flanders": William II, Count of Flanders (1224–51). It is likely, however, that this is not a historical reference, but rather an allusion to a penis.

49. "Giotto": the Florentine painter (1267–1337). Again, it is likely that this is a reference either to a lover or to the lover's penis specifically.

50. "Lelli": Gilio Lelli, with whom Nuccoli exchanged poems.

51. Heywood, *A History of Perugia*, 156–57.

52. Massèra and Marti both have "ma' lo."

53. Bonazzi, *Storia di Perugia dalle origini al 1860*, 324.

54. Heywood, *A History of Perugia*, 162–66.

55. "High wheel": the wheel of Fortune, which is continually in motion, changing people's states on earth.

56. Massèra and Marti both have "là u' vo."

57. "Hoeing the water": the phrase appears to indicate an ineffective action. Meo dei Tolomei makes a similar statement in his sonnet 16, "My mother tricked me, and Ciampolino," where he says, "I should pound water in a mortar" (v. 13).

Chapter 4. *Marino Ceccoli*

1. Massèra and Marti both have "spirte."
2. Massèra and Marti both have "Che."
3. Massèra's anthology does not contain this sonnet.
4. Marti has "fruire."
5. Massèra and Marti both have "fanno."
6. Massèra and Marti both have "Oi."

7. This sonnet was translated by Jill Claretta Robbins as "Oh, and yet I see that I will return to you anyway"; see "Marino Ceccoli," in *The Columbia Anthology of Gay Literature*, 140.

8. "Six by six": that is, in large numbers.

9. This sonnet was translated by Robbins as "Sir, I have remained so overcome"; see "Marino Ceccoli," in *The Columbia Anthology of Gay Literature*, 140.

10. See, for instance, Economou, "The Two Venuses and Courtly Love," 17–50.

11. Barolini, *Desire and Death*, 27.

12. Massèra's anthology does not contain this sonnet.

13. Marti has "ch'è conosciuto solo dopo il danno."

14. Marti has "E' mi duol forte del gabbato affanno."

15. The discussion of love as an accidental property appears in several important works of the Italian Middle Ages. Guido Cavalcanti argues that it is an accident, and not a substance, in his doctrinal *canzone* "Donna me prega." Similarly, in the *Vita Nuova*, Dante asserts, "for Love is not in himself a substance, but is an accident inherent in a substance" (chap. 25, line 1).

16. "The night's manna": that is, sleep.

17. Massèra and Marti both have "Albescit unus mons vestis."

18. Massèra and Marti both have "caderent."

19. For a translation of this poem, see Foster and Boyde, eds. and trans., *Dante's Lyric Poetry*, Vol. 1, *The Poems: Text and Translation*, 174–81.

20. Massèra and Marti both have "che l'animato."

21. Massèra and Marti both have "per che."

22. "Joyful" (*m'alegro*): the poet intends this as ironic.

23. See Giovanni Villani, *Nuova cronica*, bk. 12, chap. 2.

24. For the poetry of Adriano de' Rossi, see "Adriano de' Rossi," 901–7; for Antonio Pucci's poetry about the flood of 1333, see Morpurgo, *La grande inundation de l'Arno*. For a general study of the poetry about the flood, see Alfie, "A New Flood Was Released from the Heavens."

25. See Wack, *Lovesickness in the Middle Ages*, 151, and Cadden, *Meanings of Sex Difference in the Middle Ages*, 220.

26. Massèra and Marti both have "bene."

27. The second half of this verse is in Latin.

28. Massèra and Marti both have "voi."

29. "Farthest down rise up again": Ceccoli seems to refer to the wheel of Fortune in this verse.

30. "Pass barefoot among the thorns": other people can succeed, but only with great difficulty.

31. This line is in Latin.
32. Massèra and Marti both have "védese."
33. Massèra's anthology does not contain this sonnet.
34. Literally, "a column."
35. Massèra's anthology does not contain this sonnet.
36. "The Hebrew bull": the constellation of Taurus was associated with the Hebrew letter *aleph*.
37. Bonazzi, *Storia di Perugia dalle origini al 1860*, 324.
38. This line is in Latin.
39. Regarding the medieval stereotypes about the Jews, see chapter 1, note 37 to Meo dei Tolomei's poem 10.
40. Massèra's anthology does not contain this *canzone*.
41. Cited from Alighieri, *Convivio*, ed. Frisardi.
42. Raffa, "Love's Duplicity in the *Vita Nuova*," 16.
43. Neither Massèra's anthology nor Marti's contains this sonnet.
44. Cited from Salutati, *Epistolario di Coluccio Salutati*, 76–78.

BIBLIOGRAPHY

Alfie, Fabian. "Black Comedy: The Poetry of Nicola Muscia." *Romance Philology* 61 (Fall 2007): 193–211.

———. *Comedy and Culture: Cecco Angiolieri's Poetry and Late Medieval Society.* Leeds: Northern Universities Press, 2001.

———. "Giovanni Sercambi: Story 31." *TSQ: Transgender Studies Quarterly* 2, no. 3 (2015): 532–38.

———. "'I' son sì magro che quasi traluco': Inspiration and Indebtedness among Cecco Angiolieri, Meo dei Tolomei, and Il Burchiello." *Italian Quarterly* 35, no. 135–136 (1998): 5–28.

———. "Like She-Cats in January: An Anonymous Fifteenth-Century Misogynistic Sonnet." *Mediaevistik* 26 (2013): 207–15.

———. "Men on Bottom: Homoeroticism in Cecco Angiolieri's Poetry." *Medievalia et Humanistica* 28 (2001): 25–44.

———. "'A New Flood Was Released from the Heavens': The Literary Responses to the Disaster of 1333." In *Nature in the Middle Ages and the Early Modern Times*, edited by Albrecht Classen, 253–99. Berlin: De Gruyter, 2024.

———. "Old Lady Avignon: Petrarch's *Rerum Vulgarium Fragmenta* 136 and the Topos of *Vituperium in Vetulam*." *Italian Culture* 30, no. 2 (2012): 100–109.

———, ed. and trans. *Rustico Filippi: The Art of Insult.* Cambridge: Modern Humanities Research Association, 2014.

———. "'S'e' non ti cagia la tua santalena': Guido Cavalcanti and the Thirteenth-Century Reprehension of *Rusticitas*." *Italica* 89, no. 3 (2012): 309–21.

———. "Sinful Wives and Queens: The Medieval Concept of Sodomy in Dante's *Comedy*." *The Journal of Language and Sexuality* 11, no. 1 (2022): 101–24.

———. "The Violent Poetics of Inversion, or the Inversion of Violent Poetics: Meo dei Tolomei, His Mother, and the Italian Tradition of Comic Poetry." In *Love and Violence in Medieval Courtly Literature: A Casebook*, edited by Albrecht Classen, 207–24. New York: Routledge, 2004.

Alighieri, Dante. *Convivio: A Dual-Language Critical Edition*. Edited and translated by Andrew Frisardi. Cambridge: Cambridge University Press, 2018.
———. *Opere minori*. Edited by Alberto Del Monte. Milan: Rizzoli, 1966.
———. *Rime*. Edited by Piero Cudini. Milan: Garzanti, 1979.
———. *Rime*. Edited by Domenico De Robertis. Florence: Edizioni del Galluzzo, 2005.
Allen, Judson Boyce. *The Ethical Poetic of the Later Middle Ages: A Decorum of Convenient Distinction*. Toronto: University of Toronto Press, 1983.
Angiolieri, Cecco. *Il canzoniere*. Edited by Carlo Steiner. Turin: UTET, 1928.
———. *Il canzoniere*. Edited by Sebastiano Blancato. Milan: Il Ruscello, 1946.
———. *Le rime*. Edited by Antonio Lanza. Rome: Guido Izzi, 1990.
———. *I sonetti di Cecco Angiolieri editi criticamente ed illustrati*. Edited by Aldo Francesco Massèra. Bologna: Zanichelli, 1906.
———. *Sonnets: Cecco Angiolieri*. Translated by C. H. Scott and Anthony Mortimer. Surrey, UK: Oneworld Press, 2011.
———. *The Sonnets of a Handsome and Well-Mannered Rogue*. Translated by Thomas Caldecot Chubb. Hamden CT: Archon Books, 1970.
———. *The Sonnets of Cecco Angiolieri of Siena Done into English Doggerel*. Translated by C. H. M. D. Scott. London: Chiswick Press, 1925.
Baldassano, Alex. "Talking Back: Sodomy Laws and Transgressive Subjectivity in Medieval Venice." *MFF* 55, no. 2 (2019): 40–59.
Baldelli, Ignazio. "Lingua e letteratura di un centro trecentesco: Perugia." *La Rassegna della letteratura Italiana* 66 (1962): 3–21.
Barbi, Michele. "Un nuovo codice di rime antiche molto importante." In *Studi sul canzoniere di Dante con nuove indagini sulle raccolte manoscritte e a stampa di antiche rime italiane*, 511–27. Florence: Sansoni, 1915.
Barker, John W., and Christopher Kleinhenz. "Perugia." In *Medieval Italy: An Encyclopedia*, edited by Christopher Kleinhenz, 2:875–77. New York: Routledge, 2004.
Barolini, Teodolinda. *Desire and Death, or Francesca and Guido Cavalcanti: "Inferno" 5 in Its Lyric Context*. Binghamton NY: Center for Medieval and Renaissance Studies, 2001.
Barrett, Tracy Turner. "'Rogue,' 'Scamp': The Elusive Persona of Cecco Angiolieri." PhD diss., University of California, Berkeley, 1988.
Bayless, Martha. *Parody in the Middle Ages: The Latin Tradition*. Ann Arbor: University of Michigan Press, 1996.
Bentivogli, Bruno. "Sonetti misogini da codici quattrocenteschi." In *Studi in onore di Raffaele Spongano*, 73–93. Bologna: Boni, 1980.
Berisso, Marco. *Poesia comica del medioevo italiano*. Milan: BUR, 2011.

———, ed. *Poesie dello stilnovo*. Milan: BUR, 2006.

———. "Preistoria (mancata) del *nonsense* nella poesia medievale italiana." In *"Nominativi fritti e mappamondi": Il nonsense nella letteratura italiana. Atti del Convegno di Cassino 9–10 ottobre 2007*, edited by Giuseppe Antonelli and Carla Chiummo, 27–45. Rome: Salerno Editrice 2009.

———. *La raccolta dei poeti perugini del Vat. Barberiniano Lat. 4036: Storia della tradizione e cultura poetica di una scuola trecentesca*. Florence: Olschki, 2000.

Bertelli, Italo. *I fondamenti artistici e culturali del "dolce stil nuovo."* Milan: Bignami, 1987.

Betella, Patrizia. *The Ugly Woman: Transgressive Aesthetic Models in Italian Poetry from the Middle Ages to the Baroque*. Toronto: University of Toronto Press, 2005.

Bettarini, Anna Bruni. "Le rime di Meo dei Tolomei e di Muscia di Siena." *Studi di filologia italiana* 32 (1974): 31–98.

Blanshei, Sarah Rubin. "Perugia, 1260–1340: Conflict and Change in a Medieval Urban Society." *Transactions of the American Philosophical Society* 66, no. 2 (1976): 1–128.

———. "Population, Wealth, and Patronage in Medieval and Renaissance Perugia." *Journal of Interdisciplinary History* 9, no. 4 (1979): 597–619.

Boccaccio, Giovanni. *Decameron*. Edited by Vittore Branca. Turin: Einaudi, 1992.

Boggione, Valter, and Giovanni Casalegno. *Dizionario storico del lessico erotico italiano: Metafore, eufemismi, oscenità, doppi sensi, parole dotte e parole basse in otto secoli di letteratura italiana*. Milan: Longanesi, 1996.

Bonazzi, Luigi. *Storia di Perugia dalle origini al 1860*. Vol. 1, *Dalle origini al 1494*. Perugia: Tipografia di Vincenso Santucci, 1875.

Borriero, Giovanni. "Considerazioni sulla tradizione manoscritta della *Tenzone* di Dante con Forese." In *Antico Moderno*, Vol. 4, *I numeri*, 385–405. Rome: Bagatto Libri, 1999.

———. "'Quantum illos proximius imitemur, tantum rectius poemetur': Note sul Chigiano L.VIII. 305 e sulle 'antologie d'autore.'" In *Antico Moderno*, Vol. 3, *La filologia*, 259–86. Rome: Bagatto Libri, 1997.

Boswell, John E. *Christianity, Social Tolerance and Homosexuality: Gay People in Western Europe from the Beginning of the Christian Era to the Fourteenth Century*. Chicago: University of Chicago Press, 1980.

Botterill, Steven N. "Autobiography and Artifice in the Medieval Lyric: The Case of Cecco Nuccoli." *Italian Studies* 46 (1991): 37–57.

———. "Cecco Nuccoli." In *Medieval Italy: An Encyclopedia*, edited by Christopher Kleinhenz, 1:204. New York: Routledge, 2004.

———. "Cecco Nuccoli: An Introduction." *The Italianist* 8 (1988): 16–32.

———. "Marino Ceccoli." In *Medieval Italy: An Encyclopedia*, edited by Christopher Kleinhenz, 2:684–85. New York: Routledge, 2004.

Bragg, Lois. "Visual-Kinetic Communication in Europe before 1600: A Survey of Sign Lexicons and Finger Alphabets prior to the Rise of Deaf Education." *Journal of Deaf Studies and Deaf Education* 2, no. 1 (1997): 1–20.

Brundage, James. *Law, Sex and Christian Society in Medieval Europe*. Chicago: Chicago University Press, 1987.

Bullough, Vern L. "The Sin against Nature and Homosexuality." In *Sexual Practices & the Medieval Church*, edited by Vern L. Bullough and James Brundage, 55–71. Buffalo: Prometheus Books, 1982.

Burnley, David. *Courtliness and Literature in Medieval England*. London: Longman, 1998.

Buzzetti Gallarati, Silvia. "Onomastica equivoca nei sonetti sartirici di Rustico Filippi." In *Cecco Angiolieri e la poesia satirica medievale. Atti del convegno internazionale Siena, 26–27 ottobre 2002*, edited by Stefano Carrai and Giuseppe Marrani, 51–75. Florence: Edizioni del Galluzzo, 2005.

———. *Rustico Filippi: Sonetti Satirici e giocosi*. Rome: Carocci, 2005.

Cadden, Joan. *Meanings of Sex Difference in the Middle Ages: Medicine, Science, and Culture*. Cambridge: Cambridge University Press, 1993.

Callahan, Anne. *Writing the Voice of Pleasure: Heterosexuality without Women*. New York: Palgrave, 2001.

Calvino, Italo. *Italian Folktales*. Translated by George Martin. San Diego: Harcourt, 1980.

Capellanus, Andreas. *The Art of Courtly Love*. Translated by John Jay Parry. New York: W. W. Norton, 1941.

Cardini, Franco. "Tradizioni magiche e 'medicina popolare': Note su alcuni trattati tre-quattrocenteschi di agronomia." *La ricerca folklorica: Contributi allo studio della cultura delle classi popolari* 8 (1983): 35–42.

Casalegno, Giovanni. *Brutti, fessi e cattivi: Lessico della maldicenza italiana*. Turin: UTET, 2005.

Cavalcanti, Guido. *Complete Poems*. Translated by Anthony Mortimer. Surrey, UK: Alma Classics, 2010.

———. *Rime*. Edited by Domenico De Robertis. Turin: Einaudi, 1986.

———. *Rime*. Edited by Letterio Cassata. Rome: Donzelli, 1995.

———. *Rime*. Edited by Marcello Ciccuto. Milan: BUR, 1996.

"Cazzo." In *Grande Dizionario della Lingua Italiana*, 2:935. Turin: UTET, 1961.

"Cazzo." In *Dizionario etimologico italiano*, edited by Carlo Battisti and Giovanni Alessio, 2:833. Florence: Barbera, 1965.

"Cazzo." In *Dizionario etimologico della lingua italiana*, edited by Manlio Cortelazzo and Paolo Zilli, 1:220. Bologna: Zanichelli, 1985.

Cecchini, Giovanni. *La pacificazione fra Tolomei e Salimbeni*. Siena: Ticci editore libraio, 1942.

"Cecco Nuccoli," translated by Jill Claretta Robbins. In *The Columbia Anthology of Gay Literature: Readings from Western Antiquity to the Present Day*, edited by Byrne R. S. Fone, 139–40. New York: Columbia University Press, 1998.

Cervigni, Dino S. "Fiammetta's Song of Jealousy: Are the Young People Still at Play?" *Annali d'Italianistica* 31 (2013): 459–507.

Chiarini, Eugenio. "Ben so che fosti figliuol d'Alighieri." In *Enciclopedia dantesca*, 1:590. Rome: Istituto della Enciclopedia Italiana, 1970.

"Ciampolino." In *Grande Dizionario della Lingua Italiana*, 3:107. Turin: UTET, 1964.

Ciasca, Raffaele. *L'arte dei medici e speziali nella storia e nel commercio fiorentino dal secolo XII al XV*. Florence: Olschki, 1927.

Clark, Anna. *Desire: A History of European Sexuality*. New York: Routledge, 2008.

Cockcayne, Emily. "Experiences of the Deaf in Early Modern England." *The Historical Journal* 46, no. 3 (2003): 493–510.

Cohen, Jeremy. "Jews as the Killers of Christ in the Latin Tradition from Augustine to the Friars." *Traditio* 39 (1983): 1–27.

Collegari, Danielle. "Grey Partridges and Middle-Aged Mutton: The Social Value of Food in the Tenzone with Forese Donati." *Dante Studies* 133 (Fall 2015): 177–90.

Contini, Gianfranco. "Postilla angiolieresca." *Studi di filologia italiana* 22 (1964): 581–86.

Corbucci, Vittorio. "L'antico poeta perugino Marino Ceccoli e la dominazione dei Tarlati a Città di Castello." *L'alta valle del Tevere: Rassegna bimestrale illustrata* 1, no. 2 (1933): 3–8.

Corsi, Giuseppe, ed. *Rimatori del Trecento*. Turin: UTET, 1969.

Cowell, Andrew. *At Play in the Tavern: Signs, Coins and Bodies in the Middle Ages*. Ann Arbor: University of Michigan Press, 1999.

Crawford, Katherine. "The Good, the Bad, and the Textual: Approaches to the Study of the Body and Sexuality, 1500–1750." In *The Routledge History of Sex and the Body: 1500 to the Present*, edited by Sarah Toulalan and Kate Fisher, 23–37. Hoboken, NJ: Taylor and Francis, 2013.

Crimi, Giuseppe. "Burchiello e le sue metamorfosi: Personaggio e maschera." In *Auctor/Actor: Lo scrittore personaggio nella letteratura italiana*, edited by G. Corabi and B. Gizzi, 89–119. Rome: Bulzoni, 2006.

Damian, Peter. "Letter 31." In *Letters 31–60*, translated by Owen J. Blum, O.F.M. Washington DC: Catholic University of America Press, 1989.

D'Ancona, Alessandro. "Cecco Angiolieri da Siena, poeta umorista del secolo XIII." In *Studi di critica e storia letteraria*, 163–275. Bologna: Zanichelli, 1912.

Davidson, N. S. "Sodomy in Early Modern Venice." In *Sodomy in Early Modern Europe*, edited by Tom Betteridge, 65–81. Manchester: Manchester University Press, 2002.

Dean, Trevor. "Gender and Insult in an Italian City: Bologna in the Later Middle Ages." *Social History* 29, no. 2 (2004): 217–31.

Degli Azzi, Giustiniano, ed. *Statuti di Perugia dell'anno MCCCXLII*. Vol. 2. Rome: Loescher, 1916.

DePierre, David. *A Brief History of Oral Sex*. Jefferson, NC: Exposit, 2017.

De Robertis, Domenico. *Il canzoniere escorialense e la tradizione "veneziana" dello stil novo*. Turin: Casa Editrice Loescher-Chiantore, 1954.

———. "Censimento dei manoscritti di rime di Dante (VI)." *Studi danteschi* 42 (1965): 419–74.

Di Giovanni, Domenico, nicknamed il Burchiello. *The Poetry of Burchiello: Deep-Fried Nouns, Hunchbacked Pumpkins, and Other Nonsense*. Translated by Fabian Alfie and Aileen A. Feng. Tempe, AZ: ACMRS, 2017.

Dillon, Emma. "Representing Obscene Sound." In *Medieval Obscenities*, edited by Nicola McDonald, 55–84. York: York Medieval Press, 2006.

Dinshaw, Carolyn. *Getting Medieval: Sexualities and Communities, Pre- and Postmodern*. Durham, NC: Duke University Press, 1999.

"Diritto." In *Grande Dizionario della Lingua Italiana*, 4:541–47. Turin: UTET, 1966.

Economou, George D. "The Two Venuses and Courtly Love." In *Pursuit of Perfection: Courtly Love in Medieval Literature*, edited by Joan M. Ferrante and George D. Economou, 17–50. Port Washington, NY: Kennikat Press, 1975.

Elliott, Dyan. *The Corrupter of Boys: Sodomy, Scandal, and the Medieval Clergy*. Philadelphia: University of Pennsylvania Press, 2020.

Elsheik, Mahmoud Salem. "Scavi perugini." *Filologia e critica* 9 (1984): 284–92.

Evans, Ruth. "Introduction: What Was Sexuality in the Middle Ages?" In *A Cultural History in the Middle Ages*, edited by Ruth Evans, 1–36. London: Bloomsbury, 2011.

Falini, Irene. "Gli 'oggetti' della poesia comico-oscena del medioevo italiano (con una proposta di lettura per il sonetto *Volesse Iddio che tti paresse il vino* di Lorenzo Moschi)." *Quaderni di Palazzo Serra* 30 (2018): 35–50.

Ferm, Olle. "Form: Its Expressions and Manifestations." In *A Cultural History of Comedy in the Middle Ages*, edited by Martha Bayless, 19–37. London: Bloomsbury Academic, 2020.

Finiguerri, Stefano, detto il Za. *I Poemetti*. Edited by Antonio Lanza. Rome: Zauli Arti Grafiche, 1994.

Foster, Kenelm, and Patrick Boyde, eds. and trans. *Dante's Lyric Poetry*. Vol. 1, *The Poems: Text and Translation*. Oxford: Oxford University Press, 1967.

Foucault, Michel. *The History of Sexuality*. Vol. 1, *An Introduction*. Translated by Robert Hurley. New York: Vintage Books, 1990.

Frantzen, Allen J. "The Shadow of Sodom: Same-Sex Relations in Pastoral Prose and Poetry." In *Before the Closet: Same-Sex Love from "Beowulf" to "Angels in America,"* 184–228. Chicago: University of Chicago Press, 1998.

Fubini, Mario. "Sulla poesia del Burchiello." In *Studi della letteratura del Rinascimento*, 13–40. Florence: Sansoni, 1947.

Geremek, Bronislaw. *Poverty: A History*. Translated by Agnieszka Kloakowska. Oxford and Cambridge: Blackwell, 1994.

Goodich, Michael. *The Unmentionable Vice: Homosexuality in the Later Medieval Period*. Santa Barbara, CA: ABC-CLIO, 1979.

Gorni, Guglielmo. "Manetto tra Guido e Dante." In *Seminario dantesco internazionale/International Dante Seminar I: Atti del Primo Convegno tenutosi al Chauncey Conference Center, Princeton, 21–23 ottobre 1994*, 25–39. Florence: Le lettere, 1997.

Grigsby, Byron L. "Medical Misconceptions." In *Misconceptions about the Middle Ages*, edited by Stephen J. Harris and Byron L. Grigsby, 142–50. New York: Routledge, 2008.

Haas, Louis. "Boccaccio, Baptismal Kinship, and Spiritual Incest." *Renaissance and Reformation/Renaissance et Réforme* 13, no. 4 (1989): 343–56.

Halperin, David M. *How to Do the History of Homosexuality*. Chicago: University of Chicago Press, 2002.

Hatty, Suzanne, and James Hatty. *The Disordered Body: Epidemic Disease and Cultural Transformation*. Albany: State University of New York Press, 1999.

Hergemoller, Bernd-Ulrich. *Sodom and Gomorrah: On the Everyday Reality and Persecution of Homosexuals in the Middle Ages*. Translated by John Phillips. London: Free Association Press, 2001.

Hollywood, Amy M. "The Normal, the Queer, and the Middle Ages." *Journal of the History of Sexuality* 10, no. 2 (2001): 173–79.

Holmes, Olivia. "Doing Unto Others, or Sienese Polyamory." In *The "Decameron" Eighth Day in Perspective*, Vol. 8 of *Lectura Boccacci*, edited by William Robins, 190–204. Toronto: University of Toronto Press, 2020.

Howard, Lloyd. "An Interpretation of Cavalcanti's 'Guata, Manetto, quella scrignatuzza.'" *Canadian Journal of Italian Studies* 1 (1978): 183–87.

Heywood, William. *A History of Perugia*. Edited by R. Langton Douglas. London: Methuen & Co., 1910.

Indizio, Giuseppe. "Dante as a Florentine Lyrical Author." *Forum Italicum* 55, no. 2 (2021): 269–95.

Irvine, Judith T. "Leaky Registers and Eight-Hundred-Pound Gorillas." *Anthropological Quarterly* 84, no. 1 (2011): 15–40.

Jacobus de Voragine. *The Golden Legend*. Translated by Granger Ryan and Helmut Ripperger. New York: Longmans, Green, and Co., 1948.

Jaeger, Stephen. *Ennobling Love: In Search of a Lost Sensibility*. Philadelphia: University of Pennsylvania Press, 1999.

Jones, Malcolm. "Wicked Willies with Wings: Sex and Sexuality in Late Medieval Art and Thought." In *The Secret Middle Ages*, 248–73. Westport CT, London: Praeger, 2003.

Jones, Philip. *The Italian City-State: From Commune to Signoria*. Oxford: Clarendon, 1997.

Jordan, Mark D. *The Invention of Sodomy in Christian Theology*. Chicago: Chicago University Press, 1997.

Karras, Ruth Mazo. "The Regulation of 'Sodomy' in the Latin East and West." *Speculum* 95, no. 4 (2020): 969–86.

———. *Sexuality in Medieval Europe: Doing Unto Others*. New York: Routledge, 2005.

Killerby, Catherine Kovesi. "Practical Problems in the Enforcement of Italian Sumptuary Law." In *Crime, Society and the Law in Renaissance Italy*, edited by Trevor Dean and K. J. Lowe, 99–120. Cambridge: Cambridge University Press, 1994.

———. *Sumptuary Laws in Italy, 1200–1500*. Oxford: Clarendon, 2002.

Langer, Ullrich. "The Renaissance Novella as Justice." *Renaissance Quarterly* 52, no. 2 (1999): 311–41.

Lansing, Carol. *The Florentine Magnates: Lineage and Faction in a Medieval Commune*. Princeton, NJ: Princeton University Press, 1991.

Lanza, Antonio. *Polemiche e berte letterarie nella Firenze del primo Quattrocento*. Roma: Bulzoni, 1971.

Laqueur, Thomas W. *Solitary Sex: A Cultural History of Masturbation*. New York: Zone Books, 2003.

Larner, John. "La nobiltà." In *L'Italia nell'età di Dante, Petrarca e Boccaccio*, 147–83. Bologna: Il Mulino, 1982.

Leap, William L. "Language, Sexuality, and the Suspension of Taboo: Lessons from 'Gay English.'" *Ars Semiotica* 38, no. 3–4 (2015): 246–58.

———. "Studying a Not-So-Secret 'Secret Code.'" In *Language before Stonewall: Language, Sexuality, History*, 1–79. Cham, Switzerland: Palgrave MacMillan, 2020.

Lega, Gino. *Il canzoniere Vaticano Barberiniano Latino 3953 (già Bar. XLV. 47)*. Bologna: Romagnoli-Dall'Acqua, 1905.

Lewis, C. S. *The Allegory of Love: A Study in Medieval Tradition*. Oxford: Oxford University Press, 1936.

Lochrie, Karma. *Heterosyncrasies: Female Sexuality When Normal Wasn't*. Minneapolis, London: University of Minnesota Press, 2005.

Lochrie, Karma, Peggie McCracken, and James A. Schultz. "Introduction." In *Constructing Medieval Sexuality*, edited by Karma Lochrie, Peggie McCracken, and James A. Schultz, ix–xviii. Minneapolis: University of Minnesota Press, 1997.

Maestro Rinuccino. *I sonetti di Maestro Rinuccino di Firenze*. Edited Stefano Carrai. Florence: Accademia della Crusca, 1981.

Manca, Franco. "Dante e la poesia realistico-borghese." *Canadian Journal of Italian Studies* 8, no. 30 (1985): 32–45.

Mancini, Franco, ed. *Poeti perugini del Trecento*. Vol. 1, *Marino Ceccoli, Cecco Nuccoli e altri rimatori in tenzone*. Perugia: Guerra, 1996.

"Marino Ceccoli," translated by Jill Claretta Robbins. In *The Columbia Anthology of Gay Literature: Readings from Western Antiquity to the Present Day*, edited by Byrne R. S. Fone, 140. New York: Columbia University Press, 1998.

Marrani, Giuseppe. "La poesia comica fra '200 e '300: Aspetti della fortuna di Cecco Angiolieri fuori toscana." In *Cecco Angiolieri e la poesia satirica medievale. Atti del convegno internazionale Siena, 26–27 ottobre 2002*, edited by Stefano Carrai and Giuseppe Marrani, 101–22. Florence: Edizioni del Galluzzo, 2005.

Marti, Mario, ed. *Poeti del Dolce Stil Nuovo*. Firenze: Le Monnier, 1969.

———, ed. *Poeti giocosi del tempo di Dante*. Milan: Rizzoli, 1956.

———. "La tecnica del 'vituperium' in Meo dei Tolomei di Siena." In *Cultura e stile dei poeti giocosi*, 59–82. Pisa: Nistri-Lischi, 1953.

———. "Sulla genesi del realismo dantesco." In *Realismo dantesco e altri studi*, 1–32. Milan, Naples: Ricciardi, 1961.

———. "Tolomei, Meo dei." In *Enciclopedia dantesca*, 5:619–20. Rome: Istituto della Enciclopedia Italiana, 1976.

Martin, A. Lynn. *Alcohol, Sex, and Gender in Late Medieval and Early Modern Europe.* Hampshire, UK: Palgrave, 2001.

"Mascolino." In *Grande Dizionario della Lingua Italiana*, 9:880–81. Turin: UTET, 1961.

Massèra, Aldo Francesco, ed. *Sonetti burleschi e realistici dei primi due secoli.* Bari: Laterza, 1940.

Matthew of Vendôme. *The Art of Versification.* Edited and translated by Aubrey E. Galyon. Ames: Iowa State University Press, 1980.

Mattews-Grieco, Sara F. "Satyrs and Sausages: Erotic Strategies and the Print Market in Cinquecento Italy." In *Erotic Cultures of Renaissance Italy*, edited by Sara F. Mattews-Grieco, 19–60. Surrey, UK: Ashgate, 2010.

Menarini, Alberto. "Finocchio in senso osceno." *Lingua nostra* 24, no. 2 (1963): 57–58.

Méndez, Jerónimo. "Humor and Sexuality: Twelfth-Century Troubadours and Medieval Arabic Poetry." In *Intercultural Transmission in the Medieval Mediterranean*, edited by Stephanie L. Hathaway and David W. Kim, 119–32. London: Bloomsbury Academic, 2012.

Mengaldo, Pier Vincenzo. "Perugia." In *Enciclopedia dantesca*, 4:441–45. Roma: Istituto della Enciclopedia Italiana, 1973.

Messina, Michele, ed. *Burchiello: Sonetti inediti.* Florence: Olschki, 1952.

Metzler, Irina. *Disability in Medieval Europe: Thinking about Physical Impairment during the High Middle Ages, ca. 1100–1400.* London: Routledge, 2006.

Mieszkowksi, Gretchen. "Old Age and Medieval Misogyny: The Old Woman." In *Old Age in the Middle Ages and the Renaissance: Interdisciplinary Approaches to a Neglected Topos*, edited by Albrecht Classen, 299–319. Berlin: De Gruyter, 2007.

Miller, Paul. "John Gower, Satiric Poet." In *Gower's "Confessio Amantis": Responses and Reassessments*, 79–105. Cambridge: D. S. Brewer, 1983.

Mills, Robert. "Homosexuality: Specters of Sodom." In *A Cultural History in the Middle Ages*, edited by Ruth Evans, 57–79. London: Bloomsbury, 2011.

———. *Seeing Sodomy in the Middle Ages.* Chicago: University of Chicago Press, 2015.

Minnis, Alistair J. "Authors in Love, The Exegesis of Late-Medieval Love-Poets." In *The Uses of Manuscripts in Literary Studies: Essays in Memory of Judson Boyce Allen*, edited by Charlotte Cook Morse, Penelope Reed Doob and Marjorie Currie Woods, 161–91. Kalamazoo, MI: Medieval Institute Publications, 1992.

Minnis, Alastair, and A. B. Scott. *Medieval Literary Theory and Criticism, c. 1100–c. 1375: The Commentary-Tradition.* Oxford: Clarendon, 1988.

Mohr, Melissa. *Holy Shit: A Brief History of Swearing.* Oxford: Oxford University Press, 2013.

Mollat, Michel. *Etudes sur l'economie et la societe de l'Occident medieval XIIe–XVe Siecle.* London: Variorum Reprints, 1977.

Monaci, Ernesto. "Chigiano L.VIII.305." *Propugnatore* 10, no. 1 (1877): 128–63; 10, no. 2 (1887): 335–413; 11, no. 1 (1888): 199–264; 303–32.

———. *Dai poeti antichi perugini del Cod. già Barber. XLV-130 ora Vat. 4036.* Rome: Ermanno Loescher, 1905.

Moore, R. I. *The Formation of a Persecuting Society: Authority and Deviance in Western Europe 950–1250.* 2nd ed. Malden MA: Blackwell Publishing, 2007.

Morpurgo, Salomone. *La grande inundation de l'Arno en MCCCXXXIII: Anciens poèmes populaires italiens.* Paris: Champion, 1910.

Morrison, Susan Signe. "The Body: Unstable, Ungendered, Theorized." In *A Cultural History of Comedy in the Middle Ages*, edited by Martha Bayless, 99–119. London: Bloomsbury Academic, 2020.

Mott, Lewis Freeman Mott. *The System of Courtly Love Studied as an Introduction to the "Vita Nuova" of Dante.* New York: Haskell House, 1965.

Moulinier, Laurence, and Odile Redon. "L'Inondation de 1333 à Florence: Récit e Hypothèses de Giovanni Villani." *Médiévales* 36 (1999): 91–104.

O'Donoghue, Bernard. *The Courtly Love Tradition.* Manchester: Manchester University Press, 1982.

Orvieto, Paolo, and Lucia Brestolini. *La poesia comico-realistica: Dalle origini al Cinquecento.* Rome: Carocci, 2000.

Park, Katharine. *Doctors and Medicine in Early Renaissance Florence.* Princeton, NJ: Princeton University Press, 1985.

Pasquini, Emilio. "Il 'secolo senza poesia' e il crocevia di Burchiello." In *Le botteghe della poesia: Studi sul Tre-Quattrocento italiano*, 25–86. Bologna: Il Mulino, 1991.

Patrone, Annamaria Nada. *Il messaggio dell'Ingiuria nel Piemonte del tardo medioevo.* Cavallermaggiore: Gribaudo Editore, 1993.

"Pène." In *Dizionario etimologico della lingua italiana*, edited by Manlio Cortelazzo and Paolo Zilli, 4:901. Bologna: Zanichelli, 1985.

Percan, Josip B. *"Femina dulce malum": La donna nella letteratura medievale latina.* Rome: Edizioni Kappa, 2003.

Petrocchi, Giorgio. "Il dolce stil novo." In *Storia della letteratura italiana*, Vol. 1, *Le origini e il Duecento*, edited by Emilio Cecchi and Natalino Sapegno, 727–74. Milan: Garzanti, 1965.

———. "I poeti realisti." In *Storia della letteratura italiana*, Vol. 1, *Le origini e il Duecento*, edited by Emilio Cecchi and Natalino Sapegno, 689–725. Milan: Garzanti, 1965.

Piromalli, Antonio. "Aspetti della cultura e della poesia giocosa in Toscana nel Quattrocento." In *Dal Quattrocento al Novecento: Saggi critici*, 1–10. Florence: Olschki, 1965.

Pirovano, Donato. *Il Dolce Stil Novo*. Rome: Salerno Editrice, 2014.

———, ed. *Poeti del dolce stil novo*. Rome: Salerno Editrice, 2012.

Poe, Elizabeth Wilson. *From Poetry to Prose in Old Provençal: The Emergence of the "Vidas," the "Razos," and the "Razos de Trobar."* Birmingham, AL: Summa Publications, 1984.

Pratt, Karen. "*De vetula*: The Figure of the Old Woman in Medieval French Literature." In *Old Age in the Middle Ages and the Renaissance: Interdisciplinary Approaches to a Neglected Topic*, edited by Albrecht Classen, 321–42. Berlin: De Gruyter, 2007.

Raffa, Guy. "Love's Duplicity in the *Vita Nuova*." *Italian Culture* 10, no. 1 (1992): 15–26.

Rea, Roberto. *Stilnovismo cavalcantiano e tradizione cortese*. Rome: Bagatto Libri, 2007.

———. "Lo Stilnovo secondo Dante. Città del Vaticano, Biblioteca Apostolica Vaticana, Chigi L.VIII.305." In *"Onorevole e antico cittadino di Firenze": Il Bargello per Dante*, edited by Luca Azzetta, Sonia Chiodo, and Teresa De Robertis, 144–46. Florence: Mandragora, 2021.

Regalado, Nancy. *Poetic Patterns in Rutebeuf: A Study in Noncourtly Poetic Modes of the Thirteenth Century*. New Haven, CT: Yale University Press, 1970.

Ricettario fiorentino: Arte de' medici e degli speziali. Florence: Nella stamperia dei Giunti, 1574.

Rigo, Paolo. *Lo stilnovo*. Florence: Cesati, 2020.

Rocke, Michael. *Forbidden Friendships: Homosexuality and Male Culture in Renaissance Florence*. New York: Oxford University Press, 1996.

Rossetti, Dante Gabriel. *Dante and His Circle: With the Italian Poets Preceding Him (1100—1200—1300)*. London: Ellis, 1908.

Rossi, Luciano. "Aspetti dell'invettiva nell'Occitania del XIII secolo: Aimeric de Peguilhan e i suoi sodali." In *Cecco Angiolieri e la poesia satirica medievale. Atti del convegno internazionale Siena, 26–27 ottobre 2002*, edited by Stefano Carrai and Giuseppe Marrani, 31–49. Florence: Edizioni del Galluzzo, 2005.

Salih, Sara. "Sexual Identities: A Medieval Perspective." In *Sodomy in Early Modern Europe*, edited by Tom Betteridge, 112–18. Manchester: Manchester University Press, 2002.

Salimei, Franco. *I Salimbeni di Siena*. Rome: Editalia 1986.
Salutati, Coluccio. *Epistolario di Coluccio Salutati*. Edited by Francesco Novati. Rome: Forzani e c. tipografi del senato, 1891.
Salvestrini, Francesco. "L'Arno e l'alluvione Fiorentina del 1333." In *Le calamità ambientali nel tardo medioevo europeo: Realtà, percezioni, reazioni. Atti del XII convegno del Centro di Studi sulla Civiltà del tardo Medioevo, S. Miniato, 31 maggio–2 giugno 2008*, edited by Michael Matheus, Gabriella Piccinni, Giuliano Pinto, and Gian Maria Varanini, 231–56. Florence: Firenze University Press, 2010.
Scaglione, Aldo. *Knights at Court: Courtliness, Chivalry & Courtesy From Ottonian Germany to the Italian Renaissance*. Berkeley: University of California Press, 1991.
Schenk, Gerrit Jasper. "More Resilient with Mars or Mary? Constructing a Myth and Reclaiming Public Space, the Destruction of the Old Bridge of Florence." In *Strategies, Dispositions, and Resources of Social Resilience: A Dialogue between Medieval Studies and Sociology*, edited by Martin Andreß, Lukas Clemens, and Benjamin Rampp, 139–62. Wiesbaden: Springer VS, 2020.
———. "'Prima ci fu la cagione de la mala provedenza de' Fiorentini . . .': Disaster and 'Life World'—Reactions in the Commune of Florence to the Flood of November 1333." *Medieval History Journal* 10, no. 1–2 (2007): 355–86.
Schiaffini, Alfredo. "Influssi dei dialetti centro-meridionali sul toscano e sulla lingua letteraria. I. Il perugino trecentesco." *L'Italia dialettale: Rivista di dialettologia italiana* 4 (1928): 77–129.
The School of Salernum: Regimen sanitatis salerni. The English Version by Sir John Harington. Salerno: Ente Provinciale per il turismo, 1966.
Schultz, James A. "Heterosexuality as a Threat to Medieval Studies." *Journal of the History of Sexuality* 15, no. 1 (2006): 14–29.
Schwarts, Selby Wynn. *Rogue Poetry: Cecco Angiolieri and the Troubadour Tradition: A Study of Gender, Performance, and Comic Genres in Medieval Italian and Occitan Poetics*. Saarbrucken: VDM Verlag Dr. Muller, 2008.
Scotti-Porcelli, Giuseppina. "Dante e Cecco cantori della Maremma." *Bollettino della Società Storica Maremmana* 15 (1967): 175–82.
Sedgwick, Eve Kosofsky. *The Epistemology of the Closet*. Berkeley: University of California Press, 1990.
Sharf, Gian Paolo G. "La lenta ascesa di una famiglia signorile: I Tarlati di Pietramala prima del 1321." *Archivio storico italiano* 172, no. 2 (2014): 203–48.
Singer, Julie. "Deafness: Reading Invisible Signs." In *A Cultural History of Disability in the Middle Ages*, edited by Jonathan Hsy, Tory V. Pearman, and Joshua R. Eyler, 83–98. London: Bloomsbury Academic, 2020.

Siraisi, Nancy G. *Medieval and Early Renaissance Medicine: An Introduction to Knowledge and Practice.* Chicago: University of Chicago Press, 1990.

Smith, Alan K. "Fraudomy: Reading Sexuality and Politics in Burchiello." In *Queering the Renaissance,* edited by Jonathan Goldberg, 84–104. Durham, NC: Duke University Press, 1994.

Spitzer, Leo. "Parole di Dante: Caribo." *Lingua Nostra* 15 (1954): 65–66.

Stehling, Thomas. *Medieval Latin Poems of Male Love and Friendship.* New York: Garland, 1984.

Stevens, Hugh. "Homosexuality and Literature: An Introduction." In *The Cambridge Companion to Gay and Lesbian Writing,* edited by Hugh Stevens, 1–13. Cambridge: Cambridge University Press, 2011.

Suitner, Franco. "Dante e la poesia satirica del suo tempo." *Letture classensi* 12 (1983): 61–79. *Tesoro della Lingua Italiana delle Origini (TLIO).* http://tlio.ovi.cnr.it/TLIO/.

Todaro, Adele. *Il caribetto "A nulla guisa" di Meo di Simone dei Tolomei.* Siena: Lazzari, 1933.

———. *Sull'autenticità dei sonetti attribuiti a Cecco Angiolieri.* Palermo: Boccone del povero, 1934.

Todorović, Jelena. "Who Read the *Vita Nova* in the First Half of the Fourteenth Century?" *Dante Studies* 131 (2013): 197–217.

Trexler, Richard C. "Correre la terra: Collective Insults in the Late Middle Ages." In *Dependence in Context in Renaissance Florence,* 113–70, Binghamton, NY: Medieval & Renaissance Texts and Studies, 1994.

Trumbach, Randolph. *Sex and the Gender Revolution.* Vol. 1, *Heterosexuality and the Third Gender in Enlightenment London.* Chicago: University of Chicago Press, 1998.

———. "The Transformation of Sodomy from the Renaissance to the Modern World and Its General Consequences." *Signs: Journal of Women in Culture and Society* 37, no. 4 (2012): 832–48.

Valentini, Rosella Omicciolo. *Mangiare nelle taverne medievali tra cibo, vino e giochi.* Tuscania: Edizioni penne e papiri, 2007.

Van Arsdall, Anne. "Reading Medieval Medical Texts with an Open Mind." In *Textual Healing: Essays on Medieval and Early Modern Medicine,* edited by Elizabeth Lane Furdell, 9–29. Leiden-Boston: Brill, 2005.

Villani, Giovanni. *Nuova cronica.* Edited by Giuseppe Porta. Parma: Biblioteca di scrittori italiani, 1991.

Vinall, Shirley W., and Peter S. Noble. "Shrewd and Wanton Women: Adultery in the *Decameron* and *Heptameron.*" In *Women and Italy: Essays on Gender,*

Culture, and History, edited by Zygmunt G. Barański and Shirley W. Vinall, 141–72. Houndsmill, Basingstoke: Palgrave MacMillan, 1991.

Violante, Cinzio. "Le *noie* cremonesi nel loro ambiente culturale e sociale." In *La cortesia chiericale e borghese nel duecento*, 81–108. Florence: Olschki, 1995.

Vitale, Maurizio. *La lingua dei poeti realistico-giocosi del '200 e '300*. Milan: La goliardica, 1955.

———, ed. *Rimatori comico-realistici del Due e Trecento*. Turin: UTET, 1956.

Wack, Mary Frances. *Lovesickness in the Middle Ages: The "Viaticum" and Its Commentaries*. Philadelphia: University of Philadelphia Press, 1990.

Waley, Daniel. "A Blood-Feud with a Happy Ending: Siena, 1285–1304." In *City and Countryside in Late Medieval and Renaissance Italy: Essays Presented to Philip Jones*, edited by Trevor Dean and Chris Wickham, 45–53. London: The Hambledon Press, 1990.

Watkins, Renee. "Il Burchiello (1404–1448): Poverty, Politics, and Poetry." *Italian Quarterly* 14 (1970): 21–57.

Wheatly, Edward. *Stumbling Blocks before the Blind: Medieval Constructions of Disability*. Ann Arbor: University of Michigan Press, 2010.

Wis, Roberto. "Mito e leggenda in un sonetto di Meo dei Tolomei." *Aevum* 54, no. 2 (1980): 331–39.

Woods, Gregory. *A History of Gay Literature: The Male Tradition*. New Haven, CT: Yale University Press, 1998.

Zaccarello, Michelangelo. "Una forma istituzionale della poesia burchiellesca: La ricetta medica, cosmetica, culinaria tra parodia e *nonsense*." In *"Nominativi fritti e mappamondi": Il nonsense nella letteratura italiana. Atti del Convegno di Cassino 9–10 ottobre 2007*, edited by Giuseppe Antonelli and Carla Chiummo, 47–64. Rome: Salerno Editrice 2009.

———. "Off the Paths of Common Sense: From the *Frottola* to the *Per motti* and *Alla burchia* Poetic Styles." In *Nonsense and Other Senses: Regulated Absurdity in Literature*, edited by Elisabetta Tarantino and Carlo Caruso, 89–116. Cambridge: Cambridge Scholars Publishing, 2009.

Zancan, Diego. "Misoginia padana del Quattrocento e testi scurrili del Cinquecento: Due nuovi testimoni del *Manganus* ovvero *Manganello*." *Schede umanistiche* 1 (1995): 19–43.

INDEX

A
Abel, 170–71
Absalom, 126–27
Alighieri, Dante, xiv–xv, xx, xxiv, 58, 64–65, 192–93, 230–31, 261n11
  Inferno, xx, xxvii, xxx, xxxix, l, 11, 24–25, 27, 105, 200–201, 247n71, 258n70
  Paradiso, 115
  Purgatorio, 194, 247n71
  Tenzone with Forese Donati, 23
  Vita Nuova, 226–27, 264n15
Angiolieri, Cecco, xiv, xviii, xx, xxiii–xxvi, xxxiv–xxxv, xxxvii, xlv, xlvii–xlix, 4–9, 20, 29, 32, 54, 68–69, 89, 98, 104, 119, 130, 132–33, 162, 256n47, 258n71, 260n7, 261n16, 261n19, 262n37, 262n39
Arezzo, xliv–xlv, 152–55, 208–9, 226–27
Aristotle, 58
Arno, flood of 1333, xliv, 198–99, 251n155
Arthur (king), xliii, 108
Atalanta, 234–35

B
Baglioni, Cucco di Messer Gualfreduccio, xiii–xiv, xxv, 75, 114–29

Baglioni, Uccio di Messer Gualfreduccio, 114, 118–21, 150–51
Bandinelli, Piero Fastello dei, xli, 18–19
basilisk, 134–35
Bayless, Martha, xxii
Berisso, Marco, xvi, xxxv–xxxvi
Bernardo of Siena, xxxiii
Bettarini, Anna Bruni, xlix
Boccaccio, Giovanni, xix, xli, l, 142–43, 245n35
Boccoli, Ciuccio di Simonelli, 127–29
Boggione, Valter, xxi
Boniface VIII, 106
Books of the Bible
  John, 146
  Lamentations, 226–27
  Matthew, 11, 26, 196
Botterill, Steven, xvii

C
Campaldino, battle of, xvi
Capocchio, xxxix, 24–25, 27
Casalegno, Giovanni, xxi
Catiline, 209, 212–13
Cavalcanti, Guido, xv, xx, xxviii–xxix, xxxiv, xxxviii, 60–61, 144, 163, 166, 180, 248n82, 250n130, 264n15

Cervigni, Dino S., 245n35
Chubb, Thomas Caldecott, xlix
Cino da Pistoia, xiv–xv, xx, xliii, xlv, 66–67, 177, 184–85, 206
Ciampolino (slang term), xx–xxi
Cionello, xiii–xiv
Cola di Messer Alessandri, xxxii–xxxiii, 136–39
Collegari, Danielle, 32
comic poetry, xvii, xxii, xxxv–xl, 94–95, 200
Corso (Corzo) di Corzano, xxv, 76–79

D
Damian, Peter, xxx–xxxi
Detto del Gatto Lupesco, 142–43
disability studies, xl–xli
dolce stil nuovo, xv, xxiii, xxxv, xliii, xlv
Doria, Branca, xxxix, 27

F
fabliaux, xxviii
Faggiuola, Ranieri (Neri) della, 152, 226–27
fellatio, xvii, xxxi, 109, 122–23
Filippi, Rustico, xxix, xlvii
Finiguerri, Stefano (il Za), xlvi, xlviii, 143, 251nn162–63
First Crusade, 18–19
Fossalta, battle of, 28–29
Foucault, Michel, 248n100
Frederick I "Barbarossa," xxxv

G
Galen, 76–77
Ghinuccia, 42–43
Gianni, Lapo, xiv–xv

Giotto, 142–43, 263n49
Giovanni, Domenico di (Burchiello), xlvii–xlviii, 5, 143
Girardello, 98–101
Gratian, 262n26
Guidinelli da Castro San Piero, Gino, xiii
Guinigi family, xix
Guinizelli, Guido, 250n130

H
Henry of Luxemburg, 152
Hollywood, Amy H., xxvii
Holmes, Olivia, 245n35
Holy Face of Lucca, 10–11
homoeroticism, in medieval literature, xiv, xvi, xxvii–xxx, xxxvi–xxxvii

J
Jacobus de Voragine, xli, 255n40
Jason, 16
John the Baptist, xli, 28, 255n40
John the Evangelist, xli, 28, 255n40

L
Langer, Ulrich, 245n35
Lanza, Antonio, xlix
Latini, Brunetto, 256n48
Lelli, Gilio, xli–xlii, xlv, xlvi, 88–91, 108–9, 142–43, 226, 263n50
Lucan
Pharsalia, 196–97

M
Mancini, Franco, xx–xxi, xlix, 108
manuscripts
    Ambrosiano C 35, 252n6
    Ambrosiano O 63 supra, 252n6

Capitolare Veronese 445, 252n6
Chigiano L.VIII.305, xxiii, xxvi, xxx, xlix, 35, 64–65, 246n52, 252n6, 262n37
Escorialense e.III.23, xxiii, 246n55, 252n6, 262n39
Laurenziano Acquisti e Doni 759, 252n6
Vatican Barberiniano Latin 3953, xxiii, 245n51
Vatican Barberiniano Latin 4036, xiii, xvii–xviii, xxvi–xxvii, 234
Marie de France, xliii, 108
Marti, Mario, xiv, xix, xxiv–xxv, xlix, 12–15, 243n8, 249n117
Massèra, Aldo Francesco, xlix, 96–97, 102
Matthew of Vendôme, xxxviii
Medea, 16–17, 106
medicine, in the Middle Ages, xxxix–xl, 12–15, 30–31, 76–77, 140–41, 253n16
Méndez, Jerónimo, xxviii
Merlin, 34–35
Migo, 68–69, 259n93
Mills, Robert, xxvii
Minerva, 200
Minnis, Alistair, xxii
misogyny, in medieval literature, xvii, 23
Modena, 29
Montemelino, Bartoluccio, 122
Moore, R. I., xxxii
Morrison, Susan Signe, xxxv
Mortimer, Anthony, xlix
Moscoli, Neri, xiii–xv, 214–15, 218–21
mujūn, xxviii

Muscia, Niccola, xxix–xxx, xxxiv, 68, 248n82

O
Occitanic poetry, xiv–xvii, xlii–xliii, 40–41, 72, 74–75, 84–87, 92, 102, 108, 148, 162–67, 176–81
Oddi, Oddo degli, xxxiii, 114, 136–39, 150–51
Onesto Bolognese, xiv

P
Pasquini, Emilio, 4
Patarine heresy, 136–39, 263n41
Petroni, Mino di Peppo Accorridore, 68–69, 259n91
Perugia (fourteenth-century history), xiii–xv, xviii, xxvi, 132–33, 150–55, 194–97, 208–9, 226–27
Poe, Elizabeth Wilson, 244n32
Pucci, Antonio, xliv, 199, 264n24

R
Radda castle, besieged, xxxix, 30–31
Regimen Sanitatis Salerni, 14–15, 253n15, 255n36
Rocke, Michael, xxxiii
Rossi, Adriano de', xliv, 199, 261n20, 264n24

rusticitas, and *urbanitas*, xliv, 134–35, 168–69, 202–3, 236–37

S
Salimbene de Adam, xlii, 255n41
Salutati, Coluccio, xviii, xxvii, xlv, 238–41
Salvani, Mita di Bindino, xix

Scott, C. H. M. D., xlix
Siena (fourteenth-century history), xix, xxvi, xxxix, 25, 133
Simone da Pierile, 214–17
sodomy, xxvii–xxviii, xxxi, xxxiv, 248n91
  between women, 247n72
  and gender roles, xxxiv
  and heresy, xxxii–xxxiii, 136–39
  penalties, xxxi–xxxiii, xxxv
"Song of Gianni," 126–29
Spoleto, xxxii–xxxiii, 136–39
Sposato, Peter W., xliii
sumptuary laws, 249n109

T
Tano, 68–69, 259n91
Tarlati, Pier Saccone (di Pietramala), xliv–xlv, 152–55, 208–13, 226–27
tavern, in medieval literature, xxii, xlii, 32, 34, 41–42, 45, 47, 69, 88–89
Tese (Contese), 36–37
Thomas Aquinas, xxxi
Tiberinus (king), 96–97
Todaro, Adele, xxiii, xlix
Tolomei family, xix

Tolomei, Iacomo de', xxix, xxxiv, 68–69
Tolomei, Mino (historical), xix
Tolomei, Moco di Pietro, 68–69
Tolomei, Simone (Sorella), xix
Tristan, xliii, 99, 132–33
Trumbach, Randolph, xxxiii

U
Uberti, Fazio degli, xlii, 255n41
Uberti, Lupo degli, xxviii, xxix, xxx, xxxiv, 60
Ugolino da Fano, xliv, 109, 112–13, 170–75, 222–25
Uliva (saint), xli, 28–29

V
Villani, Giovanni, xliv, 198, 264n23
Vitale, Maurizio, xlix
vituperium in vetulam, xxxviii, xlii, 60–61, 106, 250n128

W
William of Flanders, 142–43, 263n48
Wis, Roberto, xli

Z
Zanche, Michele, xxxix, 27

FABIAN ALFIE

is a professor of Italian at the University of Arizona.
He is the author and editor of several books on the satires of
the Middle Ages and Renaissance, including *Comedy and Culture:
Cecco Angiolieri's Poetry and Late Medieval Society.*

www.ingramcontent.com/pod-product-compliance
Lightning Source LLC
Chambersburg PA
CBHW061426300426
44114CB00014B/1562